ENCYCLOPEDIA
OF TROPICAL FISHES

WITH SPECIAL EMPHASIS ON TECHNIQUES OF BREEDING

By
DR. HERBERT R. AXELROD
and
WILLIAM VORDERWINKLER

The first 21 editions of this book were dedicated to Dr. Leonard P. Schultz, who was, during that time, Curator of Fishes of the Smithsonian Institution and a great friend of the authors. Since the first edition was issued in 1958, Dr. Schultz has always been helpful in solving many of our nomenclatural problems. In 1972 Dr. Schultz retired. He died July 17, 1986.

In 1968, Bill Vorderwinkler, my constant fish companion and very close friend, suffered his ninth and most crippling stroke. This disaster put Bill into the hospital almost completely incapacitated. It took him about a year to regain some of his speech and movement powers, but a final stroke ended Bill's suffering on January 9, 1970 when he was almost 62 years old.

In the many years since Bill has been unable to contribute to the newer editions, I still find Bill's beautiful words and great ideas bouncing through the text, so that while I must assume all the responsibility for the changes, the basic ideas are just as much Bill's as mine and for that reason Bill is still deserving of being listed as the co-author of this book.

Dr. Herbert R. Axelrod

Distributed in the UNITED STATES by T.F.H. Publications, Inc., One T.F.H. Plaza, Neptune City, NJ 07753; in CANADA to the Pet Trade by H & L Pet Supplies Inc., 27 Kingston Crescent, Kitchener, Ontario N2B 2T6; Rolf C. Hagen Ltd., 3225 Sartelon Street, Montreal 382 Quebec; in CANADA to the Book Trade by Macmillan of Canada (A Division of Canada Publishing Corporation), 164 Commander Boulevard, Agincourt, Ontario M1S 3C7; in ENGLAND by T.F.H. Publications Limited, Cliveden House/Priors Way/Bray, Maidenhead, Berkshire SL6 2HP, England; in AUSTRALIA AND THE SOUTH PACIFIC by T.F.H. (Australia) Pty. Ltd., Box 149, Brookvale 2100 N.S.W., Australia; in NEW ZEALAND by Ross Haines & Son, Ltd., 18 Monmouth Street, Grey Lynn, Auckland 2, New Zealand; in SINGAPORE AND MALAYSIA by MPH Distributors (S) Pte., Ltd., 601 Sims Drive, #03/07/21, Singapore 1438; in the PHILIPPINES by Bio-Research, 5 Lippay Street, San Lorenzo Village, Makati Rizal; in SOUTH AFRICA by Multipet Pty. Ltd., 30 Turners Avenue, Durban 4001. Published by T.F.H. Publications, Inc. Manufactured in the United States of America by T.F.H. Publications, Inc.

CONTENTS

Brown discus *Symphysodon aequifasciata axelrodi* with a Black-lace Angelfish in the background. Both ot these fishes are difficult to sex; only the full belly of a ripe female and the intense drive and slimness of a male are reliable indications of sex differences.
Photo by M. Kocar.

Preface

THE REAL SECRET OF SPAWNING FISHES

"I don't know why it is, but that Joe Smith seems to be able to spawn any fish he wants to!"

You've often heard that statement made about some fellow aquarium society member or other. If you are the fellow they are enviously talking about, this book is not for you; however, if you are one of the ones who wonder how he does it, keep reading.

In the first place, a breeder who says he "spawned" a certain species of fish is guilty of a gross misstatement. What he should say is that a certain species of fish spawned *for him*. He may have helped by creating conditions which were to the fish's liking, but the credit for spawning still belongs to the fish. So much for that; now let us see how these conditions may be created.

No matter what conditions you create, it will still do you no good if the fish you work with are not capable of reproduction. So your first task is to be certain of a few things.

The first thing to be sure of is the question of whether you have a pair or not. This may sound silly, but a busy clerk in a store anxious to make a sale could easily be tempted to catch two immature fish and assure the buyer that he has a pair, meaning two fish rather than a male and a female. Some fishes are difficult to sex when full-grown, and impossible when half-grown.

Another thing which is important is the *age* of the fish. If you were given the choice of picking a human couple to produce offspring, you certainly would not pick grandma and grandpa; you would select a young, healthy couple in the prime of life. It is just as silly to expect good results from a feeble old pair of fish. Even a mature pair might have trouble adapting themselves to the new environment which your tank would provide for them. The way to avoid this is to avoid purchasing mature fish for breeding purposes. Rather than getting a large pair, try to get a half dozen or so youngsters which are only half to three-quarters grown. You are then in a position to observe them and become acquainted with their habits and food preferences. When they are ready for spawning, the best specimens may then be selected. In the case of cichlids, there is a tendency for the males to choose the females of their preference and "pair off." Your chances of spawning in these cases are usually almost certain.

Now we come to the point where a little knowledge and observation comes in very handy. Do your fish prefer to swim in the open, or are they always hiding? Do you find them in the sunny spots, or do you have to look for them in the dark corners? What is the nature of the terrain from which they come? Are they native to clear, running streams or sluggish, mud-bottomed ponds? Do they come from far inland, or from coastal waters?

How can the aquarist duplicate these conditions? The answer is, he cannot. However, they can be approximated. First of all, it must be kept in mind that the bottom of a pond or stream does not resemble an aquarium. The glass sides let in a great deal of light where Mother Nature does not. The mistake is often made of forcing a timid fish to show himself by taking away some of his hiding places. This increases his timidity and keeps him in a constant state of terror. How can a fish spawn under these conditions? It is better to provide such a fish with *more* plant thickets into which he can dodge. You may be pleasantly surprised to see that he puts in an appearance often when he knows that there are places where he *could* hide if something frightened him. Some fishes love sunlight, while others instinctively avoid it. A simple observation on this point will tell you whether it is better to select a bright location or not. A fish which is native to running streams, such as our danios and White Clouds, will not tolerate dirty water or very high temperatures. On the other hand, pond and lake-dwellers, such as the cichlids, might pick a spot in shallow water near the shore for spawning, like sunfishes do. Here the sun is bright and water warm. In the case of some other cichlids, the presence of enemies forces them to hide in pockets along the shore, or in reed growths, or in rock piles. If we approximate these conditions, or in other words if we make our fishes feel at home, our battle is usually won. As for the water itself, it will be found that a fish which comes from brackish, coastal water will require the addition of a little salt for its well-being. Rain-fed inland streams have an almost neutral, very soft water, while fishes from swampy regions would require water of definitely acid character.

Don't be misled by the apparently careless procedure of the successful breeder who declares that he has no trouble; just uses tap-water. There are all kinds of tap-water, and his kind may be just right. However, he generally knows the characteristics of his tap-water and whether or not it is right for the fish he is breeding. He also is well aware of the

6

of the fish in question, and supplies them too.
t the successful breeder will tell you of his successes;
ar the failures mentioned. Don't let your failures
n the "experts" have them too!

many ways that the same fish may be induced to
ssional fish farmer will tell you stories of breeders
uccessfully in their basement that they invested their
v facility to raise tropical fishes commercially. Most
e doomed to failure! They could not even raise the
sed so easily in their old basements.

the fish you wish to spawn. Learn all you can about
any people as you know who may have kept them or
ie time or another and read some of the many books
pecially the series of books *"Breeding Aquarium*
d co-authors) which shows step-by-step photographs
ilar aquarium fishes as they spawn. Pretty soon you
is possible about the particular fish and you can then
to breed them. If one set of conditions doesn't suit
hances are if the fish are healthy, if they eat properly
e on the right track.

l fish, try to breed prettier, healthier and larger
i contribution to tropical fish keeping. Tell your
ow about fish if they ask you, and above all:
i't try to breed every kind of fish you can get your
hands on at the same time. Buy a dozen young fish of one species, raise
them up properly and learn all their secrets. Then YOU are the expert
on that particular species!

The senior author has bred more than 100 species of fishes, yet there
are several hundred he has not yet bred, and knows very little about
personally. Share your knowledge with the world and have your information published in a magazine. The pages of *Tropical Fish Hobbyist*
magazine are open to everyone who wishes to publish an accurate,
authenticated story of the breeding of any fish not bred before.

Dr. Herbert R. Axelrod
and the Late
William Vorderwinkler
September, 1974

7

The albino Walking Catfish, *Clarias batrachus* (above) and the Pike Livebearer, *Belonesox belizanus*, gobbling up a male Guppy (below) are fishes which have become established in Florida as undesirable introductions. The release of non-native fishes into any natural body of water is potentially harmful and in many cases illegal. Any unwanted fishes should be returned to your local pet shop or public aquarium or, if neither is available, the fishes should be humanely killed. Upper photo by Peter Tsang; lower photo by Rudolf Zukal.

INTRODUCTION

Numerous technical and non-technical journals have featured articles in which the breeding of many tropical and subtropical aquarium fishes is described accurately. Some of these have been written by outstanding ichthyologists, many of whom have had first-hand experience from studying fishes in their native habitat and in laboratory and home aquaria.

A number of the written reports are available only in the German, French, and Dutch languages. The pages of "Tropical Fish Hobbyist" magazine, as well as other publications, carry many translations of these articles; they represent only a small percentage of the material at hand. Some of the information presented in this book has been obtained from articles in these foreign language publications. Much of our own first-hand information and that of other aquarists form the background of this work. There are also many books on breeding aquarium fishes at your pet store, bookshop or library.

What we are recommending in this book are methods of breeding aquarium fishes that have been used successfully by others . . . in some cases by ourselves. Following our suggestions, we feel, will at least increase your chances of success. However, if you think that you can do better, and find that you actually can, let the world know by writing about your findings. We are far from the end of the road when it comes to knowledge about things aquatic. A great deal of practical information about aquarium fish keeping has come from the published writings of aquarists at all levels of experience.

A WARNING

Most local laws prohibit the introduction of "exotic" fishes, and whilst I was chairman of the Exotic Fishes Committee of the American Fisheries Society, the entire membership of some 5,000 scientists, fishery biologists and fishery management people voted overwhelmingly in favor of the following "position statement" relative to such introductions.

Position of American Fisheries Society on Introduction of Exotic Aquatic Species

Our purpose is to formulate a broad mechanism for planning, regulating, implementing, and monitoring all introductions of exotic aquatic species.

Some introductions of species into ecosystems in which they are not native have been successful (e.g., coho salmon and striped bass) and others unfortunate (e.g., common carp and walking catfish).

Species not native to an ecosystem will be termed "exotic." Some introductions are in some sense planned and purposeful for management reasons; others are accidental or are simply ways of disposing of unwanted pets or research organisms.

It is recommended that the policy of the American Fisheries Society be:

1. Encourage exotic fish importers, farmers, dealers and hobbyists to prevent and discourage the accidental or purposeful introduction of exotics into their local ecosystems.

   a. Support legislation prohibiting all ornamental aquarium fish importers, exotic fish importers, hobbyists, breeders, dealers, governmental employees and fish farmers from releasing living, dead or dying fishes into any water system, but encouraging dry-wells, dikes and moats for the preservation of the ecosystem from accidental introduction of exotic fishes and fish diseases.

   b. Urge the establishment of four Federal Fish Disease and Fish Culture Stations, similar to that already established as the Eastern Fish Disease Laboratory in Leetown, West Virginia, in or near Miami and Tampa, Florida, Los Angeles, California and New York, New York where the majority of exotic fish businesses are located, to assist exotic fish dealers, importers, etc., in the control of fish diseases and the culture and identification of exotic species, and to evaluate, control, and monitor exotic introductions into these areas.

   c. Urge the accurate completion of existing Federal documentation for compliance with Customs and Interior Department regulations. Form 3-177 "Declaration for Importation of Fish or Wildlife" is grossly abused, with deflated costs and generally incorrect information.

2. Urge that no city, county, state or Federal agency introduce, or allow to be introduced, any exotic species into any waters within its jurisdiction which might contaminate any waters outside its jurisdiction without official sanction of the exposed jurisdictions.

3. Urge that only ornamental aquarium fish dealers be permitted to import such fishes for sale or distribution to hobbyists. The "dealer" would be defined as a firm or person whose income derives from live ornamental aquarium fishes.

4. Urge that the importation of exotic fishes for purposes of research

10

not involving introduction into a natural ecosystem, or for display in public aquaria by individuals or organizations, be made under agreement with responsible governmental agencies. Such importers will be subject to investigatory procedures currently existing and/or to be developed, and species so imported shall be kept under conditions preventing escape or accidental introduction. Aquarium hobbyists should be encouraged to import rare ornamental fishes through such importers. No fishes shall be released into any natural ecosystem upon termination of research or display.

5. Urge that all species of exotics considered for release be prohibited and considered undesirable for any purposes of introduction into any ecosystem unless that fish shall have been evaluated upon the following bases and found to be desirable:

a. RATIONALE. Reasons for seeking an import should be clearly stated and demonstrated. It should be clearly noted what qualities are sought that would make the import more desirable than native forms.

b. SEARCH. Within the qualifications set forth under RATIONALE, a search of possible contenders should be made, with a list prepared of those that appear most likely to succeed, and the favorable and unfavorable aspects of each species noted.

c. PRELIMINARY ASSESSMENT OF THE IMPACT. This should go beyond the area of rationale to consider impact on target aquatic ecosystems, general effect on game and food fishes or waterfowl, on aquatic plants and public health. The published information on the species should be reviewed and the species should be studied in preliminary fashion in its biotope.

d. PUBLICITY AND REVIEW. The subject should be entirely open and expert advice should be sought. It is at this point that thoroughness is in order. No importation is so urgent that it should not be subject to careful evaluation.

e. EXPERIMENTAL RESEARCH. If a prospective import passes the first four steps, a research program should be initiated by an appropriate agency or organization to test the import in confined waters (experimental ponds, etc.). This agency or organization should not have the authority to approve its own results or to effect the release of stocks, but should submit its report and recommendations for evaluation.

f. EVALUATION OR RECOMMENDATION. Again publicity is in order and complete reports should be circulated amongst interested scientists and presented for publication in the *Transactions of the American Fisheries Society*.

g. INTRODUCTION. With favorable evaluations, the release should be effected and monitored, with results published or circulated.

Because animals do not respect political boundaries, it would seem that an international, national and regional agency should either be involved at the start or have the veto power at the end. Under this procedure there is no doubt that fewer exotic introductions would be accomplished, but quality and not quantity is desired and many mistakes might be avoided.

A stickleback, *Gasterosteus aculeatus*, infected with *Glugea* and *Schistocephalus*. Photo by Dr. E. Elkan from his *ATLAS OF FISH DISEASES*.

A Neon Tetra, *Paracheirodon innesi*, showing signs of *Plistophora* infection. Photo by S. Frank.

Spinal curvature in two female Guppies. Upon closer examination these two fish were found to have fish tuberculosis.

A Goldfish with a fungus infection. Usually fungus is a secondary invader which attacks areas which have initially been penetrated by bacteria or a wound.

THE FISH BREEDER'S TEN COMMANDMENTS

Make a list of these "Ten Commandments" which follow and hang them up in your fish room. Every time you decide to put up a pair of fish to breed, run down the list and make sure that you observe each one. If you do, you should have very little trouble.

1. Make sure they are healthy.
2. Make sure they are a pair.
3. Make sure they are properly conditioned.
4. Make sure they have enough room.
5. Make sure they have the proper temperature.
6. Make sure they have the proper water conditions.
7. Make sure they have the proper lighting.
8. Make sure they have a clean aquarium.
9. Make sure they have the proper planting.
10. Make sure they have the proper shelter.

First Commandment: *MAKE SURE THEY ARE HEALTHY*.

You cannot expect a good spawning from a pair of fish unless they are in the best of health. If it comes to a choice between purchasing prime

Proper conditioning of potential breeders is to a great extent dependent on the type of food they're given. Today there is such a great variety of good foods available to hobbyists (shown below are just few of the many flake foods on the market, for instance) that it is possible *to guarantee* good nutrition.

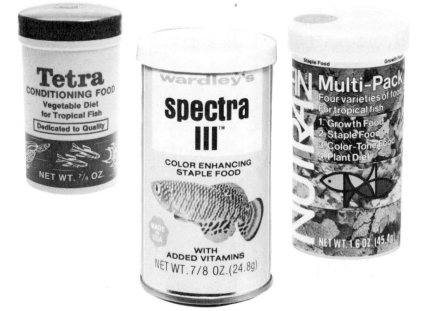

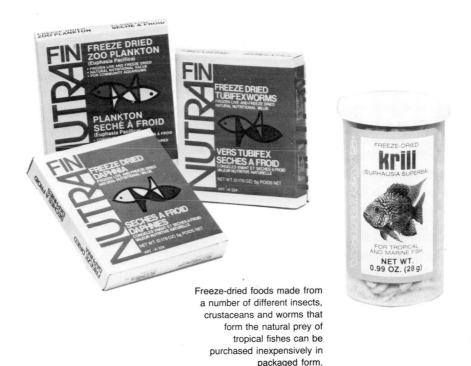

Freeze-dried foods made from a number of different insects, crustaceans and worms that form the natural prey of tropical fishes can be purchased inexpensively in packaged form.

specimens and so-called "bargain fishes," remember that misplaced economy on your part can mean not only the loss of your purchased pair, but also others with which they were kept. When you make a purchase, make sure that not only the fish you buy are in good shape, but that none of the others in the same tank show pinched, hollow bellies, spots on the body or fins, or folded fins. A fish once ill and treated with any of the usual aquarium remedies is useless as a breeder in nearly every instance.

A good way to arrive at a healthy spawning pair of fish is to get about a half-dozen young specimens and raise them to full size. This requires a bit more patience, but eliminates the possibility that your fully grown purchases might be old and past their useful breeding age. In this way you may also encourage the fish to pair "naturally"—having chosen each other's company. Chances of obtaining a good breeding pair in this fashion are greater than if you make the selection yourself.

Second Commandment: *MAKE SURE THEY ARE A PAIR.*

Sex is difficult to ascertain in many cases, but it is sometimes practically impossible. Many species of fishes, however, have sexual characteristics which can be spotted with a little close observation. The male usually has the edge on the female in color and fin size, and is usually the more slender of the two. In some of the transparent species, the male has a more pointed swim-bladder, while the female's is more rounded. In live-bearing species males are easy to distinguish: the anal fin of the male is pointed and is the means by which he introduces his sperm into the body of the female. When ready to spawn, the female develops a heavy belly, but it is still possible to make the mistake of identifying the perpetually slender females of some species as males.

Third Commandment: *MAKE SURE THEY ARE PROPERLY CONDITIONED.*

"Proper conditioning" in this case means feeding generously with the proper foods, and assuring good health. It is usually a good practice to keep the males and females in separate aquaria while this conditioning process is going on. This insures the ripeness of the females as well as the males and gives us a control over the time spawning is to take place. It is a good idea to put out a pair for spawning when you are at home for a day to keep an eye on them (starting them the evening before is suggested). If they belong to a species which is fond of eating its own eggs, remove them as soon as spawning is over and before the egg-hunt has a chance to start. There are some fishes which lay only a few eggs every day over a period of time. Separating the male and female beforehand will give the eggs a chance to accumulate in the female's body, resulting in a more generous spawning when the male is put back with her.

Some barbs are easily sexed, since the female (to the left) is usually fatter and less colorful than the male (the fish on the right is the male.) Photo of a spawning pair of Tic-Tac-Toe Barbs by Hans Joachim Richter.

Pencilfish are easy to sex since a female in good condition is always fat and rotund. The upper fish in this photo is the female. Photo by Dr. Stanislav Frank.

In annual fishes like these *Cynolebias whitei* from southern Brazil, the male (lower fish) is so different from the female that sexing is simple. Photo by Dr. K. Knaack.

Fourth Commandment: *MAKE SURE THEY HAVE ENOUGH ROOM.*

A pair of large, active fish cannot be expected to spawn in a small space..It is like expecting a ballerina to give a performance in a telephone booth. There is a sort of sixth sense which tells a fish that a small space is not right to have a family grow up in, but mostly it is because there is also a sense of claustrophobia. This fear of enclosed places becomes quite evident when a fish is placed in a jar for transportation purposes. He will bang his head against the glass sides not only from fear, but from a sense of panic caused by being hemmed in. A caged wild bird will show the same panic.

Fifth Commandment: *MAKE SURE THEY HAVE THE PROPER TEMPERATURE.*

In their natural environment fishes generally spawn when certain stimuli prompt them to. One of these stimuli frequently is a rise in temperature. This does not mean a rise of 10°, or anything as drastic as that. Many spawning attempts are unsuccessful because the water temperature is just a little bit too low. In the wild state, the natural spawning period may correspond to springtime in the temperate zones. In the months of May and June in the northern hemisphere, great hordes of natural foods have made their appearance in many bodies of fresh water. The fishes feed on them to their heart's content, and their bodies gradually become full of spawn. The warm spring sun raises the water temperature, and increases the activity and general feeling of well-being, and Nature takes its course.

Vibrator air pumps can be used with different types of air-powered filtering and aerating devices in the aquarium; a good air pump is a sensible investment.

Undergravel filters can be powered by either an air pump or one of the "power head" devices now available; the power heads tremendously increase the rate of water flow through the gravel.

In the aquarium, we must duplicate these conditions to the best of our ability to achieve similar results. A partial change of water gives some of this stimulation, and a slight rise in temperature will give the same effect as the sun shining down on the water after a rain. If the fish are in proper condition and all else is to their liking, they will spawn.

Sixth Commandment: *MAKE SURE THEY HAVE THE PROPER WATER CONDITIONS.*

Coming as they do from all corners of the world, aquarium fishes are found under all sorts of water conditions. What these conditions are and what should be done to approximate them is so important that there is an entire chapter devoted to it.

Seventh Commandment: *MAKE SURE THEY HAVE PROPER LIGHTING.*

In an effort to see our fishes at their best, most of us are inclined to illuminate our show tanks a little too brightly. An aquarium lets in light from four sides as well as the surface. We wouldn't want it any other way, but the fish might. Look into a pond where there are fishes; the light comes in through the surface, and you will notice that the fish tend to congregate where there is the least amount, in the shadows below overhanging banks or among vegetation. A fish which likes to stay out in the sunlight is the most likely candidate for a larger fish's gullet, and they instinctively feel uneasy when exposed.

These instincts are intensified at spawning-time, with few exceptions. The tendency for most fishes is to seek out the darkest corner for their spawning activities. If an aquarium is lighted brightly and planting is not heavy, you will find that spawning is not easily encouraged.

There is an entire book on the subject of *"Light in the Aquarium."* Read it!

Eighth Commandment: *MAKE SURE THEY HAVE A CLEAN AQUARIUM.*

This gives rise to the old adage: "A clean aquarium is a healthy aquarium." It is only a small extra precaution when designating a tank as one to be used for breeding purposes to give it a thorough cleaning. Many aquarists are successful in getting their fishes to spawn for them, only to have the eggs fail to hatch or to have the fry disappear mysteri-

A view from below. This shows a pair of Siamese Fighting Fishes, *Betta splendens,* as they circle immediately prior to their nuptual embrace. The bubblenest floats on the surface of the water and the light is reflected in the bubbles. Bettas always prefer to spawn under light, so give them top-lighting when they prepare their bubblenest. Hansen photo.

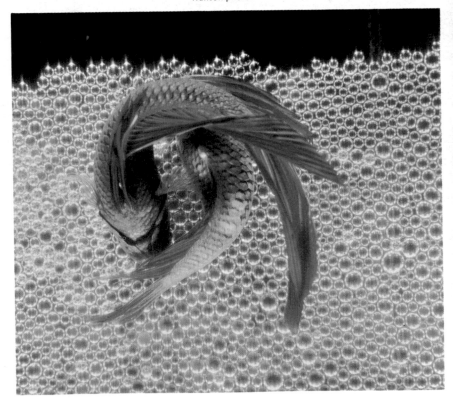

A female *Apistogramma trifasciata* which has been crossed with another species of *Apistogramma* guards her hanging pink eggs in the dark seclusion of a coconut shell. The light has been introduced by a strobe for photographic purposes only; usually the coconut shell shades the fish and the eggs from all light. Photo by Hans Joachim Richter.

The power filters now available to aquarists are efficient units capable of straining out suspended matter and recirculating the water in a tank many times each day—and they do it without consuming much electrical power.

ously. The mystery is not so great if the tank has been neglected and is dirty. A newly hatched fish's struggle for existence is hard enough without having it combat parasites as well.

Ninth Commandment: *MAKE SURE THEY HAVE THE PROPER PLANTING.*

Plants or plant substitutes are indispensable in almost every breeding tank. Many egg-laying fishes deposit their eggs in finely leaved plants, while others attach them to the surface of broad leaved plants. Some weave plants into a nest, while others use bits of plants as part of their bubble-nests. Plants serve as a refuge for newly born live-bearing fishes, protecting them from the voracity of their own parents. Another important job done by plants is to provide shade, which we have mentioned as being important in proper lighting. It is important to be acquainted with the breeding habits of the fish which we are attempting to spawn, and providing the proper plants for the purpose.

Mention has been made of "plant substitutes." Many aquarists have replaced spawning plants with other media. One of the favorites is Spanish moss, which may be used in many cases to replace bushy plants. The advantage is that it can be used over and over, and can also be used where the location of the aquarium gets so little light that plants will not grow properly. For fishes which spawn at or near the top, bundles of nylon yarn tied to a small cork serve very well. When it contains eggs, the yarn may be removed and placed in another container where the eggs will hatch. After use, it may be sterilized by boiling.

Tenth Commandment: *MAKE SURE THEY HAVE THE PROPER SHELTER.*

Plant shelter is not the only shelter which must be considered. Some fishes require rocks as well. These are the species which fasten their eggs to a rock or some other firm object on the bottom. Some prefer the confines of a small cave for their spawning activity. An excellent medium which provides them with this is an old flower-pot, laid on its side, preferably with the open side away from the light. If this is not artistic enough for the decor of the tank, some rocks may be arranged in such a manner as to provide natural-looking retreats. Many species of fishes not only use rocks in spawning, but seek protection among them when being pursued.

One of the functions performed by plants in the tank—whether those plants are living or artificial—is to provide shelter. The artificial plants available to hobbyists today are remarkably lifelike.

Glowlight Tetras, twisting upside down in a spawning ritualistic orgy, spray eggs among the Java moss. Note the eggs hanging from the plants in the background. Photo by Hans Joachim Richter.

Polycentrus schomburgki spawning upside down under a sturdy Amazon Sword Plant leaf.
Photo by Rudolf Zukal.

In Lake Tanganyika, in about 40 feet of water *Cyphotilapia frontosa* selects rocky areas near
which to spawn and hide. Obviously providing them with plants in an aquarium would be
useless. . . they must have rocks! Photo by Dr. Herbert R. Axelrod.

A Firemouth Cichlid, *Cichlosama meeki*, spawning inside a flowerpot. You must present your fishes with the proper spawning site if you expect them to spawn readily. Photo by Rudolf Zukal.

So much for rules and regulations; let us now see what can be done in the way of following some of them in the proper manner.

PLANTS IN THE AQUARIUM

The function of plants in the aquarium has been fully and completely discussed in many articles by the author (HRA) and by such noted authorities as Charles M. Breder, Jr. and James W. Atz of the American Museum of Natural History in New York.

Most writers agree that plants have seven main functions in the aquarium:

1. Aesthetically, plants decorate an aquarium and make it suitable as a "piece of furniture" in the home.

2. Plants can be used to test water conditions. Certain plants, if they grow well in water, prove that certain fishes will also grow well in this same water. An example of this is *Nitella* and most livebearing fishes.

3. Aquarium plants inhibit the growth of algae by competing with these lower forms of plant life for food and vital light.

4. Plants serve as a food for fishes both directly and indirectly as food for certain organisms which the fishes will feed upon.

5. Plants serve as a hiding place for small fishes and other fishes which are too timid to "fight the bullies."

6. Plants serve as a spawning medium for nearly all fishes except cichlids.

7. Plants serve to acclimate the fishes to their aquarium environment by making them feel "at home."

Certain fishes actually require specific plants in order for them to spawn. In these cases the specific plants required will be mentioned in the discussions of the fishes in question. But nearly every aquarium fish requires some kind of plant or other substitute spawning medium.

Plants are as important to the display aquarium as the fish themselves. Plants with varied forms of foliage, together with other decorations like driftwood, can greatly enhance the appearance of a tank.

Echinodorus andrieuxi; the flower above, the growing plant below. Photos by Rudolf Zukal.

Echinodorus latifolius above; *Echinodorus cordifolius* below.

Plants, if properly utilized, make shy fishes like most of the dwarf cichlids come out in the open, for they seem to sense that security in hiding behind the plants is close at hand and their danger is limited by short excursions into the open.

It is not meant to be inferred that plants are an absolute necessity for the well being of fishes. This is not true. Many of the commercial breeders maintain their fishes without plants and truly the only time they come into contact with any plants at all is when they arrive in the home aquarium. The reason that plants are not used is two-fold: They get in the way when the fishes must be netted, and secondly, they hinder a close look at the fishes when they are inspected for size and health. Small parasites are harder to see in the planted aquarium too.

Plants and fishes do have something like a symbiotic relationship. The fishes' wastes are excellent fertilizer for the aquatic plants and they are utilized as such. This in turn helps rid the aquarium of an otherwise useless by-product of maintaining fishes. Though plants do give off oxygen during their photosynthetic process, their more important function lies in absorbing and utilizing dissolved carbon dioxide in this same process. Photosynthesis can only take place in the presence of light and it is necessary to give the plants either direct exposure to daylight, or substitute an equivalent amount of artificial light.

Aquatic plants in general are divided into three main groups: *rooted* plants, *floating* plants and *bunch* plants. Rooted plants are those which require individual planting, have long roots and are purchased in a rooted condition. Bunch plants are a type of rooted plant; they are purchased without roots, by the bunch, and are best planted by the bunch. They will usually develop roots as they grow. Floating plants are those which normally float upon the surface of the water and are not planted into aquarium sand.

Special plant lights are available at your pet store.

AMAZON SWORD PLANT, *Echinodorus brevipedicellatus*

The most popular of the rooted plants is the Amazon Sword Plant, *Echinodorus brevipedicellatus*. It is a rooted plant that may have from 30 to 40 leaves coming off the main stem, much like a stalk of celery. It is a rather delicate plant and must not be subjected to plant-molesting cichlids or plant-eating snails. It reproduces by runners which should be weighted into the sand at the various points at which baby plants begin to sprout. It does well with moderate to heavy light, and gets along well on 12 hours of daily electric light. As the leaves turn brown they should be removed. If other than outer leaves begin to discolor, the plant is not getting enough light and it should be exposed to either more light, or stronger light.

Fertilizers are not necessary to propagate this beauty, but they will do a bit better in a large flower pot ½ full of fertilizer loam or garden potting soil topped with coarse gravel; fill the rest with sand.

Once the plant has been set it shouldn't be removed unless absolutely necessary. When planting make sure the crown of the plant is above the sand level, though all the roots must be buried beneath the sand. If algae grow upon the leaves the plant is receiving too much light. This algae must be removed by rubbing leaves gently between your fingers, or by the use of an algacide.

This Amazon Sword Plant has a medium-size leaf. In the aquarium the leaves are not expected to grow more than about 11 inches.

This is the broad-leaf type of Amazon Sword Plant. In the wild the leaves grow as much as 15 inches long and 3 inches wide.

CAPE FEAR SPATTERDOCK, *Nuphar sagittifolia*

The Cape Fear Spatterdock is one of the more popular of the American plants. It has beautiful green, delicate leaves, not too disimilar to the Amazon Sword Plant leaf. Propagation is both vegetative and sexual. The root or rhizome (like a tuber) is usually purchased from the store and this is planted in the sand. Most of the time it will grow beautifully into a grand, 8 inch high plant; other times the root begins to rot and the plant is worthless. When purchasing these plants be sure that a luxurious growth of leaves has already been started. Squeeze the root to be sure that·it isn't soft and mushy. Smell the root. If it has a foul odor keep on looking. If possible dip the end of the plant (root) into some

31

Cryptocoryne legroi. Photo by Rudolf Zukal.

A closeup of the inflorescence and
seed pod of *Cryptocoryne legroi.*

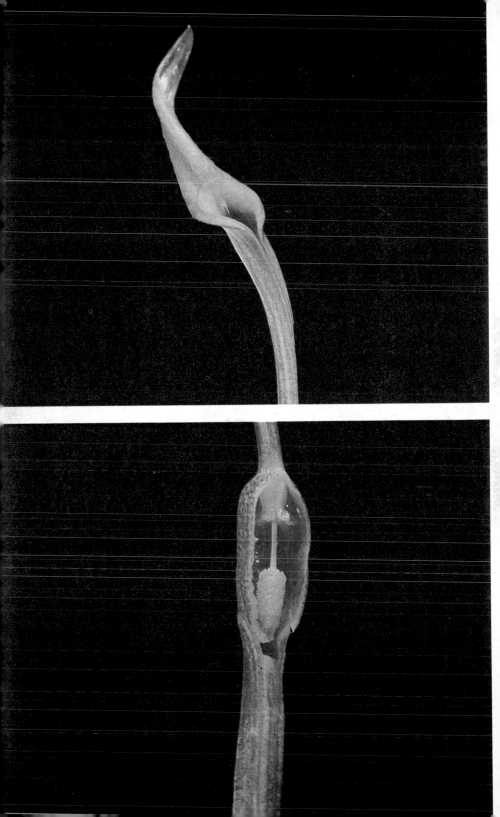

Cape Fear Spatterdock, *Nuphar sagittifolia.* Photo by Dr. Herbert R. Axelrod.

plant hormones manufactured just for this purpose. This seems to stimulate the growth and cut down on decay. Does best in acid water.

CRYPTOCORYNE species

There are many, many species of *Cryptocoryne* plants now available to the aquarist. Not too long ago these Far Eastern plants were a rarity. Now that local breeders have gotten the knack of raising them they are in profusion. The plants do well in a slightly acid environment (6.8 to 6.4) with OVERHEAD light. Side lighting doesn't seem to suit this group of plants and they never seem to do well in this type of situation.

On an expedition to Singapore and Malaysia, the author (HRA) photographed Yeok Ong and his assistant as they were collecting *Cryptocoryne* plants in a shallow ditch. Ong ships millions of these plants annually.

Propagation is usually by runners, and a good plant will produce 20 plants a year without any trouble provided they are not overcrowded. The plant requires little light, indeed many profess that the plant does better in the darker situation. Thus, if limited light is available, try one of this variety of plants.

It is not uncommon for a single plant to grow two different kinds of leaves. Several single plants of the author (HRA) have some mottled underside leaves, while on the same plant other leaves are a bright, unmottled green. Since these plants have not been raised in the tank it must be attributed to a change in conditions. New plants are all uniform.

If kept in the large aquarium some species will tend to grow large, while other species will always be small. The popular smaller species are

Three species of *Cryptocoryne*: from right to left, *willisii*, *beckettii* and *cordata*. Photo by Dr. Herbert R. Axelrod.

C. beckettii, C. willisii, C. cordata, while *C. griffithi* and *C. ciliata* grow to 8 or 10 inches in length. New species of *Cryptocoryne* arrive every year as the plant ships easily if kept in moist newspaper.

Breeders use a soil-sand mixture in propagating the 'Cryp's'; this is not necessary for the home aquarium.

EEL GRASS, *Vallisneria spiralis*

Vallisneria is oftentimes called Eel Grass or Italian Val. It is a straight grass type plant which reproduces rapidly by runners when in a well lighted environment. It does well when planted densely close to a glass which has to be shaded in order to cut down on the amount of light reaching the aquarium. It isn't too long before this plant covers the floor of the aquarium.

Planting should be carried out with care as the crowns of the plant must be above the soil level.

Echinodorus subulatus, above. Cryptocoryne petchii, below. Photos by Rudolf Zukal.

Echinodorus major is only one of the newer and more rare imports. The keeping of rare aquarium plants is just as rewarding as keeping rare fishes. Some aquarists make more money raising scarce plants than scarce fishes. Photo by Rudolf Zukal.

Corkscrew Vallisneria,
V. spiralis. This is a
very beautiful species.

Vallisneria blossom showing
a seed coming out of
the seed pod.

Common Eelgrass,
Vallisneria torta.

Several varieties of *Vallisneria* are available. The Corkscrew variety is the same as the Italian variety except the leaves curl around like a corkscrew. Giant Val is a Florida variety which grows two feet long and the leaf is over ½ inch wide. These plants are widely used by breeders in pools of livebearers. They harvest both fishes and plants at the same time.

Echinodorus radicans

Another member of the very large genus *Echinodorus* is this beautiful plant, *E. radicans*. At one time the plant was mistakenly called a *Sagittaria*, but it since has been correctly identified. It is not recommended for the large aquarium for it tends to grow into a lily-like plant with aerial and floating leaves, leaving nothing much except stems below the water level. If there is little light given to the plant, thus retarding its growth there is a fair chance that the plant will maintain its leaves below the water mark, but this is only fairly easy to accomplish. Many aquarists grow the plant well in the small aquarium and when it has many leaves they will transfer it to the larger aquarium where the longer leaves are still submerged and the plant shows up very well. This plant flowers very easily and the seeds are easily propagated. It requires little light.

Aponogeton undulatum

The Madagascar Sword Plant is a real beauty. Propagation is very easy. Though the plant flowers easily, very few seeds develop. Most of the plants in the home aquarium came to this country as small bulbs imported from the Far East. Actually the plant comes from Ceylon. The bulbs are fairly large and may develop into as many as three separate plants. The plant does well in a well lighted aquarium and soon fills the whole aquarium with its many leaves. Unfortunately the leaves tend to float on the surface and the stems tend to get longer and longer. By constantly transplanting the plant may be kept in a semi-constant state of flowering.

Echinodorus radicans, one of the rare aquarium beauties.   *Aponogeton fenestralis x undulatum* (accomplished by Albert Greenberg).

Brown outer leaves should be removed as soon as possible. The plant should always be kept trimmed. It is fast growing and does well without any added fertilizers. The plant grows to 24 or 30 inches in length in an 18 inches high aquarium.

THE MADAGASCAR LACE PLANT, *Aponogeton fenestralis*

This beautiful plant is only now becoming a 'medium' priced item, and it is gradually creeping into the 'most popular' class of aquarium foliage. Leaves are tough, yet the stems are delicate and snap easily. The plant requires moderate light, slightly alkaline water, a bit of fertilizer or aquarium dirt to enrich the sand and a few snails to help it maintain clean lattice-work. The Madagascar Lace Plant is, without a doubt, one of the most beautiful of aquarium plants. It is usually imported directly from Madagascar in a bulb form.

PIGMY CHAIN SWORD PLANT, *Echinodorus intermedius*

The Pigmy Chain Sword Plant, *Echinodorus intermedius*, is a miniature of the larger Amazon Sword Plant to which it is closely related.

A very rare and difficult to find plant is *Aponogeton echinotus*. Photo by Rudolf Zukal.

Aponogeton ulvaceus, above; below Cryptocoryne lucens. Photos by Rudolf Zukal.

Closeup of the leaf of the Madagascar Lace Plant, *Aponongeton fenestralis*. According to the best authorities, all that you need to grow these very delicate plants is alkaline gravel and lots of light. The photo below shows a mature Madagascar Lace Plant.

Though it has a tendency to greater and faster reproduction than the larger plant, it makes an ideal center piece plant for the 1, 2 or 5 gallon aquarium as it rarely gets higher than 4 inches. Runners should be cut as soon as they start growing if the plant is used for a center piece. This will make the plant grow more bushy instead of being extended. In the larger aquarium, if left uncut, it will cover the whole bottom of the tank in a few months. It does as well in relatively weak light as in strong light. It is very variable in its needs and is hardy. It should be planted, as all rooted plants, with its crown above the sand level.

WATER ORCHID, *Spiranthes odorata*

A native plant of Florida, this bog-plant has only recently been adapted to the aquarium. Not really an aquatic plant, it grows on bogs, marshes, semi-submerged, fully submerged and even wholly above water.

The Pygmy Chain Sword Plant, *Echinodorus intermedius*. This plant makes an ideal foreground plant and, with plenty of light, it can carpet the whole bottom of your aquarium with a beautiful short, thick growth. Photo by G.J.M. Timmerman.

Its well-being in the aquarium seems totally dependent upon the amount of light it receives. At least 8 hours of good strong light is required. The heavy, fleshy roots are necessary for the plant to live; don't buy this species unless it has a fully developed root system.

Undoubtedly the Water Orchid does best in a soil-sand medium. A well aged aquarium with plenty of fish waste on the bottom is a fair substitute. In this environment the plant will flower upon occasion.

Sagittaria species

Another favorite grassy type plant is *Sagittaria*. Several species of this plant are cultivated for the home aquarium. They all have the same requirements, other than size of aquarium, and differ only in their size. All reproduce principally by runners and are a fast growing plant when

The Water Orchid, *Spiranthes odorata*. Photo by Dr. Herbert R. Axelrod.

Echinodorus horemani, named to honor Thomas Horeman of London, above. *Echinodorus berteroi*, below. Photos by Rudolf Zukal.

Echinodorus quadricostatus showing a mother plant with runner, above. *Echinodorus aschersonianus*, below. Photos by Rudolf Zukal.

Sagittaria gigantea.

Comparison of three types of Sagittaria, from left to right: S. subulata, S. natans, and S. microfolia.
Gene Wolfsheimer Aquaphoto.

in a suitable environment. Their needs are simple: clean, clear, aged, water, plenty of light and they prefer a well stocked tank (stocked with fish that is!!).

Giant Sagittaria, *Sagittaria gigantea*, is the largest species. It grows to two feet long and over $\frac{1}{2}$ inch wide, and it is best suited for the larger aquarium, over 200 gallons. Its growth is less rapid than the smaller varieties and it is harder to maintain. This is undoubtedly due to its being cultivated in the wild and not under aquarium conditions.

S. natans is the familiar, popular 'Sag' which grows about 8 inches long and is easily cultivated. It has long been an aquarium favorite and is usually found in most aquaria.

A string of *Sagittaria microfolia.*

Sagittaria subulata.

S. subulata is a similar species though its leaves are narrow and much thicker. It takes on a much greener and more sturdy appearance than *S. natans*.

S. microfolia, sometimes called 'Dwarf Sag' is much like the 'Pigmy Chain Sword Plant.' It is seldom over 3 inches high and it takes on an attractive bushy appearance.

All *Sagittaria* should be carefully planted being sure that the crowns of the plants are not buried beneath the sand. With proper lighting this species makes a beautiful arrangement. Many aquarists set up an aquarium simply with varieties of this single genus of plants, the tall grass in the background and the shorter species in the foreground.

WATER SPRITE, *Ceratopteris thalictroides*

Water Sprite is one of the in-between plants which does equally well as a rooted plant or as a floating plant. It grows and propagates when planted, but as the leaves get longer and float to the surface, baby plants appear on the floating leaves and pretty soon the top is covered with the floating Water Sprite. Once this happens the bottom plant begins to die and must be replaced.

The plant is fast growing and is a favorite with many of the advanced hobbyists.

The general appearance reminds the author of a carrot top!

Left: Water Sprite, *Ceratopteris thalictroides.* Right: Water Sprite, *Ceratopteris thalictroides.* Depending upon the depth of water, amount of light and whether the plant is floating or planted, the shape of the leaf may vary.

Sagittaria subulata. Photo by Rudolf Zukal.

Sagittaria platyphylla. Drawing from the *Encyclopedia of Water Plants* by Dr. Jiri Stodola.

HAIR GRASS, *Eleocharis acicularis*

Hair Grass, sometimes called Needle Grass, is 'something different' for the aquarium. The plant looks much like ordinary grass except that the 'blades' are cylindrical rather than flat. A good growth is nearly entirely dependent upon sufficient light, and unless light is available at least 8 hours a day there is little use in even attempting to utilize this plant.

When purchased, the grass is bunched and tied together with a lead strip or rubber band. The brown stems should be removed and the grass should be planted in clumps. It makes excellent spawning grass both for live bearers and for egglayers.

The plant originates in Georgia and Florida where it grows wild on the exposed banks of ponds and streams. Most of the commercial grass available is from wild stock so examine it carefully for parasites and other harmful organisms.

Hygrophila polysperma

This plant, very often mistakenly called *Hydrophilia*, is only now becoming an aquarium favorite. It is a rooted plant which does well when planted in bunches. Small rootlets come out of every leaf-stem junction and the lower leaves begin to fall off when the plant is first introduced into a new environment. After a week or so of settling down, the plant begins to come into its own and before long it has become a magnificent growth.

Interestingly enough this plant is the only member of its genus that isn't terrestrial.

Cabomba caroliniana

Cabomba is one of the oldest friends of the aquarist. It is one of the most versatile too. A fast growing plant, needing 8 hours of strong light a day, the plant may reach lengths of 2 to 3 feet.

Planting should be accomplished by cutting off the lower inch of the bunch as it comes from the dealer. Next strip off the leaves from the bottom inch of the plant and press it firmly into the gravel, in a bunch. Do not fasten at the base with a strip of lead or with a rubber band. In no time at all it will take hold and grow beautifully in 2 to 3 inches of gravel.

The plant is a popular 'spawning grass' and is very useful in breeding both egglaying species and the livebearers. Inspection of the bunch prior to purchase should reveal crisp, green stems and leaves, without odor and not slimy to the touch. If the plant is turning brown, it should not be used.

A comparison of *Cabomba caroliniana* and *Cabomba aquatica*.

Hair grass, *Eleocharis acicularis*.

Hygrophila polysperma.

Eleocharis acicularis. Drawing from the *Encyclopedia of Water Plants* by Dr. Jiri Stodola.

Cryptocoryne pontederifolia. Photo by Rudolf Zukal.

Sagittaria graminea. Photo by Rudolf Zukal.

Fanwort, *Cabomba caroliniana*, is less demanding with respect to light requirements than other species.

A cultivated form of *Elodea* popularly called Giant Anacharis. It comes from South America.

ANACHARIS, *Elodea*

Elodea is in the same category as *Cabomba*. It comes in bunches and should be planted in clusters with the lower parts of the plant being treated as per *Cabomba*. It requires at least 8 hours of good light or it will grow into a stringy mess. If the leaves are turning brown when the plant is first purchased, the plant will soon perish and the leaves will foul the tank in short order. Only very crisp, dark green plants should be selected. If possible, try to obtain tank-bred varieties, even if the price is a little higher.

When breeding livebearers some bunches may be planted while others should be allowed to float about on the surface of the water. Most fishes seem to enjoy picking at the leaves a bit, but the plant is so fast-growing that there never seems to be much of a permanent damage to the plant.

MILFOIL, *Myriophyllum spicatum*

The long, fine leaves of this plant afford maximum efficiency in catching the eggs of the egg-laying fishes. It needs plenty of strong light to maintain its closely knit leaves. When such light is available, the plant will grow astoundingly fast, sometimes as much as 3 or 4 inches per week.

Myriophyllum should be planted the same way as *Cabomba*, and many inexperienced aquarists might even mistake this plant for *Cabomba*, so closely do they resemble each other. Should growth be too rapid, the plant may be trimmed and the lower parts disposed of, using the upper part to replace it.

The leaves of *Myriophyllum* are much finer and more closely knit than those of *Cabomba*.

Two stems of *Myriophyllum spicatum*, right, and one stem of *M. prosperinacoides*.

HORNWORT, *Ceratophyllum demersum*

This submerged aquatic plant is one of the best spawning grasses available to the aquarist. The plant itself has weak stems and grows to 8 feet in length in Nature. There are never any roots. The plant does well in hard water with little light. It gives off an odor at times and for that reason isn't too welcome in most aquaria, but its fine knit leaves and dense growth make it a superior plant for spawning fishes.

If the bottom is stuck deeply into the gravel the plant will grow beautifully up to the surface of the water in a magnificent spray.

The plant is found in Cuba and southern United States.

Myriophyllym scabratum. Photo by Rudolf Zukal.

Echinodorus cordifolius. Photo by Rudolf Zukal.

Cabomba is one of the most beautiful aquarium plants. However, it requires plenty of light in order to show its best appearance. Photo by Rudolf Zukal.

Hornwort, *Ceratophyllum demersum*.

Another species of *Ceratophyllum*. This type is excellent spawning grass.

Fontinalis gracilis

For a breeding grass easily found in the temperate climates, needing very little light, and ideal for breeding the *"Panchax"* fishes, there is none better than *Fontinalis*.

The plant is commonly known as Willowmoss and is easily collected. It attaches itself to any kind of base, be it an old water-soaked log, a bit

Ambulia is often mistaken for *Cabomba* or *Myriophyllum*.

Fontinalis gracilis, one of the best spawning grasses. It requires little light and is very hardy. A Gene Wolfsheimer Aquaphoto.

of stone or even a tin can, it is easily picked up by the handfuls. Wild plants should be thoroughly washed and sterilized.

LUDWIGIA

Though not a true water plant, *Ludwigia* has, nevertheless found its way into those aquaria where light and richly fertilized sand is available.

Ludwigia, like the other bunch plants, tends to become very stringy and dies if sufficient light is not available. The beautiful red under-leaf species, grown so successfully in greenhouses and ponds in Florida, rarely ever maintains itself in a home aquarium.

Eleocharis vivipara. Drawing from the *Encyclopedia of Water Plants* by Dr. Jiri Stodola.

Hygrophila polysperma. Drawing from the *Encyclopedia of Water Plants* by Dr. Jiri Stodola.

Ludwigia natans, also called L. mullertii, is distributed mainly from North Carolina to Florida and Mexico. Photo by G. J. M. Timmerman.

The fact that *Ludwigia* does best in a rich soil culture bears out the fact that it is primarily a bog plant. Reproduction can be accomplished vegetatively, that is, the parent plant may be divided into smaller plants by merely snipping off a piece and planting it in a suitable environment.

BACOPA, *Bacopa caroliniana*

Bacopa is a plant much like *Ludwigia*. It requires more light than the latter and its leaves are slightly fragrant. The plant isn't quite as popular as it has a right to be, for it does well in 6 hours of light-per-day aquaria.

The reason for its lack of popularity is possibly due to the growers who don't favor the plant much because it is a slower grower and doesn't do well in the brightly lit pools in which other plants are raised.

WATER HYACINTH, *Eichhornia crassipes*

One of the pest plants in the South is Water Hyacinth. So rapidly and densely do they propagate that they usually make waterways impassable in a matter of weeks. The plant has use in the outdoor pool for the shading effect it has for other submerged plants and as a spawning medium. Its dense fine roots suit the purpose of many fishes, especially the bubble-nest builders and goldfish.

Needle Leaf Ludwigia or Purslane, *Ludwigia natans* (?). This is not a common aquarium plant.

Green Ludwigia, incorrectly called *L. mullerti*. Probably *Ludwigia palustris*, the Water Seed Box.

Water Hedge, *Didiplis diandra*, from North Carolina. A delicate little plant.

Aquatic Baby Tears, *Helxine* species. This is a beautiful aquarium decoration.

Ludwigia palustris. Photo by Rudolf Zukal.

Ludwigia brevipes. Photo by Rudolf Zukal.

Close-up view of the flower of *Bacopa amplexicaulis*. Photo by Rudolf Zukal.

The ever-popular Banana Plant.

Najas microdon, a tropical species, does well in breeding tanks even in the absence of bottom soil. Photo by G.J.M. Timmerman.

Two very popular plants that float. Left, Water Hyacinth and right, Water Lettuce. These are excellent plants for bubblenest builders and Goldfish. Baby Livebearers also find refuge among the dense roots. Photos by Dr. C.D. Sculthorpe.

It is impossible to maintain this plant in the home aquarium for any length of time for it needs many hours of direct sunlight every day.

When it blooms, the flowers are beautiful and grow to a foot in height. It is not to be considered as a valuable aquarium plant though it is quite commonly sold in most pet shops. As a pool plant it is ideal.

Flowers only last one day in the aquarium.

SPANISH MOSS, *Tillandsia usneiodes*

Here is an aerial plant which is used in the aquarium only after it is dead and cured. The plant itself is several feet long and is found hanging in irregular profusion from all sorts of projections be they tree limbs, telephone wires or what have you. The plant is common from Virginia south to Florida and west to Texas.

Spanish Moss is commercially valuable to the furniture industry where it is used as upholstery stuffing. Some packers even use it for insulation. Aquarists use it after the outer skin has been taken off and only the fine, dark inner strands are left. The color is then boiled out of it and the plant makes the best known breeding grass, for after each use it can be washed out and hung up to dry until it is needed again. Since the plant is dead when it is being used it requires no light and doesn't seem to decay even after many years of usage.

Eichhornia azurea growing in great masses in its native waters in South America. Photo by Harald Schultz.

A cluster of flowers of the Water Hyacinth, *Eichhornia crassipes*. Photo by Paul Stetson.

A dense growth of Water Hyacinth can affect the normal circulation and aeration of natural waterways. Photo by Harald Schultz of *Eichhornia crassipes* in the jungles of the Amazon.

Members of the genus *Anubias* are best suited for terrariums. These plants grow best partially out of the water and in temperatures higher than 77 degrees F. Photo by Rudolf Zukal.

Spanish Moss hanging from the trees in Florida's citrus groves.

If used without a series of boilings, it will discolor the water and tend to make the pH slightly lower, toward the acid side. This has a certain value, and American aquarists are finding it a suitable substitute for peat moss.

Nitella

Nitella is a form of stonewort, or Charales, one of the groups of plants forming the connecting link between the algae and the flowering plants. It looks much like emaciated *Cabomba*. It has a fine, long main stem from which very fine filaments protrude in all directions. It doesn't root and is excellent for use when spawning egg-layers and livebearers. Most fishes enjoy eating the plant: *Scatophagus*, barbs, swordtails and some cichlids go for it in a big way.

This is one of the best plants for aging and testing aquarium water. If a handful of crisp, green *Nitella* is placed into the newly set-up aquarium and it flourishes for a few days, then the tank may be assumed to be safe for fishes. If, however, the *Nitella* starts to turn brown and decay, then another clump of *Nitella* must be introduced, for it is sure that when the first clump was put in, the water was unsafe for fishes, but that first clump might have treated the water sufficiently for it to be safe for fishes.

Nitella is a fast growing plant and should be kept thinned out.

70

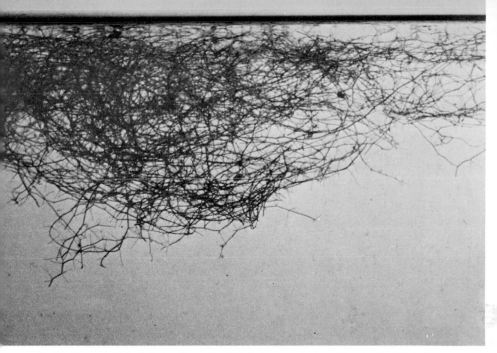

The Bladderwort, *Utricularia*, is often sold as *Nitella* by many dealers. Photo by Dr. C.D. Sculthorpe.

Some nest-building fish such as the Dwarf Gourami, *Colisa lalia*, generally prefer to incorporate plant material like *Nitella* or *Utricularia* in their nests. Photo by Rudolf Zukal.

Water Wisteria, *Synnema triflorum*, is a good-looking, fast-growing, and easy to keep aquarium plant. The leaves are also very variable, ranging from very feathery types to almost undivided forms. Photo by Rudolf Zukal.

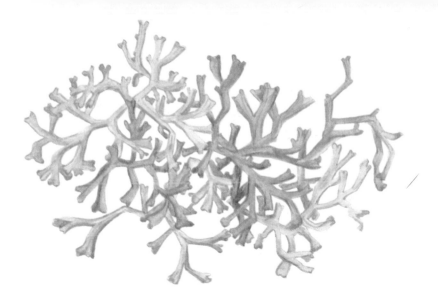

Riccia fluitans, Crystalwort. Drawing from the *Encyclopedia of Water Plants* by Dr. Jiri Stodola.

Two species of floating plants. *Salvinia* (larger leaves with fine hairs) and *Lemna* (small oval leaves) with a bubblenest in the central part of the picture.

CRYSTALWORT, *Riccia*

Riccia is a floating plant with many and varied uses. It is ideal for the bubble-nest builders, it is soft enough for newborn livebearers to creep into for protection, it may be used as a food for the vegetarians among the fishes, it can be used as a shading plant and it can also be used in breeding certain egglaying species if it is held down under the water in some manner.

Riccia needs plenty of light and unless it gets at least 6 hours of strong light a day it will stop growing and start to decay. The plant is found throughout the eastern Atlantic states from Virginia south to Florida in nearly all of the shaded pools and lakes. Care should be taken when collecting the wild plants to insure that no parasites are introduced with the plants.

DUCKWEED, *Lemna minor*

Duckweed appears as one or more egg-shaped thin floating plants with only a single root. It is found in Nature floating on the top of stagnant waters or washed up on shores of slow moving bodies of fresh water, from Nova Scotia to Florida and westward to the Pacific.

The plant propagates vegetatively at terrific speeds and in a sunny, humid environment it will cover the surface of the water. The plant serves as a food for ducks and pheasants in the wild, and when introduced into a *Daphnia* pond they greatly increase the yield of the 'bugs' but make them difficult to separate from the plants.

Dried Duckweed when ground up makes an excellent culture medium for Infusorians. Merely add a few pinches to aged aquarium water and place it in the sun.

SALVINIA

Salvinia is a South American version of Duckweed. Its leaves are a bit more circular but it certainly isn't to be considered better than the American plant by any means. It requires the same care as Duckweed and propagates exactly in the same manner.

WATER LETTUCE and WATER LILIES

Water Lettuce, like water lilies, has little value in the home aquarium. In Nature they are considered as pests, but for ponds they are attractive and controllable. Many hybrids of the water lily have been developed and some of the flowers are extremely beautiful.

In the breeding pool during the summer months these plants may be used for shade and for hiding grass, but other than that they have little value for aquarists.

Water Lettuce, *Pistia stratiotes*, can be grown to provide some shade for outdoor pools. However, the plants have to be thinned out before the whole pond is overgrown by this very fast-growing species. Photo by Dr. C.D. Sculthorpe.

An example of a well-planned planted aquarium which can be used as a community fish tank. There is ample space for the fish to swim about, including some hiding places (beneath the root decorations) for shy fishes. Photo by Rudolf Zukal.

The water of Lake Malawi in Africa is so clear that at a depth of 20 feet Dr. Herbert R. Axelrod was able to photograph a school of *Haplochromis* feeding in the grassy areas of the lake.

This is the typical habitat of the rock-dwelling Mbuna Cichlids along the shores of Lake Malawi. The upper layers of the lake are rich in oxygen in contrast to the lower depths, where oxygen is absent and the water incapable of supporting life. Photo by Dr. Herbert R. Axelrod.

WATER

One of our first lessons in chemistry is that water is composed of two parts of hydrogen and one part of oxygen. This definition holds good for water in its purest form, and the only way we can arrive at water as pure as this is to manufacture it chemically or to get it by distilling impure water.

Pure water is of little practical use to the aquarist because it does not occur naturally; however, it provides a convenient base line from which to begin. Having no chemical components whatsoever besides the elements which make it up, it is neither acid nor alkaline, but perfectly neutral. As there is no calcium content, it has no hardness, and our scale of "degrees of hardness" begins here. As for acidity, there is a scale known as the pH scale, which is a method of measuring the percentage of hydrogen ions in a liquid. This scale begins with the strongest acids, which would measure pH 1, and ends with the strongest alkalis, which go as high as pH 14. Water in its pure state, being neutral, comes in the center of the scale, pH 7. Waters which harbor fish life usually range between pH 4 and pH 9, so our aquarium water readings should occur within this range.

A freshwater stream in Camatagua, Venezuela. Note the presence of "white water," indicative of the rapid rate of flow of water. The speed of water flow influences the oxygen content of the water. Photo by Dr. Herbert R. Axelrod.

There are pH kits available at your dealers which are accurate and quite inexpensive. Every aquarist who expects better than mediocre success should be able to analyze his water both as to pH and DH (DH is the abbreviation for Deutsche Hartgrad or "Degrees of Hardness"). Probably the simplest pH kit consists of a strip of sensitized paper which comes with a color chart. A reading is obtained by dipping the paper into the water and then comparing with the color chart for a reading. This is a good rough test, but sometimes the paper changes slightly due to weather conditions or age. A better kit provides a small vial, with a set of colors and a bottle of indicator fluid, usually bromthymol blue. The water is brought to a mark in the vial and a specified amount of indicator is added. This tints the water. Neutral water would show green, shading to yellow on the acid side or blue on the alkaline. A comparison with standard colors tells what the reading is.

A simple but effective kit for testing the pH of the aquarium water.

Aquarists can purchase products that keep the pH of the water at a fairly constant reading by chemically buffering the water against changes in pH away from the level chosen as desirable; they can be tailored to maintaining the water at a neutral, acidic or alkaline level.

Hardness in the water usually results from the presence of dissolved calcium and magnesium salts. Some fishes simply refuse to breed, nor do they remain healthy, unless the water is fairly soft. Others require a certain amount of hardness in the water. Therefore it behooves the aquarist to know how he stands in regard to the water hardness in his aquaria, and to know as well what the requirements of his fishes are. Until the last decade or so, this phase of water chemistry was ignored by aquarists, and since its importance has become evident, the spawning of certain 'problem fishes' has become a relatively simple matter. There are two types of water hardness testing kits available to aquarists; both are fairly accurate and inexpensive. One consists of a vial and a special liquid soap. A measured amount of water to be tested is put into the vial, and a drop of soap is added and the water shaken. Then the process is repeated drop by drop until a lather is produced. The number of drops used tells us the hardness of the water. Another kit consists of three bottles and a vial. The water to be tested is placed in the vial until it reaches a specified mark. Then a drop of ♯1 solution is added and shaken in, to be followed by a drop of ♯2 solution, which turns the water to a wine-red color. The third solution is then added, shaking it in drop by drop. The number of drops it takes to turn the solution from wine-red to blue is equal to the degrees of hardness of the water. A check of the water in your aquaria may result in some surprises. Your petshop will be able to show you many water test kits.

Generally the recommended type of water for keeping Mollies such as this black *Poecilia mexicana* is hard, alkaline water with temperature between 78° and 84°F. When kept too long in acid water mollies are likely to develop fin rot. Photo by Stanislav Frank.

Many Rivulins like this Red Spotted Aphyosemion, *Aphyosemion cognatum*, do best when kept in soft, acid, and well-aged water. However, some hobbyists prefer to maintain their fish in slightly alkaline water for hygenic reasons. Bacteria tend to increase faster in acid water.

The Butterfly Barb, *Capoeta hulstaerti*, from the Congo. Be sure this fish is kept in neutral to acid water only, for they are very delicate. Photo by Dr. Herbert R. Axelrod.

The Scat, *Scatophagus argus*, is a well-known estuarine and marine fish frequently found in river mouths, estuaries, and even in coral reefs of the tropical Indo-Pacific. Although Scats can live in fresh water, soft water is not suited to them. Photo by Dr. Herbert R. Axelrod.

One of the most important sources of water to be tested is your tap water. If this water is nearly neutral and measures less than 8 degrees of hardness, you may call yourself a lucky individual; after it has been allowed to stand for a week or so, very little adjustment is necessary for most fishes. Most tap water will be found to be quite hard and also alkaline, especially when the water comes from a region which is rich in limestone. Fortunately it is possible to soften hard water quite easily. There are several commercial brands of acrylic resin water softener crystals. Most pet dealers are able to supply these crystals packed in a convenient nylon bag. This bag may be hung in the aquarium, or better still, placed in a filter where a constant stream of water will circulate through it. This will bring down the water hardness in a day or two, depending on the amount and hardness of the water. When a test shows that the water coming through the filter is of the same hardness as the water in the aquarium, it may be assumed that the crystals have become discharged. Do not throw them away; they may be recharged again by rinsing the bag in clean water and then placing it in a solution of two tablespoons of table salt in a pint of water and allowing it to stand overnight. The bag is then rinsed out again in clean water and is ready for action once more.

A word of caution should be injected here: do not change too abruptly the pH or hardness of water in which fish are being kept. Your fishes must experience these changes gradually. A sudden change could easily cause death. When changing fishes from one aquarium to another, make sure that the two aquaria contain water with approximately the same pH and DH readings. Many mysterious fish deaths, where an apparently healthy specimen is transferred to another aquarium and then dies, is attributable to failure to observe this simple precaution. If a fish shows distress, such as gasping at the surface and inability to maintain balance when changed from one aquarium to another, a test will usually show a wide dissimilarity of water values, and the fish is in great danger if the water is not adjusted. Acid water may be adjusted by adding some sodium bicarbonate or mixing with alkaline tap water. Alkaline water may be acidified by adding sodium biphosphate or by filtering it through peat moss. The latter method supplies the more natural humic acid and is preferable because the method of adding it makes the transition more gradual.

Requirements vary for different fishes, and will be discussed under the general requirements for each fish species or group.

AQUARIUM GRAVEL AND ROCKS

The use of gravel in a breeding aquarium has often been the unsuspected cause of annoyance to an aquarist. He sets up his aquarium and adjusts the water to the necessary value of whatever fish he is trying to breed. All seems well, but there is a lack of cooperation on the part of the breeding fish when they are added. The water is tested again and found to be strongly alkaline and hard. Why? Many gravels are rich in mineral content; some of this is washed away when the gravel is cleaned, but the sad truth is that much is released gradually. This can be highly annoying when we are working with a fish which requires soft, acid water.

It is possible to work with a minimum of gravel when breeding most fishes. When plants are used, such as bushy plants which serve as a spawning medium, they can be replaced by such substitutes as Spanish moss or a bundle of nylon yarn. We are inclined to favor the nylon yarn, as it is soft and does not break down like Spanish moss; it has the added advantage that it can be sterilized by boiling and used over and over. Some fishes prefer to spawn in an aquarium which is too dark to support plants properly, and the use of plant substitutes obviates the necessity of providing enough light for plants to grow well. Of course, this is not to say that plants cannot be used where there is enough light and where appearance must be taken into consideration. Here also, a minimum of gravel may be used; a bundle of floating plants makes an excellent refuge for newly born live-bearers, and these plants require no anchorage, having no roots. Where the spawning habits of fish are such that plant stalks or leaves are used to hold the eggs, these plants may be planted in small pots. There is also a group of fishes which do a lot of digging in the gravel for the purpose of providing safe spots for their young. Here we would be upsetting their natural habits by not providing gravel for them, so it must be provided; in this case a few simple precautions may be taken. If a sample handful of gravel is placed in some soft water for a day or two and does not harden it, it may be assumed to be safe for use. If however the hardness becomes greater, the gravel should be either discarded for another lot or it may be treated by leaving it in a mild solution of hydrochloric acid and then rinsing it thoroughly.

Many cichlids like the Jack Dempsey (*Cichlasoma octofasciatum*), above, and the Convict Cichlid (*Cichlasoma facetum*), below, usually fight each other and dig the bottom, especially during breeding. The gravel bottom chosen should be free of noxious materials and should consist of particles which are neither too large for the fish to mouth nor too fine to injure their gills. Upper photo by Rudolf Zukal, lower photo by G. Marcuse.

The addition of some spawning grass (natural or artificial) for breeding annuals like the Golden Pheasant, *Aphyosemion* (*Roloffia*) *occidentalis*, is extremely helpful. It not only protects the eggs from possible mechanical injury but also makes the retrieval of individual eggs very easy. Eggs laid directly on gravel bottom could very well get lost and crushed between the gravel particles. Photo by Hans Joachim Richter.

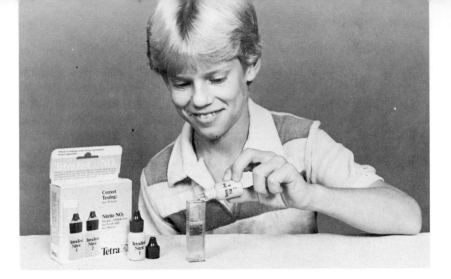

Kits that make it possible for the aquarist to test for nitrite levels as well as kits for testing for pH and hardness levels are available at pet shops and aquarium specialty stores.

All that has been said about gravel also applies to decorative rocks. Of course, rocks need not be used in a breeding aquarium; fishes which normally breed on rock surfaces or rock caverns will accept such substitutes as an old flower pot or a cracked teacup. However, as a matter of general information, rocks should be of a non-metallic nature, and should be free of limestone. The best rocks are those of a basaltic nature. A rock suspected of undesirable chemical properties may be treated with hydrochloric acid solution as outlined for gravel. Many times we hear the complaint that "My tank is very pretty, but I just can't seem to keep fish alive in it!" This mystery can often be cleared up by testing the water. If it is very hard, the culprit can usually be traced to either the gravel or the rocks used.

A number of manufactured products do a very good job of simulating rocky ledges and caves and can be used to good advantage with fishes that like to hide.

FOOD

It is truly amazing how many people who own fish are very diet conscious and dose themselves regularly with vitamins, and at the same time will feed their fish entirely with a single commercial preparation.

This preparation may contain a scientifically prepared fish food which has great quantities of nourishing ingredients incorporated in its formula; the fact remains that they are only a substitute, and often a poor one, for what the fish would get in its natural habitat. We are not running down the prepared foods; far from it. One thing must be made clear, however: these prepared foods are usually adequate for sustenance, but the addition of living foods or their frozen or freeze-dried form is practically a "must" for fish conditioning if spawning is to be expected. Every successful breeder knows and makes use of this fact.

In the large hatcheries in Europe, Hong Kong and Singapore, they have a boy who walks up and down among the rows of tanks, carrying a bucket of live *Tubifex* or *Daphnia*. His job is to inspect each tank and make sure there are *Daphnia* hopping in it. If there are none, he must add a supply which is adequate but not enough to crowd the tank. In this way there is a constant supply of living food at hand at all times for all fish, and they can eat all they want at any time. And woe betide the boy if he overfeeds and a tank fouls!

How does this constant temptation to gorge themselves affect the fish? They gorge, and grow at a terrific rate. A tropical fish is not adversely affected by eating too much; he knows when to stop. What does the harm when the fish are overfed is that there is uneaten food left, which decays, clouds the tank and provides food for huge swarms of unwanted organisms, which in turn attack the fish. For this reason, it is always recommended to give several small feedings per day. Feeding three times as much at one time is no substitute for three lighter feedings. If your fish do not clean up whatever prepared food you give them in five minutes, you are feeding too much. This uneaten food deteriorates very quickly in a heated aquarium, and once it decays most fish will no longer touch it. Of course, when we are dealing with live foods such as *Daphnia*, we can be a bit more generous. This is the principle used by the commercial breeders. They feel that if a tank is not crowded and there is living food on hand at all times, a fish is getting better than natural conditions.

Atlantic marine worms spawning on the surface of the sea off the coast of New Jersey. Most of these worms ultimately become food for other animals in the area. Photo by Dr. Herbert R. Axelrod.

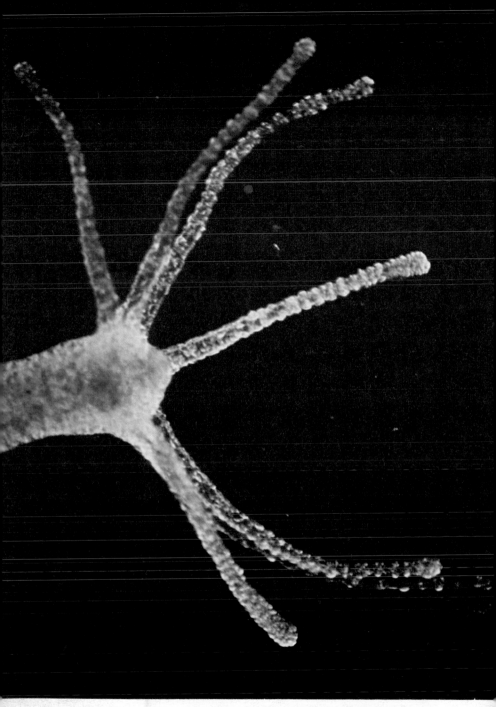

Under the proper conditions, Hydras accidentally introduced into an aquarium can increase in numbers rapidly and can endanger the fish. Small fishes and the fry in particular can both become victims of these coelenterates, which are equipped with prehensile tentacles armed with paralyzing stinging cells. Photo by Dr. H. Reichenbach-Klinke.

It may safely be assumed that a high percentage of fry from egg-laying fishes which hatch from breedings by inexperienced aquarists die of starvation. A newly-hatched fish which has used up all of the sustenance in its yolk-sac is in a very critical stage of development and will waste away and die in a short time if there is no food to be had. This is the one time in a fish's life when it cannot stand the slightest deprivation.

Adult brine shrimp showing eggs.

In their natural state, most fishes do not breed indiscriminately the year round. The urge generally comes upon them at the first weeks of the rainy season, when food is plentiful and the water is clean. At this time, the waters cover more territory than they do usually, washing a great deal of vegetation and other organic matter into pools, river and stream beds. This periodic organic enrichment of natural bodies of water encourages the growth of many organisms that are a fish's food supply. The simultaneous appearance of tiny food organisms and newly hatched fry always seems to be coincidental, but it is an essential part of nature's design in providing adequate food for the youngsters.

These are conditions we must strive to create in the aquarium; fortunately this is not always difficult. The first food we will discuss in this section consists of the microscopic creatures that our tiny fry prefer.

INFUSORIA. Every body of water which is capable of supporting life harbors a certain amount of protozoan animalcules which we group here under the title of "infusoria." These creatures depend upon decaying organic matter for their sustenance.

In their natural state, fishes can move about seeking areas rich in natural foods. In the aquarium, things are quite different; our fish cannot move around when things are not satisfactory; they must accept them, and if things go badly, they suffer. Many aquarists have abandoned the use of infusoria and substituted newly hatched brine shrimp as the first food for egg-laying fry, but in the case of very small fry, such as those of the Gouramis, the young must have infusoria at first or most of them will die.

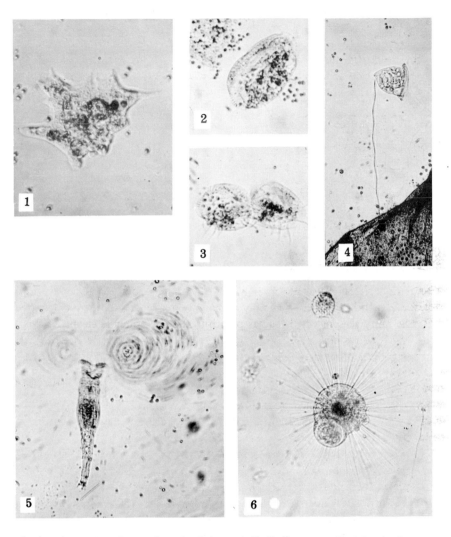

1. *Amoeba proteus* is excellent food for larger newborn fry.

2. A small ciliate sometimes found in infusoria cultures.

3. Same as 2 except showing the cell reproducing.

4. *Vorticella,* an excellent fry food.

5. A Rotifer showing the vortices formed by ciliary action.

6. The Sun animalcule, *Actinophrys sol,* a good food. Photomicrographs from Dr. C. W. Emmens.

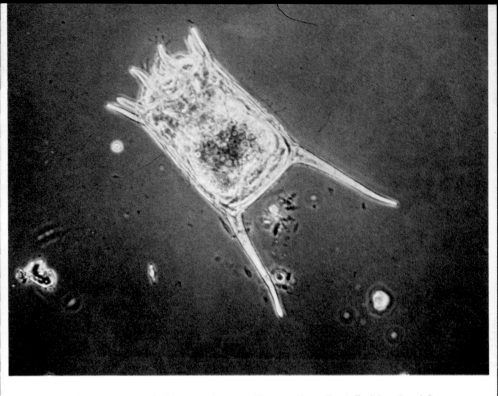

Rotifers are easy to find in natural waters. These rotifers, *Keratella* (above) and *Brachionis* (below), can be collected in ponds and pools where water lillies grow. Rotifers are not protozoans, but it is not unusual to see them among infusorians. Photos by Frickhinger.

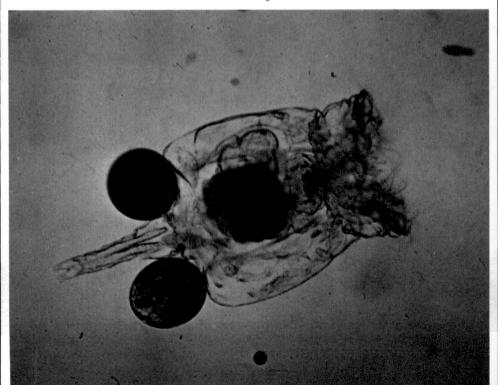

Diaptomus female with eggs. *Cyclops* and *Diaptomus* comprise most of the freshwater copepods found in nature.

There are many methods of culturing infusoria. Practically all of them work well, and we will list some of the favorite media. The principle is always the same: to break down some vegetable matter by decomposition in water, thereby providing bacterial food for swarms of infusorian life. Microscopic though they may be, infusoria can be seen easily with the naked eye when they form dust-like clouds in the water.

Some of the media used may vary from banana peels, hay, lettuce leaves, potato peels, peas, beans or the like. There are also infusoria tablets available containing powdered and pressed vegetable matter which breaks down rapidly in water.

The method usually recommended is to start an infusoria culture with 4 or 5 one quart jars. Place a bit of culture medium in each jar after filling with clean aged water and add a few drops of aquarium water. This culture should be set up at about the time the fish spawn. When the fry begin to swim, the culture jars should contain cloudy water. If there is a strong odor, you are using too much culture medium. The water should be dumped and a fresh culture started. This is the reason for a number of culture jars; if one goes bad, there are others. Feed by adding a pint of culture to the aquarium which contains the fry, being careful that the water is of the same temperature. Refill the culture jar by replacing the water removed with fresh aged water. Rotate your good cultures. Your fry will soon grow to a size where they can consume larger foods.

Several mail order firms offer starting cultures of most live foods. See a current issue of *Tropical Fish Hobbyist* magazine for a good selection of these firms.

BRINE SHRIMP. This wonderful food was made available to aquarists during the late 1940's, when it was found that the eggs of *Artemia salina*, the Brine Shrimp, could be gathered in quantity and made commercially available to aquarists the world over. The amazing thing about them is that the eggs withstand drying for long periods of time, retaining their viability like plant seeds. This makes it possible for the aquarist to provide himself with a quantity of small, living crustacea at any time he needs them. These newly hatched shrimp do not have a hard shell, and can readily be torn to bits by most small fishes.

There are two prime sources of supply, one from the vicinity of San Francisco, Cal., and the other from Ogden, Utah. In time there may be more; this shrimp has a wide range, and it is not at all impossible that there are heavy concentrations elsewhere. The Utah variety seems to be a bit larger than the other, and contains more DDT. Get San Francisco shrimp eggs if possible.

Hatching the eggs is simplicity itself: a gallon jar is filled with tap water; to this is added 4 tablespoonfuls of non-iodized table salt. (If you are using Utah eggs, the addition of 2 level tablespoonfuls of bicarbonate besides the salt is recommended). Then add half a teaspoonful of eggs and agitate vigorously by putting in an air releaser. Eggs will hatch in 36 to 48 hours. To remove the shrimp, take out the air releaser and allow the jar to stand for a while, giving the unhatched eggs a chance to settle. Then siphon out about half the water into an empty jar, allowing it to filter through a clean cloth. The shrimp gather in an orange-colored mass, and are fed into the tanks from this mass. The salt water is replaced into the original jar, the air releaser replaced and a small amount of eggs is added again, to make up for the shrimp removed. If you do not have facilities for aeration, the shrimp may be hatched by using a shallow enameled pan, such as is used for roasting. Enclose about one-quarter of the pan with a thin wooden slat, but leaving a space of about $\frac{1}{4}$ inch at the bottom. The eggs are placed in this smaller section, and the shrimp when they hatch will swim through the open space at the bottom into the clear section, which will contain no eggs or shells, only water and shrimp. Separate and feed by the same method as before.

Hatch the eggs in total darkness for best results. Intermittent aeration, one minute every hour is best if the shrimp are not overcrowded.

Ocean water is highly preferable to the substitute article, and those who live near the seashore will find that by using this, the percentage of hatched eggs will increase.

Quick-frozen Brine Shrimp may at times be purchased in two sizes: newly hatched and adult. The adult size, about $\frac{1}{2}$ inch in length, makes an acceptable food for medium-sized or larger fishes. However, we find that newly-hatched Brine Shrimp makes a more nourishing food for fishes of all sizes. It can be swallowed or picked to pieces by most fry, and the larger fishes seem to prefer it too. There is more food value in the smaller-sized shrimp. The shell, gills and swimmerets of the larger ones offer little in the way of nourishment; these are much less developed in the young stages, and the body is almost 100% nourishment.

The frozen baby Brine Shrimp make an excellent first food for some fry, but it must be kept in mind that, being dead, they sink to the bottom. Fish which feed near the middle of the water or just under the surface would get little benefit from the frozen Brine Shrimp. However, bottom-feeding fry of barbs or catfishes would get them concentrated right where they would look for them, and would do very well.

Better than frozen shrimp is freeze dried Brine Shrimp. Freeze dried

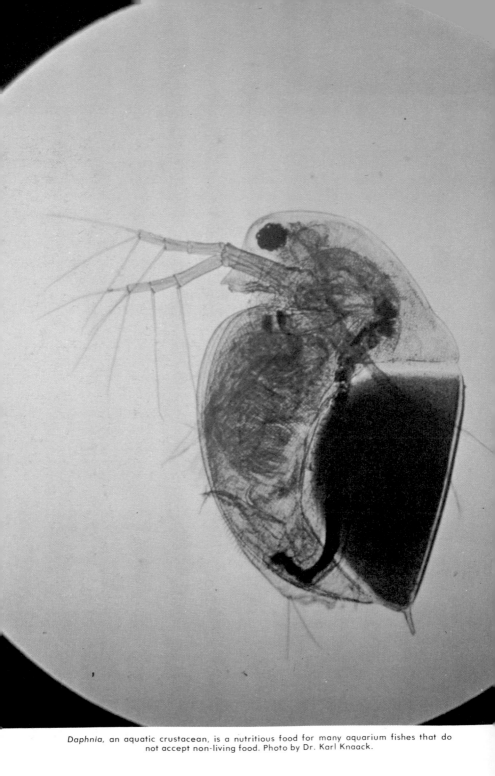

Daphnia, an aquatic crustacean, is a nutritious food for many aquarium fishes that do not accept non-living food. Photo by Dr. Karl Knaack.

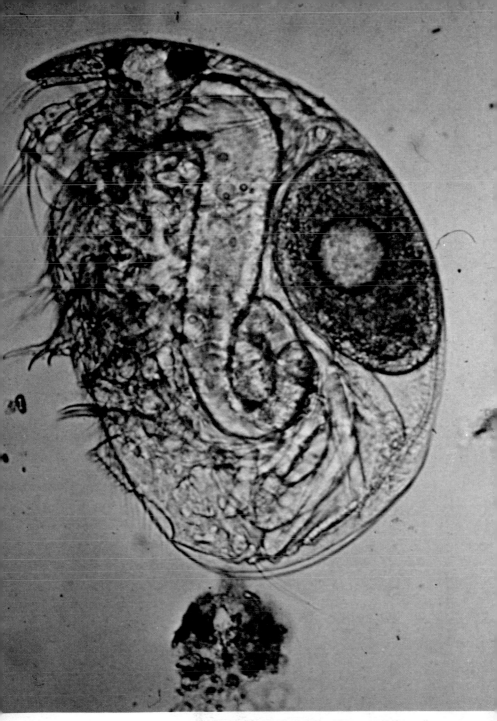

Bosmina is another popular water flea used as food of fishes. They are much smaller than *Daphnia* and are thus excellent food for newly hatched fry. Photo by Dr. H. Reichenback-Klinke.

Brine Shrimp is undoubtedly the best prepared food available for all tropical aquarium fishes.

DAPHNIA. The aquarist who is within collecting distance of a reliable source of *Daphnia* may well consider himself fortunate. This has always been deemed to be one of the choicest items on the aquarium fish's menu.

Daphnia occur in numbers in partly stagnant waters where there is an abundance of decaying vegetable matter and not too much fish life. They are small crustaceans, averaging about the size of a pin-head, and are sometimes bright red in color. The popular name "water fleas" suggests their shape and their hopping manner of swimming, but they are not insects. They are crustaceans.

When conditions are right, they occur in swarms near the banks; the swarms are so dense that they appear as orange or red blotches in the water. A long-handled cheesecloth net is used to sift them from the water. The amount gathered should not be too great, or they will die and be useless before they get to their destination. In hot weather, put a chunk of ice into the collecting pail, which should be covered and just large enough that it can be carried without too much effort. This slows down the body processes and permits the *Daphnia* to stay alive without consuming too much oxygen. When you get back home, feed your fish generously and store the rest in as large a container as you can give them. If you can aerate them, so much the better. The excess can be frozen.

BOSMINA . In your search for *Daphnia,* you may come upon another valuable living food which resembles *Daphnia* to a great extent, except that it is about half the size. These crustaceans are black in color. Look along the shores, near bridge abutments or in the vicinity of weed clusters for swarms of these organisms. They will look like a cloud of black pepper in the water. Being smaller than *Daphnia,* a rather fine net is required. They withstand very little crowding in the collecting can, and do not keep well, but they make one of the finest foods available for young fishes, which consume them greedily and grow at a great rate as a result. Spring and early summer is the time when *Bosmina* are most numerous.

MOSQUITO LARVAE. Here we have what doubtless forms the bulk of the food consumed by most tropical fishes in nature. Many regions in the tropics would be practically uninhabitable to man if the larvae of these pests were not eaten by fishes. An active fish can consume its own weight in mosquito larvæ in the course of a day. Many of our well-known prolific fishes have been introduced into waters which are far from their homes for the purpose of mosquito control, and collectors are often astonished to find a fish in some far-off country which does not belong to that part of the world at all. The author (HRA) found Guppies in Ethiopia and Singapore!

The aquarist who does not mind running the risk of having some of them developing to maturity in his home will find that mosquito larvæ are among the finest foods for aquarium fishes. Development from the larval through the pupal stage to their adult form is much more rapid in a heated aquarium than in the great outdoors, and if feeding is too generous or the larvae too far developed, there is sure to be some unpleasant swatting afterwards.

The eggs of the common mosquito are laid in masses of 20 or 30, all stuck together in a bunch which floats. These are known as "rafts," and soon hatch into tiny larvæ which swim with a wriggling motion and feed on infusoria. Growth, especially in warm weather, is very rapid, and they soon reach the third stage of development, the pupal stage. The forward half of the body becomes round, and instead of swimming with the wriggling motion, they propel themselves much more rapidly with a series of lobsterlike kicks with the tail. If you feed any of these to your fishes, beware! In a short time they are destined to have their skins split open at the head, and a fully grown mosquito will emerge. Your only consolation at this time will be the knowledge that only the females bite!

Despite all these disadvantages, the fact remains that an occasional feeding with mosquito larvæ will do wonders. They lack the hard shell of *Daphnia,* and are more easily digested by a fish. Learn to recognize the little "rafts" and float them in your tanks whenever you find some; in this way you may be fairly sure that the mosquito larvæ will be eaten before they attain maturity.

BLOODWORMS. These are not worms, but the larval form of *Chironomus,* a species of fly. They are a bright red in color and are sometimes found in pools with decaying leaves. Even though they have a somewhat hard shell, they form an excellent food for mature fishes. They are easily recognized by their color and their method of propulsion—snapping their body in and out of an "S" shape. Do not trust them in a tank which contains small fry; they are capable of catching and killing them.

GLASS WORMS. These are the larvæ of *Chaoborus plumicornis,* a fly which greatly resembles a mosquito. They are sometimes found in ponds and ditches, in company with *Daphnia.* Very transparent, the most noticeable part of their bodies is the black eyes. They can be found at almost any time of the year, and this fly spends the winter in its larval form; they may be netted through the ice in places, if you are

A female *Cyclops* with egg sacs. Adult *Cyclops* are known to attack fish, so it is not advisable to give them to very delicate fish or newly hatched fry. Photo by Dr. H. Reichenbach-Klinke.

A swarm of *Cyclops* represented by individuals of varying lengths. In deep lakes, under certain conditions, these crustaceans exhibit vertical migration. At night they ascend towards the surface and at the approach of daylight they move deeper into the lake.

of a rugged constitution and care to go in for that sort of thing. Like the Bloodworm, they are also capable of harming small fry.

OTHER FOODS. There are of course many other crustacean and larval foods which are available to aquarists. The trouble is that they are usually not numerous enough to make them practical. They are, however, worth mentioning.

There is a fresh water shrimp whose habits and appearance are very similar to those of the Brine Shrimp. This is *Chirocephalus grubei,* the Fairy Shrimp. Generally found in woodland pools which are normally dry in the summer, Fairy Shrimp are most apt to show up in the spring months. They are bright red in color, with a black stripe down the back and rather large black eyes. The females attain a length of about 1 inch, and the males are slightly smaller. The under part of the forward half of the body contains rows of feathery swimmerets, which are waved in an undulant motion for propulsion. Strangely enough, they always swim on their backs. The life span is very short, and the females drop bundles of eggs near the shore. Soon the warmer, drier months cause the pools to dry up; the adult shrimp die, and the eggs remain viable in the dry state until the pools are flooded again the following spring. As a food, they are excellent. Larger fish swallow them whole, and the smaller ones tear them to bits.

Netting for *Daphnia* is likely to produce some other even smaller crustaceans which are also suitable for fish food. A common one is Cyclops. It usually shows up a bit earlier in the year than *Daphnia,* but does not swarm, making its collection a tedious task. Fish do not relish them very greatly either; they are capable of rapid locomotion, and most fishes find them difficult to catch. German aquarists rate Cyclops highly as a food and state that immature specimens make the finest food for the fry of most fishes. At the same time, they warn about using mature ones where there are fry present. They do not tell us what to do to prevent uneaten immature ones from growing up in the presence of fry and *becoming* dangerous.

WORMS

TUBIFEX WORMS. We begin the section on worms with the most used of the group. Tubifex worms are red in color, about the diameter of horsehair, and attain a length of about 1½ inches. Most dealers stock them all year, and this is the way we recommend that you get them. If you prefer to try for them yourself, by all means do so. Tubifex worms are found in bodies of water which are rich in organic and vegetable

A close-up view of a mass of live *Tubifex* worms. To forestall possible pollution, the worms should be thoroughly rinsed with water and given in small portions. Uneaten worms can get buried in the gravel, die and pollute the water. Photo by Robert E. Gassington.

wastes. Look for shallow spots where the bottom is muddy. Where the worm population is thick, they form colonies which can be seen as red patches waving in the water. If you are lucky and the colonies are so closely packed that they form a firm bundle, they may then be picked up, rinsed out and be transported home. Usually the colony is not packed, and then it is necessary to remove the worms along with their accompanying mud and debris. Enough water in a pail is then added to slightly more than cover the mud and the smelly mess is allowed to stand in a warm spot for about 2 to 3 hours. By this time the worms find it necessary to avoid suffocation by coming up to the top, and if the mud contains a good percentage of worms, they will form a ball which can be removed. If you have a surplus after feeding, put them in a wide-mouthed jar under a cold-water faucet which is set so that it drips slowly. Properly kept in this manner, they will remain alive for a week; if they begin to die and give off a strong odor, throw them out. Freeze dried worms are excellent, too.

Photographs of fish feeding. Freeze-dried worms are convenient to give and safe to use (the process kills all living organisms), and they are accepted by many fishes like the Cardinal Tetras, Angelfish, Gouramis, etc. Photos by Herbert R. Axelrod.

MICROWORMS. In 1939, a tiny worm was discovered which could be easily cultured and made an excellent food for small fishes. These became known scientifically as *Anguillula silusiæ* and to the aquatic world as "Microworms." They resemble fine threads about $\frac{1}{8}$ inch in length. Culturing them is simplicity itself: 3 parts of oatmeal are mixed with 1 part of yeast, adding enough water to form a thin paste. This is poured into a refrigerator jar of about 1-quart capacity until about $\frac{1}{2}$ inch deep. A small amount of worms is then added and the jar covered and allowed to stand for a couple of days at room temperature. The worms will then be seen clinging to the sides, where they can be removed by running the finger along and picking them up. When the worm population begins to wane, save enough for another culture and start anew with a fresh mixture of culture medium.

GRINDAL WORMS. This is a dwarf form of the White Worm, which was successfully brought from Sweden. A wooden box is filled with an equal mixture of humus and peat moss. This is dampened and the culture of worms is introduced. A thin layer of cooked oatmeal is put in and lightly covered. After 3 to 4 days, the oatmeal will be consumed and feeding should be repeated. Worms are found in clusters, which can be lifted out and fed to the fish. In order to keep the moisture in the earth, cover it with a close-fitting glass cover. If it does become dry anyway, sprinkle lightly with water, but do not drench the soil.

WHITE WORMS. These small cousins of the common earthworm may be cultured in the same manner as the Grindal Worms, which they resemble in every way except that they attain about an inch in length, twice the size of their smaller cousins. We know a very successful breeder of these worms who feeds them any leftover vegetables from his table. He digs a shallow trench across the box and pours in whatever peas, beans, carrots or other vegetables he may have on hand, and gets terrific results.

It must be remembered that these worms are a very rich food, and should not be fed to the exclusion of everything else. Alternate with other foods.

EARTHWORMS. An excellent source of food for fishes is the common earthworm. They are readily available in all but the winter months, and may be kept for a long time during these months by the method described for White Worms, but with a larger box. Of course, it is not advisable to feed a worm in its entirety to any but very large fishes; for most of them it is necessary to cut them up. A sharp pair of scissors is the tool recommended for the job. If you just can't stand having the worm squirming in your fingers while you are trimming away at him, try this: place several worms in a covered plastic refrigerator dish

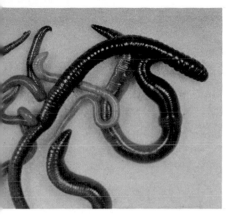

Young and adult earthworms. Some serious aquarists prefer to kill the worms by boiling. They are then chopped and fed to larger fishes like cichlids, gouramis, catfish and other carnivorous fish. Photo by Paul Imgrund.

White worms as they look in their culture medium. Special worm separators are available to force the worms out of the earth. These separators utilize a light bulb on top of the culture. The bulb heats the earth, forcing the worms to go deeper. Under the earth is a screen over some cold water. The worms fall into the water through the screen in an effort to get away from the heat.

and quick-freeze them. When you are ready to feed, take out the amount of worms required and cut off slices with a razor blade on a block of wood. Replenish your supply whenever necessary.

When collecting worms, do not mistake the dungworm for an earthworm; dungworms are dark red in color and smaller than earthworms. They have a foul odor and are usually found in manure piles. Your fish, unless they are almost starved, will refuse to have anything to do with them. The earthworm, *Lumbricus terrestris,* has a pink color, becoming darker at the pointed end, which is the head. The color fades out at the tail, which is somewhat flattened. An easy method of collecting earthworms, known to most fishermen, is to sprinkle the lawn just before dark. After dark, the worms may be seen crawling about when a flashlight is turned on them.

SUBSTITUTES FOR LIVE FOODS. Although there are actually no real substitutes for living fish foods, there are some things which form acceptable items on the menu until live foods are available. If you live near the seashore, you have little need for anything besides what the bays, inlets and creeks have to offer. Bits of crab meat, clams, oysters, shrimp, fish, marine worms, or almost anything else which salt-water fishes might feed on are also acceptable to our fresh-water species. One of the very finest foods along these lines are the small, inch-long grass shrimp which are so numerous in most inlands tidal waters. Crush

Most unpolluted streams, ponds and lakes may contain a small or even a large population of small shrimp like this Grass Shrimp. If fed and aerated sufficiently shrimp can live for a while in captivity also.

one or two and drop them into your aquarium and watch the fish go for them.

Frozen or freeze dried liver, beef heart and shrimp are excellent for almost all fish over one inch long.

There are two things to remember when feeding the above items: they are better raw than cooked, and they will spoil quickly and foul the water if fed in too large amounts. Find out what your fish will clean up in a short time, and never feed any more than this amount.

Swatted flies are another excellent food in your aquarium. Do not make the mistake of picking up flies which have been killed by an insecticide; they will poison whatever unfortunate fish might eat them.

SNAILS IN THE BREEDING AQUARIUM

The question often arises among aquarists as to whether snails are a blessing or a nuisance in the aquarium. Certainly there is no place for them in the breeding aquarium when there are eggs present. There are few things which are as great a delicacy to a hungry snail (and they are almost always hungry) as a freshly laid batch of fish eggs. It would not be so bad if they satisfied their hunger by devouring a few eggs completely, but they seem to take a special delight in breaking as many shells as they can.

On the other hand, snails can and often do find an important job to do in an aquarium where young fishes are being raised. It is sometimes difficult for the aquarist to judge exactly how much to feed his growing fishes. If he underfeeds, his fishes are greatly retarded in growth, a condition which will keep them from becoming large, healthy specimens in later life. If he overfeeds, a much more serious and quicker catastrophe may overtake him: the water fouls, and most of his youngsters will be found lying on the bottom in a very short time. If there are snails to cope with the surplus food, the dangers attendant to overfeeding are greatly minimized.

Snails have been accused of producing more droppings than they pick up. To expect a snail to clean up droppings left by fish is just as ridiculous as expecting the *Corydoras* catfish to do the same. Both will do an excellent job of cleaning up food left by other fishes, but to expect them to eat feces is just a little too much.

Shown here is a type of aquarium snail frequently handled and sold in many pet shops. To a very limited extent some snails may be desirable in certain fish tanks. Excess snails can always be used as food of large carnivorous fishes. Photo by J.A. Cavalier.

Up to the 1920's, a number of snails was considered a very necessary and desirable thing for the "balanced" aquarium. The theory was that the fish leavings would support the snails, that the droppings of the snails would provide the plants with a supply of nitrogen, and that the plants in turn would give off oxygen, replacing the oxygen consumed by the fishes. This was accepted for many years, and was finally exploded when it was proven that an aquarium without plants got almost as much oxygen as a heavily-planted one, and that in the hours of darkness the plants competed with the fishes for oxygen by also consuming it, rather than giving it off.

So now we ask ourselves, what is the function, if any, of the snail in the aquarium? A good filter keeps the aquarium clean by sifting out the dirt from the water, and helps to boost the oxygen content by circulating the water as well, so why use snails? The one function which a snail performs is to convert left-over food into droppings which are readily broken down and then either absorbed by the plants or sifted out by the filter. Another use to which they are put by many aquarists is as food for the larger fishes, to whom they are fed crushed or chopped up into "bite size" when smaller fishes are being fed.

There was still another use for snails which has since fallen by the wayside, but which might be of some interest to our younger readers, who would not have heard of it: there was a large, sluggish snail which grew to almost the size of a man's fist if given plenty of food and room. These were known as "Nurse-maid" or "Infusoria Snails"; the scientific name is *Ampullaria gigas*. They were given a tank to themselves and fed plenty of lettuce. Their gluttony soon resulted in a goodly amount

Pond snail of the genus *Melania*. Snails help keep the aquarium glass clean by eating the algae, but some may also eat other larger living plants in the tank.

Ampullaria cuprina on the left, and *Ampullaria gigas* on the right, photographed at close view. Photo by Dr. Herbert R. Axelrod.

As the eggs hatch, the newborn snails drop into the water. The empty egg case dries up eventually.

Eggs of *Ampullaria* are laid above the water level. They are either pink or white in color.

Ampullaria eggs attached to a tree trunk in the Amazon. The presence of a thick egg case around each egg effectively protects the embryo from dehydration. Photo by Harald Schultz.

Ampullaria gigas, the giant apple snail, comes from South America.

Ampullaria eggs laid in the midst of marsh plants in the Amazon. Note the characteristic pink color of these eggs. Photo by Harald Schultz.

of droppings which contained partly digested lettuce and provided a wonderful source of infusoria. These snails could not be placed in a planted tank, or there would soon be no plants left. They would often crawl out of a tank which was left uncovered and end their mortal span in a corner of the room where a ripe odor betrayed their presence if they were not found. The modern aquarist has less messy methods of culturing infusoria than this one, but it worked well.

For those who want to make use of them, we will go briefly into the various species of snails available today.

The most common snail, which we are most likely to find as a "stowaway" on plants or with live food is the Pond Snail. It is dark brown in color and its shell comes to a point. It is seldom more than ½ inch in length, and its small size has the advantage of permitting it to squeeze into many nooks and crannies, where it does a good job of scavenging. It is a very prolific breeder, and will soon overrun a tank if not thinned out occasionally. Many fishes will eat them if crushed, and they crush easily. The generic name is *Physa*, and there are several species, all of which are very difficult for the layman to distinguish.

The most popular of the aquarium snails is the Red Ramshorn, *Planorbis corneus*. The flat spiral shell of this snail grows to about an inch in diameter, but this size is exceptional. The body is bright red, and the partly transparent shell lets the red color through. As the shell gets thicker, it loses its transparency and becomes brown. Very prolific, and easily raised.

Another snail which is sometimes seen, and quite pretty, is the Colombian Ramshorn, *Marisa rotula*. This one also has a flat spiral shell, and attains a diameter of 1½ inches. The shell is light brown, and has a series of dark brown stripes running lengthwise along the shell. This species and the other two will eat an occasional hole in plants.

We mentioned the supreme glutton among snails, *Ampullaria gigas*. There are several others of the same genus, and one other is worth mentioning. This is the *A. cuprina*, known as the "Mystery Snail." They are not as vegetarian in their appetites as their cousins, confining their table manners to other tidbits in the aquarium. These snails have an interesting manner of spawning: they crawl out above the surface of the water, usually at night, and attach a large pink or white cluster of eggs to the glass or the top of the aquarium, which should be kept covered to discourage further pilgrimage on their part. The eggs, if kept warm and not too dry, hatch in 2 weeks and the young snails fall into the water. This snail is a dark brown in color and grows to the size of a golf ball.

Some freshwater snails: 1, 2 and 3. *Planorbis corneus*, 4. *Ancylus*, 5. *Radix auricularia*, 6. *Limnaea stagnalis*. Photos by Knaack.

A live freshwater crab *(Platythelphusa)* collected from Lake Tanganyika, Africa, shown in three different positions in the home aquarium. Crabs never fail to amuse and fascinate observers. They are not too difficult to keep, but they generally require a tank of their own to keep them from devouring smaller fish or being eaten themselves by much bigger fish. Photos by Dr. Herbert R. Axelrod.

There are many other species of snails, which we do not mention here because of some objectionable trait: some of them spend most of the time burrowing in the gravel, and others have an intolerance to warm water, which makes them unfit for tropical fish aquaria.

THE HABITS OF FISHES

There are three general classes of fishes, when we consider their eating habits: the carnivores or flesh-eaters, the herbivores or plant-eaters, and the omnivores, which eat both plants and animals. Among the aquarium fishes there are no true herbivores, but there are some omnivores with a preference for a herbivorous diet. *Poecilia* [*Mollienesia*] species are a good example of this type of fish, and these fishes do not thrive well if they cannot be fed a good proportion of green food. Most of the other livebearing toothcarps also like a percentage of plant food, but not as much.

117

A pair of Green Sailfin Mollies. They are distributed from Florida to Louisiana, thriving in ditches and canals that are mostly heavy with plant growth. Mollies are omnivorous and apparently cannot live well for long on a steady diet of animal food alone. Vegetable food is indispensable for their normal survival.

The carnivorous fishes have a wide range of foods, all the way from large mammals, which are attacked and skeletonized by huge swarms of the vicious and well-known pirhanas, the *Serrasalmus* species, to the small-mouthed eaters of small plankton like the *Nannostomus* species and many others.

We must cater to the eating habits of our fishes if we are to have any success in propagating them, so it is important to know their eating habits as well as their mode of life in their natural environment.

A fish's habits are very often a good clue to its diet. Take for instance a fish which spends most of its time at the surface: it generally feeds upon insects which fall into the water, or fly near enough to the surface of the water to be captured by jumping, or on smaller fishes which are wont to inhabit the upper layers of the water. The jumpers which catch insects are characterized by large, upturned mouths and well-developed pectoral fins and tail muscles, which give them the needed push to drive them out of the water. On the other hand those which feed on small fish life near the surface have a long, streamlined form; the dorsal fin is set quite far back on the body, and is not very conspicuous; the head is flattened in form and the mouth large. Teeth are usually small and fine, designed to hold the prey previous to swallowing it whole. The caudal muscles are well developed, enabling the fish to propel itself forward rapidly in a vicious lunge when it has stalked its prey. A good example of the fishes which leap out of the water for their prey is the hatchet fishes (*Gasteropelecus, Carnegiella*). The others which stalk their prey and pounce upon it might be typified by the "Panchax" species (*Epiplatys, Aplocheilus*, etc.), and the livebearers.

We now come to the fishes generally found in the middle zone. In flowing waters, we have the well-formed, streamlined fishes which are active swimmers, like the danios (*Brachydanio, Danio*). The middle zone of the quieter waters is generally inhabited by the fishes such as the tetras, which have a tendency to travel in schools (*Hemigrammus, Hyphessobrycon*, etc.). Then there is a group which is more apt to

Close-up photo of a dead Piranha with the lips removed to expose its sharp teeth. . . no wonder piranhas are considered as being the most dangerous fish in the world. They are strictly carnivorous and require live animal food (other fishes mostly) to survive. Photo by Harald Schultz.

Loaches like this *Botia beauforti* are bottom feeders. They are constantly probing the ground for small bits of food with the help of several sensitive barbels around the mouth. Photo by Klaus Paysan.

A rare characid fish, *Synaptolaemus cingulatus* from Upper Xingu River, Brazil. Notice the unusual superior position of the mouth and the striking similarity of this fish to *Leporinus fasciatus*. Photo by Harald Schultz.

Leporinus fasciatus, the Banded Leporinus, is a very attractive bottom-feeding fish. It subsists partially on algae growing on the surfaces of plants and walls of the tank. Photo by Rudolf Zukal.

This dainty little Pencilfish has a tiny mouth. Obviously it would be impossible to raise on large particles of food. They must be fed sifted *Daphnia* or newly hatched brine shrimp. They also relish bits of fine-grained dry food. Photo by Rudolf Zukal.

inhabit the reedy or heavily weeded regions. The species found among reeds are usually strongly compressed laterally, permitting them to move easily among upright stalks. Our well-known angel fish, *Ptero-phyllum scalare*, and the discus fish, *Symphysodon*, are examples here. Others like to browse among the leaves of bushy plants, nibbling on the food which gathers there. These have long, thin bodies and comparatively small fins. The pencil fishes, *Nannostomus* and *Poecilobrycon* species, are good examples.

The next zone we come to is the very bottom of the water. Here there are fishes which get their food by picking it up when it lands there, or by grubbing for living foods. These fishes are provided with underslung mouths, often accompanied by barbels. These "whiskers" are sensory organs, and may be used for locating nutriment. The *Cory-doras* catfishes and the barbs are good examples here.

Other fishes live near the bottom, not because of their feeding habits, but because they find shelter there. They prefer to remain in the neighborhood of rocks and other rubble, and here they raise their families. Many of the cichlids (*Pseudotropheus, Cichlasoma, Aequidens, Apisto-gramma,* etc.) lead this sort of life.

There are also some unusual environments in which fishes are found; one of these is the subterranean cave. Cave fishes sometimes are deprived of all sight, or they may be without functional eyes. These fishes have highly developed organs of taste and touch; they even seem to be provided with a sort of "radar" which prevents them from colliding with obstructions in their path. *Anoptichtys jordani* is one of these fishes.

Parts of South America and Africa have bodies of water which dry up completely during the several months of the dry season. Fry appear in these places as if by magic almost as soon as the water reappears, and grow at a terrific rate, attaining maturity in a very short time. Eggs are laid in the mud bottom and shortly thereafter the holes dry out; the incubation period of these eggs is long and like the brine shrimp eggs, they withstand drying. The parent fishes, their life span at an end, of course die when the water is gone. Most of these fishes are brilliantly colored and of a proper size for aquaria. With a little patience, they are not too difficult to propagate (*Cynolebias, Pterolebias, Nothobranchius*, etc.).

This *Phago* is a very vicious character. With his sharp teeth he has chewed off all the fins on this Head and Tail Light Tetra. It gradually killed the fish and ignored it after it was dead. Photo by G. J. M. Timmerman.

In Africa, there is a fish having another method of withstanding periods of drought. It goes into what the scientists call "estivation," which in some ways is like hibernation. When the waters begin to recede this fish, which is provided with lungs, buries itself in the mud, forming a cocoon, pushing out a hole through which it breathes, and

The elongate body of *Julidochromis ornatus* from Lake Tanganyika enables the fish to move in and out of the crevices of rocks. They are also territorial, and openings or holes in the rocks are fiercely guarded from intruders. Photo by Hilmar Hansen.

A rare carnivorous fish from the Amazon called *Boulengerella*, or Pike-Characin. The close-up view of the fish above shows that the mouth can be opened very wide. It also has the characteristics of a surface-feeding fish. Photos by Harald Schultz.

Ventral view of the Sucker Catfish. The underslung mouth surrounded by a sucker, the flat abdomen, and laterally directed fins are modifications suited for a bottom existence. Photo by Dr. Herbert R. Axelrod.

goes into a state of stupor under which its body processes almost stop. This faint spark of life persists, sometimes over a period of years. When the water returns, some estivating fishes must break out of their shells of mud so that they can come up for an occasional gulp of air or, strange as it seems, they will actually drown! One such is the African Lungfish, *Protopterus*.

Breeding habits vary greatly among different genera, in some cases among different species of the same genus. The various fishes will be treated individually, but it will be a help at this point to review some general features of the breeding habits of all aquarium fishes.

There are three general groups:

The first group of fishes lays its eggs and then allows them to hatch unattended:

1. The eggs are released and either adhere to plants or other objects or fall to the bottom. Most of the barbs and characins spawn in this manner. Some fishes release buoyant eggs, which float at the surface. This is characteristic of the kissing gourami, *Helostoma temminckii*.

2. The eggs are hung individually or in groups from plant leaves. Many of the so-called "Panchax" group spawns in this manner.

3. The eggs are laid in depressions and buried. The *Cynolebias* and *Pterolebias* species do this.

4. The eggs are laid within another animal, which acts as a host until they hatch. The best known fresh-water fish which does this is the European bitterling, *Rhodeus sericeus*. Eggs are laid within the mantle of the fresh-water mussel, where they hatch and then swim out, causing no damage to the mussel.

The second group guards the eggs. This duty is performed by one or the other of the parents, often both:

1. The eggs are laid on a firm object, such as a rock, plant leaf or plant stem, and are subsequently attended by one or both parents. Most of the cichlids and nandids use this method.

2. The eggs are laid on the under surface of an overhanging leaf above the surface, after which the parents splash water on them to keep them moist until the fry hatch and drop into the water. We have records of only one fish, the splashing tetra (*Copeina arnoldi*), spawning in this unusual fashion.

3. The eggs are laid in hidden places and guarded. The only difference between this and the first method is that here the eggs are hidden, rather than laid on an open surface. Some of the African cichlids and nandids prefer to hide their eggs in this manner.

4. The eggs are laid in a depression and guarded. *Tilapia* does this, as well as some American sunfishes, and other cichlids, such as *Geophagus*.

This is *Hoplias malabaricus*. Its sharp teeth and strong body typify the vicious type of aquarium fish that should not be mixed with other fishes regardless of size. Notice the sharp pointed teeth. Photo by G. J. M. Timmerman.

This is a *Barilius* species. They have large mouths and feed on mosquito larvae, small fishes and other living organisms. They are not to be trusted with any long-finned fish.

The cichlid *Geophagus balzani* guarding a clutch of eggs. Photo by Hans J. Richter.

A pair of Orange Chromides, *Etroplus maculatus*, guarding the nest of eggs hanging on the rock. A cave-like situation is created by the presence of an excavation below the rock. Photo by Hans J. Richter.

Above: These Clown Loaches, *Botia macracantha*, are bottom dwelling fish; if they are to prosper at all they should be given some sort of cave to hide in. A coconut shell will suffice. Photo by G. J. M. Timmerman.

Left: one of the headstanding fishes, *Abramites microcephalus*. It spends all of its time looking for food on the bottom. Photo by G. J. M. Timmerman.

Bottom: these Dwarf Cichlids, *Apistogramma ramerizi*, have mouths located in the midline of their bodies. Thus they can be expected to feed in the middle layer of the water. Photo by Gunter Senfft.

Copeina arnoldi, the Splashing Characin, shown with the eggs laid on a piece of glass outside the water. Illustration from *Exotic Aquarium Fishes* by Wm. T. Innes.

5. The eggs are placed in a nest, usually prepared in advance by the male. These nests vary from the underwater structures of the stickle-backs (*Apeltes, Gasterosteus*) to the floating bubble-nests made by some of the anabantids, such as *Colisa, Betta* and *Trichogaster* species.

Now we come to the third group, in which the eggs remain in direct contact with one of the parents:

1. The eggs remain suspended from the female's vent after they are released and fertilized. They do not usually remain there until they hatch, but are brushed off at some time or other. The *Cubanichthys* and *Oryzias* species are examples.

2. The eggs are incubated within the mouth cavity of one of the parents. After hatching, the fry are given further protection by the parent opening the mouth and allowing them to swim in if there is danger. These fishes include *Geophagus, Haplochromis* and some *Tilapia* species.

3. The eggs develop within the body of the female. The fry hatch and are released as free-swimming, fully formed young. These, of course, are the popular livebearing fishes, the poeciliids and the half-beaks.

It now remains to sort the many species now known to aquarists the world over and examine their ways of life, thereby enabling us to give them the conditions they require to keep them in the best of health and enable us to witness the many different ways in which they propagate.

BREEDING PROCEDURES

The aquarium fishes are grouped in the following pages according to their methods of reproduction. The fishes in each group are listed alpha-betically by scientific name at the head of their special section, as well as in the index. These listings are far from complete and the fishes selected as examples are merely those most popular. Consult your pet store or library for the scores of books available on the subject of breeding aquarium fishes.

A pair of Siamese Fighting Fish spawning beneath the bubblenest previously built by the male. The male attempts to retrieve the eggs before they touch the bottom and blows them to the nest above. Since the nest is fragile, aeration should not be applied in their breeding tanks. Photo by Hans Joachim Richter.

A brood of fry leaving the mouth of a female *Geophagus balzani*, a mouthbrooding cichlid from South America. When frightened the fry can get back to the safety of the mouth cavity for a short while. Later the protective instinct diminishes and the young might be eaten. Photo by Hans Joachim Richter.

Another very popular bubble-nesting fish is the Pearl Gourami (*Trichogaster leeri*). The eggs are light and tend to float to the surface, and the male simply pushes each egg into the nest. Pearl Gouramis are very prolific and can keep as many as 1000 eggs in the nest. Photo by Hans Joachim Richter.

Some fishes have very strange eating habits. This South American fish, *Catoprion mento*, relishes eating the scales of unwary fishes. It is equipped with very fine teeth. Photo by Harald Schultz.

Some fishes are very difficult to acclimate to aquarium conditions and, while they may be kept alive and in fairly good health, there is some little element missing which, if provided, would prove a solution to the mystery. In some cases we have a fairly good idea as to what the missing piece in the jig-saw puzzle might be, but it could be something which the average aquarist would find impossible to provide. A fish, for instance, might spawn readily in its native habitat, but only at pressures encountered at the bottom of a lake which is 50 feet deep. Others might become sterile under average shipping conditions. Others might require much more water surface than the aquarist can provide. Still others might subsist on a diet which consists of some insect or plant, or even other fish life native only to their natural environs. These are all hypothetical examples, intended to show how aquarium conditions sometimes do not even come close to approximating natural conditions.

There are some fish which eat only the scales of other fishes (*Catoprion mento*) while still others eat other fish's eyes!

It has been said often that once a fish has been bred in captivity, the ensuing generations which grow up in aquaria are much easier to breed. It may therefore be surprising to a reader who picks up this book a few years hence that certain species are listed as "breeding habits unknown." This does not mean that the species under discussion has never been bred; it merely means that whoever *did* breed it has not at this time made the information public. In a surprisingly short time, a fish which is a brand-new importation at the time of writing can become widely bred and almost commonplace.

Fishes with known breeding habits must be discussed individually. Coming as they do from the far corners of the earth, they have many individual requirements, and it would be impossible to generalize as to what those requirements are.

To a certain extent we may economize on words, however, by making some collective remarks on the care of young. Most fry which are lost are either starved to death or killed with kindness. *There is no excuse for either.* It was once quite an accomplishment for the average amateur breeder to raise a large spawning to maturity. In the old days, not so many of us had aeration and micro-worms and brine shrimp were unknown. First feedings for egg-layers were with infusoria, cultured in

A bunch of frightened Tilapia fry rushing into the safety of the mouth of the mother fish. These two-day old fry are not yet too big to be accommondated in her large buccal space. Photo by Gerhard Marcuse.

the time-honored way with dried banana peels or lettuce; the result was often a smelly mess which contained little infusoria and much bacteria. When the fry became larger, sifted *Daphnia* were fed, followed by bigger *Daphnia*. There is nothing wrong with this method, but today the culturing of infusoria has been greatly simplified with prepared tablets which, used according to directions, give a rich infusoria culture. Sifted *Daphnia* is a wonderful food to follow with; the only drawback is that live *Daphnia* are not always available. In the northern hemisphere *Daphnia* are available in quantity for only 6 months in the year. During the other months, newly hatched brine shrimp or micro-worms serve as substitutes until the youngsters are large enough to take chopped tubifex and white worms.

The newly hatched fry of most egg-layers are quite helpless. They resemble a tiny hairlike thread with a glass bead attached. This bead is the yolk-sac, from which the fish gets its first nourishment. Never feed them while they are in this stage, helplessly hanging from the plants and glass sides or squirming on the bottom. This is the time to fill your quart

Three-day old eggs of *Pseudotropheus auratus*, the Nyasa Golden Cichlid, one of the more popular African imports today. Photo by Dr. D. Terver.

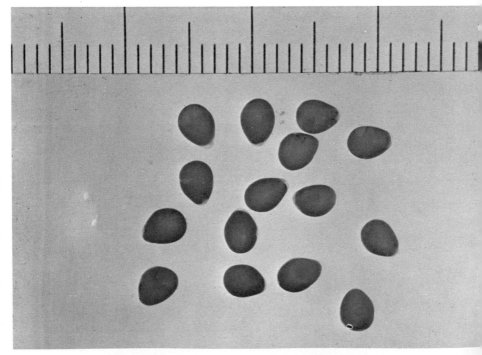

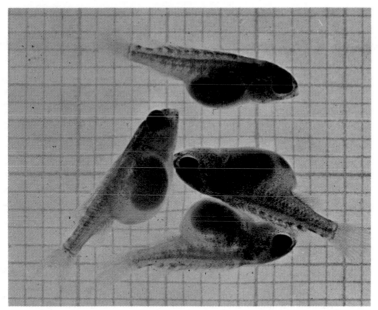

While incubating in the mouth of the mother fish the *Pseudotropheus* fry obtains nutrition from its yolk sac. Photo by Gerhard Marcuse.

With the yolk almost totally consumed, these *Pseudotropheus* fry are ready to feed independently outside the mouth of the female. Photo by Gerhard Marcuse.

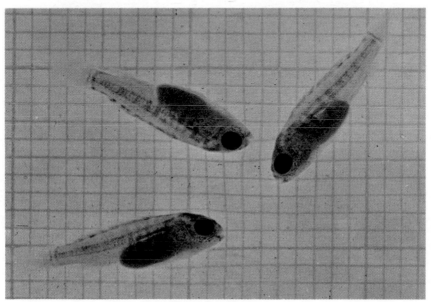

jars and begin the infusoria culture. Some aquarists believe in merely dropping a few infusoria tablets into the aquarium with the newly hatched fry; this is the easy way, but by no means the safe one. When infusoria are cultured with the fry, there is a certain amount of decay, which could be harmful.

Infusoria cultures are much richer and the presence of bacteria is greatly minimized if the water is put into motion gently by aeration.

Do not run any kind of a filter which picks up foreign matter and passes it through glass wool or charcoal. The intake will pick up the fry as well, and many will be lost in this way. The only filter which is safe with small fry is one of the sub-gravel filters, which pulls the water through the bottom gravel. If a youngster should find his way through the gravel into the intake, he will merely be lifted to the surface and released. The usual filters are safe to use again when the fry have grown to a size where they will no longer be pulled in.

When the fry have absorbed their yolk-sacs, they begin to swim, a bit awkwardly at first, but soon with agility. This is the time when food must be provided. There is a certain amount of infusoria always present in the breeding tank, or any other tank for that matter, but this scant population must be greatly augmented if there is to be enough for a good-sized batch of fry.

There are several types of filters available for your aquarium. Shown here are sponge filters, a corner filter and an outside power filter.

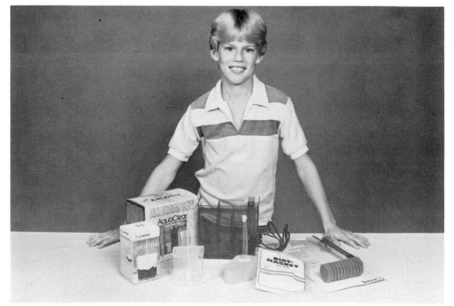

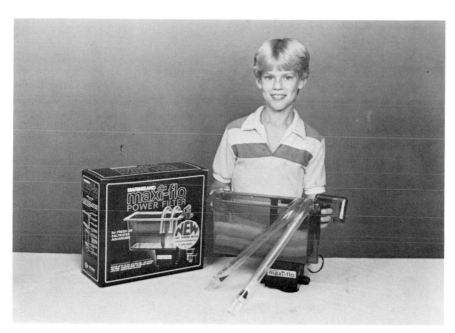

Although an outside filter is efficient in keeping your tank clean, it is definitely not proper to use one in breeding tanks with very young fry which can be trapped helplessly within the filtering mechanism.

After a few days to a week of infusoria feeding, you will find that your fish have grown to such a size that something larger in the way of food is required. Now is the time for micro-worms or newly-hatched brine shrimp. An even better food at this time is *Bosmina* if available, or fine live *Daphnia*. These foods have the advantage of remaining alive in fresh water if uneaten. Avoid feeding so much that the *Daphnia* will compete with the fish for oxygen. Don't worry if there are some *Daphnia* which are too large to be swallowed; they will produce small ones regularly, which will in turn be eaten.

Once your youngsters have really begun to grow, feeding is no more of a problem than taking care of your older fishes. A growing fish should be well fed; as he reaches maturity, his appetite tapers off a bit.

It has been found that infusoria is unnecessary for all but the tiniest fry. The newly hatched or nauplius stage of brine shrimp has such a soft shell that it resembles a tiny counterpart of a crab which has just gone through the "shedding" stage. The body is soft and helpless, and a fish whose mouth is so small that he cannot swallow it whole can easily tear it to bits. Only a few fishes are exceptions and must be started on infusoria; these will be discussed as we come to them.

FIRST GROUP

A. THE EGG SCATTERERS

Anabas testudineus. The Climbing Perch or Walking Fish.
Anoptichthys jordani. The Blind Cave Fish.
Aphyocharax rubripinnis. The Bloodfin.
Astyanax bimaculatus.
    mexicanus.
    mutator.
Brachydanio albolineatus. The Pearl Danio.
    frankei
    nigrofasciatus. The Spotted Danio.
    rerio. The Zebra Danio.
Carassius auratus. The Goldfish.
Carnegiella strigata. The Marbled Hatchetfish.
Chanda buruensis. The East Indian Glassfish.
    ranga. The Glassfish or Glass Perch.
Channa asiatica. The Snakehead.
Characidium fasciatum. The Darter Characin.
Cheirodon axelrodi. The Cardinal Tetra.
Copeina callolepis. The Beautiful-scaled Characin.
Copeina eigenmanni. The Redlined Pencilfish.
Corydoras aeneus. The Bronze Catfish.
    hastatus. The Dwarf or Pygmy Catfish.
    nattereri. The Blue Corydoras.
    paleatus. The Peppered Corydoras.
    rabauti. Rabaut's Corydoras.
Corynopoma riisei. The Swordtail Characin.
Creagrutus beni. The Gold-striped Characin.
Crenuchus spilurus. The Sailfin Characin.
Ctenobrycon spilurus. The Silver Tetra.
Curimatopsis saladensis. The Rose-colored Curimatopsis.
Cyprinodon variegatus. The Sheepshead Minnow.
Cyprinus sp. Koi.
Danio devario.
    malabaricus. The Giant Danio.
Esomus danrica. The Flying Barb.
    malayensis. The Malayan Flying Barb.

A group of Japanese ornamental carp, Koi, spawning in a garden pool. A female Koi can produce a phenomenally large number of eggs (100,000 - 400,000) which are slightly adhesive and are trapped mostly by the feathery roots of the floating plants present, like the Water Lettuce in these photos by Glenn Takeshita.

Exodon paradoxus.
Gephyrocharax atracaudatus. The Platinum Tetra.
Glandulocauda inequalis. The Croaking Tetra.
Gymnocorymbus ternetzi. The Black Tetra or Blackamoor.
Helostoma temminckii. The Kissing Gourami.
Hemigrammus armstrongi. The Golden Tetra.
    caudovittatus. The Tetra from Buenos Aires.
    gracilis. The Glow-light Tetra.
    nanus. The Silver-tipped Tetra.
    ocellifer. The Head-and-tail Light.
    pulcher. The Pretty Tetra or Garnet Tetra.
    rhodostomus. The Rummy-nosed Tetra.
    unilineatus. The Featherfin Tetra.
Hyphessobrycon bifasciatus. The Yellow Tetra.
    callistus. The Jewel Tetra.
    eos. The Dawn Tetra.
    flammeus. The Red Tetra or Tetra from Rio.
    herbertaxelrodi. The Black Neon.
    heterorhabdus. The Flag Tetra.
    innesi. The Neon Tetra.
    pulchripinnis. The Lemon Tetra.
    rosaceus. The Rosy Tetra.
    scholzei. The Black-lined Tetra.
    simulans.
Melanotaenia maccullochi. The Black-lined Rainbow Fish.
    nigrans. The Australian Rainbow Fish.
Metynnis lippincottianus.
Mimagoniates microlepis. The Blue Tetra.
Moenkhausia oligolepis. The Glass Tetra.
    pittieri. The Diamond Tetra.
Nannaethiops unitaeniatus. The African Tetra.
Nannostomus anomalus. The Golden Pencilfish.
    aripirangensis. The Brown Pencilfish.
    marginatus. The One-lined Pencilfish.
    trifasciatus. The Three-lined Pencilfish.
Neolebias ansorgei.
Otocinclus affinis. The Dwarf Otocinclus.
Pantodon buchholzi. The Butterfly Fish.
Petitella georgiae.
Phenacogrammus interruptus. The Congo Tetra.
Phoxinopsis typicus.
Poecilobrycon unifasciatus. The One-lined Pencilfish.

Pristella riddlei. Riddle's Pristella.
Pseudocorynopoma doriae. The Dragonfin.
Puntius conchonius. The Rosy Barb.
    cumingi. Cuming's Barb.
    filamentosus. The Black-spot Barb.
    gelius. The Golden Dwarf Barb.
    nigrofasciatus. The Black Ruby Barb.
    phutunio. The Dwarf Barb or Pygmy Barb.
    sachsi. The Golden Barb.
    stoliczkai. Stoliczka's Barb.
    terio. The One-spot Barb.
    ticto. The Two-spot Barb.
    vittatus.
Barbodes binotatus. The Spotted Barb.
    callipterus.
    dorsimaculatus.
    dunckeri. Duncker's Barb.
    everetti. The Clown Barb.
    fasciatus. The Striped Barb or Zebra Barb.
    hexazona. The Tiger Barb.
    lateristriga. The T-Barb.
    pentazona. The Five-banded Barb.
    trispilos. The African Three-spot Barb.
    unitaeniatus. The Red-finned Barb.
Capoeta arulius.
    chola. The Swamp Barb.
    hulstaerti. The Butterfly Barb.
    oligolepis. The Checkered Barb.
    partipentazona. The Banded Barb.
    semifasciolatus. The Half-banded Barb.
    tetrazona. The Sumatran Tiger Barb.
    titteya. The Cherry Barb.
Rasbora daniconius. The Slender Rasbora.
    einthoveni. The Brilliant Rasbora.
    elegans. The Yellow Rasbora.
    maculata. Spotted Rasbora.
    meinkeni. Meinken's Rasbora.
    trilineata. The Scissor-tail.
Tanichthys albonubes. The White Cloud Mountain Fish.
Telmatherina ladigesi. The Celebes Rainbowfish.
Thayeria obliquua. The Penguin.
    boehlkei.

Well known examples of egg-scattering species of aquarium fishes. Upper photo: Checker Barb, *Capoeta oligolepis*. Lower photo: Pearl Danio, *Brachydanio albolineatus*. Opposite page: Emperor Tetra, *Nematobrycon palmeri*. Photos by Rudolf Zukal.

Group 1a, the egg-scattering fishes, is by far the largest group of fishes with known breeding habits. It includes most of the characins, some of the catfishes, most of the barbs, some of the minnows, as well as some of the smaller families.

Breeding is accomplished by a more or less haphazard scattering of the eggs in all directions; sometimes this is confined to heavily planted sections, and with the *Corydoras* species, the eggs are not scattered but are pasted here and there by the female. The one thing all the fishes in this group have in common is lack of parental care. The eggs are laid and forgotten.

To discourage egg-eating, we must take steps to prevent the eggs from being found. Usually very few are eaten while spawning is going on. A sudden interest in the eggs as caviar is a good indication that spawning is completed. The eggs laid by this group vary in degrees of stickiness to none at all; some are even buoyant and float on the surface. Unlike the floating eggs laid by some of the Bubblenest-Builders, however, they are not given any attention by the parents.

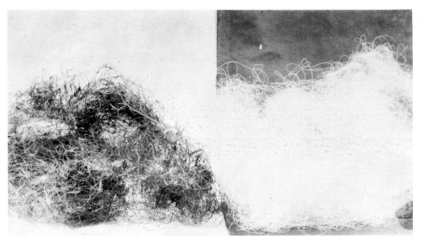

Two types of spawning grass. On the right is a man-made plastic material and on the left is cured Spanish Moss.

One thing we can do to prevent some egg-eating is to cut down on the light. If this source is daylight, shade the tank from the side where sunlight enters. If the light source is artificial, either cut down the wattage if incandescent lighting is used, or shade the fluorescent light source to cut down the brightness. Bright light may show up your fishes in all their gorgeous colors, but it is a detriment when the fishes are spawning.

146

The fishes which spawn among plants can be kept from excessive egg-eating by making the planting so dense that they can just swim through it but cannot readily explore it later when egg-hunting.

Those fishes which lay non-adhesive eggs may be curbed from egg-eating in several ways, all of which result in the eggs falling through some device near the bottom which does not permit the fish to get to them. The simplest of these is a layer of pebbles or glass marbles on the bottom, between which the eggs will settle. The same result can be attained with a grid made of plastic rods which sit on the bottom. This is easily made: get a bundle of round plastic rods and cut enough of them so that they will fit across the long dimension of the bottom of the aquarium. The diameter of the rods should be about $\frac{1}{8}$ inch, and the spaces between about $\frac{1}{16}$ inch. The rods are held in place by cementing them to a plastic strip $\frac{3}{4}$ inch wide and long enough to fit across the narrow part of the aquarium bottom. This results in a grid which will cover all of the aquarium bottom. Use silicone cement to fasten the rods, and allow it to dry thoroughly for several days before using. Another method is to place a layer of Spanish moss or soft nylon knitting yarn on the bottom; an inch of it is enough.

The choice of a breeding tank is also important. The usual rule of thumb is that the smaller varieties do not require as large an aquarium for breeding as the bigger ones. This does not mean that the smaller

An ideal combination for breeding egg-scatterers is to use Spanish Moss over marbles. Usually the fish will shake the moss up a bit during spawning and knock some of the eggs out of the moss. When the eggs fall to the floor of the aquarium they might be easily spotted and the fish would eat them. The marbles prevent them from doing this.

Note the eggs between the fins of this female Bronze Catfish, *Corydoras aeneus*, which is about to attach them on the broad leaf below. Photo by Rudolf Zukal.

In the absence of plants, the eggs are attached to any solid object on hand like the aquarium wall and filter, as this female albino *Corydoras* has just accomplished. Photo by Giovanni Padovani.

Brood care after spawning is not characteristic of the Bronze Catfish or any other *Cory-doras* species. It will be quite practical to remove the parents as soon as they are no longer occupied in spawning. Photo by Dr. Karl Knaack.

A pair of Golden Pencilfish, *Nannostomus anomalus*, almost ready to come side by side and scatter the eggs. The female is on the left and the darker male on the right. Photo by Rudolf Zukal.

Miss Michelle Bolly, A Belgian fish hobbyist and resident of Burundi, Africa, photographed by Dr. Herbert R. Axelrod beside her breeding tanks. These are situated in that part of the dwelling with the least traffic and light.

The well known fish collector Pierre Brichard in Burundi, Africa, keeps his fish in isolation in heavy-duty plastic vats for observation prior to shipment. A record of all deaths and possible causes are also recorded. Photo by Dr. Herbert R. Axelrod.

varieties *should* have smaller tanks. Always use the largest aquarium at your disposal. The advantages of a larger tank are manifold: the fish do not feel cramped and have more areas for spawning to choose from. If the tank is heated, temperature fluctuations are not as great or as rapid in a larger tank. There is less likelihood that as many eggs will be devoured after spawning, because the eggs are spread over a larger area. The fry also stand a greater chance for survival and rapid growth in larger quarters; there is more food in a larger volume of water and less chance that there will not be enough to go around.

Temperature also plays a very important part. A difference of only a few degrees often changes a pair of listless, inactive fish into a glowing, lively pair anxious to begin spawning. Some, of course, require higher and some lower temperatures.

Unless you heat the room in which your tanks are kept, a good thermostatically controlled heater is an excellent investment. The temperature can be held wherever needed, and there is very little fluctuation. The correct wattage is important: reckon 5 watts for each gallon of water to be heated. A heavy duty thermostat can take care of a number of heaters; this can be a disadvantage, too; if the heater in the tank where the thermostat is immersed burns out, the thermostat remains closed and

Rows of molded cement tanks set on very strong supports for holding the bulk of the fish collected by Pierre Brichard from Lake Tanganyika, one of the deepest lakes in the world. Photo by Dr. Herbert R. Axelrod.

Despite the absence of eyes in the Blind Cave Fish, *Anoptichthys jordani*, these fishes are still able to find eggs they have laid earlier with their very keen sense of smell. Photo by Dr. Herbert R. Axelrod.

Anabas testudineus, the Climbing Perch, shown above with normal coloration and in xanthistic form below. Upper photo by Dr. Herbert R. Axelrod.

the other tanks will be overheated. Otherwise, a single thermostat is preferable because it causes less radio and television interference.

Anabas testudineus, the Climbing Perch, has a wide range from southern China throughout southeastern Asia. Chiefly it is kept as a curiosity, being able to wobble along on its fins in a walking motion when taken out of the water. Its color is a dirty olive-green, and it attains a size of 10 inches. It will spawn at about half this size. Water characteristics are unimportant, and the temperature should be about 80°. The male can be distinguished by his slightly larger dorsal and anal fins. A large tank is required, about 30 gallons in capacity, at least. Large numbers of eggs are released, which immediately float to the surface. The young are easily raised and can be started on brine shrimp. Do not keep this fish with smaller fishes in the community aquarium; it is very likely to attack them. A breeding population has, unfortunately, become established in Florida. Hopefully this dangerous fish can be eliminated from Florida's water. Never release *any* fish into *any* natural body of water.

Anoptichthys jordani, the Blind Cave Fish, is another curiosity. It comes from Mexico, where it is found in caves. It is without functional eyes and spends its life in darkness. It is of an overall pinkish color and grows to $3\frac{1}{2}$ inches, becoming mature at $2\frac{1}{2}$ inches. The female is deeper-bodied than the male, and spawning is easily accomplished at a temperature of about 78°. Eggs are scattered in all directions and will be eaten if the parents are not removed immediately afterwards. The young are easily raised and will find every bit of food, even though they are blind. After a few days of infusoria, give them brine shrimp, micro-worms or sifted *Daphnia.*

Aphyocharax rubripinnis, the Bloodfin, is aptly named. This little characin has a silvery body with deep red fins. Its full length is 2 inches, and its disposition peaceful. Being a jumper, the tank should be covered at all times. The only way to distinguish the females is by their heavier bodies and the absence of a tiny reversed hook on the anal fin. Native to South America, the body shape of the fish, elongated and streamlined, tells us that it lives in flowing water. This fish should, there-fore, be provided with a little less heat than most, and will spawn at a temperature of about 75°. Here is a chance to use the grid described previously, or the layer of pebbles or glass marbles. The eggs are non-adhesive and drop to the bottom. Use a long tank of about 8 gallons capacity and put in about $\frac{1}{3}$ aged water of about 10° of hardness. Then add enough fresh water to half fill the tank. If the fish are properly con-ditioned, they will begin chasing actively in a short while. Spawning is

This is the ideal breeding setup. It is a view down one of the aisles in Tutwiler's Tropical Fish Hatchery in Tampa, Florida.

In another section of Tutwiler's fish hatchery you will note that there are large pools under the tanks. These pools receive the fish from the spawning aquaria. After the fishes have reached a fair size, they are transferred to the pools and graded by size prior to shipment. Photos by Dr. Herbert R. Axelrod.

Astyanax bimaculatus. This fish was collected and photographed by Dr. Herbert R. Axelrod in Venezuela.

Astyanax mexicanus, the fish believed to be the ancestor of the Mexican Blind Cave Fish, *Anoptichthys jordani.* Photo by Dr. Herbert R. Axelrod.

A pair of Bloodfins; the female is the heavier lower fish. Photo by Dr. Herbert R. Axelrod.

Aphyocharax axelrodi is a tetra discovered by the author in Trinidad and named in his honor by Dr. Haroldo Travassos. It is popularly called the Calypso Tetra or Red-tailed Pristella. Photo by Dr. Herbert R. Axelrod.

accomplished even while leaping out of the water, the eggs being scattered all over the surface and sinking to the bottom. Incubation period lasts 36 hours, and the fry should be fed on infusoria after they begin swimming. When they begin to grow, follow with brine shrimp, microworms or small *Daphnia*.

Astyanax bimaculatus is a characin which is native to a wide area which includes Trinidad, eastern Venezuela, Guyana, Brazil and even parts of Argentina. This fact tells us that it withstands varying water conditions and is not sensitive in this respect. It is a large fish for the average aquarist, attaining 6 inches in length. Because of this size, it is not advisable to keep it with other fishes which are much smaller. The female has a deeper body, which is just about the only indication of her sex. A breeding tank of about 30 gallons is recommended, water temperature 78°, and a group of bushy plants on one side, into which they will spawn. Young grow rapidly, and should be fed generously. Its size and lack of colors, the two black spots on a silvery body being its only adornment, makes this one of the less popular aquarium fishes.

Astyanax mexicanus is a smaller species of this family and as the name indicates, comes to us from Mexico. It is fully grown at 3 inches, and is distinguished from the preceding species by having two spots on the sides as well as one on the caudal peduncle. Being a smaller fish, it can be bred in a tank of as little as 15 gallons capacity; otherwise what has been said for *A. bimaculatus* holds good. Many states in the U.S.A. prohibit the importation and possession of this characin because it can survive cold waters and is potentially harmful to native fishes by competing with them for food.

Brachydanio albolineatus, the Pearl Danio, comes from Sumatra, Burma, and Thailand. It ranks high in popularity the world over and is one of the hardiest of aquarium fishes, as well as one of the easiest to breed. Its scales all have an iridescent mother-of-pearl sheen and a horizontal orange stripe begins just behind the dorsal region and continues through the middle rays of the caudal fin. A golden color variation of this pretty fish has been developed which has a yellow overcast. The maximum length is $2\frac{1}{2}$ inches, and the slender form again informs us that this fish is native to running water. It is a very active swimmer, and catching them in a heavily planted aquarium can be quite a task.

This fish lays non-adhesive eggs, and some provision should be made to prevent the parents from getting at the eggs after they fall to the bottom. A tank of about 3 gallons capacity may be used, and the water should be brought only about 3 inches above whatever you are using on the bottom. The females may be distinguished by their heavy bellies; the males are considerably more slender, and have slightly more color.

While not absolutely necessary, the use of 2 males to 1 female will result in a higher percentage of fertile eggs. Water conditions are of very little importance, but the addition of ⅓ fresh water to ⅔ aged water will help to induce spawning, if indeed there is any inducement needed. The best breeding temperature is in the neighborhood of 75°. There is a mad chase when breeding activities begin. Every once in a while the female hesitates long enough to let a male catch up, and they assume a side-by-side position and tremblingly the female drops a few eggs which are immediately fertilized by the male. The chase is then resumed with further halts until the female's spawn is depleted. When there is no more chasing and the slenderized form of the female shows that there are no more eggs, the breeders may be removed. The eggs hatch in 2 days and the fry begin to swim in 2 more days. Copious amounts of infusoria are then given for the first 2 days, followed by newly hatched brine shrimp. Feedings of fine-sized prepared foods may also be interspersed; appetites are positively gluttonous, and growth is rapid.

Professional breeders have a very effective method for breeding large numbers of these fish: they separate sexes and feed well until the females are loaded with eggs. They then prepare a box with a screen bottom and float it in a trough, into which a number of breeders are placed. When spawning activities are at their height, there is a regular rain of eggs through the screen bottom.

Brachydanio frankei is a mystery fish. No one knows where it comes from in Nature. Probably it appeared as a sport or as the result of a cross between *B. nigrofasciatus* and *B. rerio*. It is very pretty, easily bred, hardy and peaceful. It breeds true, is very inexpensive and does well in a community aquarium. It breeds like the Pearl Danio and reaches about 2½ inches in length. The scientific name *"frankei"* is not valid.

Brachydanio nigrofasciatus, the Spotted Danio, is the small member of this genus. Its size when fully grown is only 1½ inches. The color is bluish green, becoming lighter toward the belly. The upper half of the body is adorned with darker blue stripes, which break up into rows of dots below. Again, the best way to distinguish the female is by the plumper shape of her body. Breeding and other care is similar to that for the Pearl Danio. This fish has a limited natural range, being found only in Burma.

Brachydanio rerio, the Zebra Danio, is native to Burma. It reaches a size of 2 inches, and is beautifully marked with a series of alternating silver and blue lines which cross the body horizontally and even extend through the caudal and anal fins. Besides the difference in body form, this fish may be sexed in another manner: the female has blue stripes on

Brachydanio frankei, also known as Leopard Danio.

Brachydanio albolineatus, the Pearl Danio. Photo by Dr. Herbert R. Axelrod.

Brachydanio rerio, the Zebra Danio. Photo by Stanislav Frank.

Brachydanio nigrofasciatus, the Spotted Danio. Photo by Dr. Stanislav Frank.

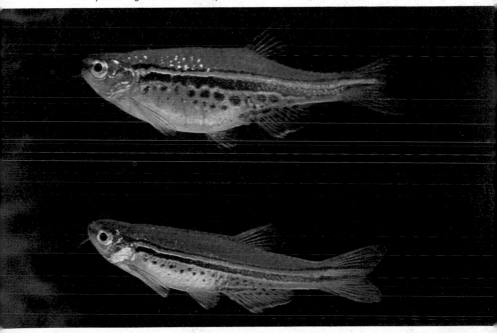

To keep and breed Koi a modest garden pool like this is a must. The broad leaves of the water lilies can provide the fish some protection from too much sunlight while the other plants are purely decorative. Photo by J. Francis Michajluk.

her anal fin with silver stripes interspersed; in the male these lighter stripes are gold.

This is often the first egg-laying fish to be bred by the budding aquarist; methods are exactly as for the Pearl Danio. The eggs hatch in 24 hours.

The Pearl Danio and Zebra Danio have been successfully cross-bred; the results, however, are a fish which looks washed-out and what is more, such hybrids have proven sterile.

Koi, *Cyprinus* species, are Japanese colored carp and are available in many color varieties and color patterns. While small young specimens might survive in the home aquarium, they do much better in an outside pool. Spawning is identical to Goldfish but has never been accomplished in a small home aquarium. There are many Koi books available at your local petshop.

Carassius auratus, the Goldfish, is the granddaddy of all aquarium fishes. It has thrived on more abuse at the hands of uninformed people than any other aquarium fish; we have all seen how they are often kept in small bowls which do not give them any more than a small fraction of the water surface which they require; in spite of this, they keep on living under conditions which would quickly kill any fish less rugged.

This beautiful fish has been bred in captivity by the Chinese since the seventh century A.D., and it stands to reason that in this time many varieties have been developed.

A large aquarium is necessary for breeding Goldfish, the larger the better. This should be well stocked with bushy plants; some breeders use the roots of the Water Hyacinth, which floats on the surface, for catching the eggs. This plant can be removed easily when spawning is over and placed in another container for hatching. To encourage breeding, the water in the aquarium should be raised gradually by about 5 to 10° above that in which the fish were kept. Three males to one female is the usual proportion, and will result in the largest number of fertile eggs. The males soon give chase, and eggs are scattered all over the tank, most of them on the plants. Spawning is usually completed in about 3 hours, after which the parents are removed. Eggs hatch in a week to 10 days, depending on the temperature. Once the yolk-sac has been absorbed and the fry begin swimming, you will usually find that you have been copiously rewarded. A large spawning must be fed regularly and generously. After a week of infusorian diet, which can be helped along somewhat with extra fine prepared food, they must be given something more substantial, such as brine shrimp, small daphnia or bosminae. As the young grow, they will soon become crowded and should be given more roomy quarters.

Carnegiella strigata, the Marbled Hatchetfish, is found in Guyana as well as in the Amazon Basin. This fish is easily distinguished by its deep, slender body and large pectoral fin. The *C. strigata* is small, attaining only 2 inches in length, and is nicely colored: the back is a rich brown, and a black lateral line runs from the gill-cover to the tail base. The fore part of the body is a golden tan, shading to silver in the latter half. The entire lower part of the body is covered with uneven black lines, giving a marbled effect. The males may be distinguished by their slightly larger fins, and are somewhat narrower when viewed from above.

This fish spends most of its time at or near the surface; for this reason, it is particularly difficult to approach its normal conditions. Food which sinks cannot be seen, and the upturned mouth makes it difficult for the fish to pick things off the bottom. Swatted flies are considered a particularly tasty morsel, and *Daphnia* can be made to float by netting

163

Bubble-eye Calico Goldfish.

Variegated Oranda.

Different varieties of Koi. Photograph from *Koi of the World* by Dr. Herbert R. Axelrod.

some and whipping out the water, causing the shells to dry partially. Another excellent food when available is mosquito larvae, which must come up to the surface at intervals to breathe.

This difficulty in feeding makes the *C. strigata* a hard fish to condition properly. It has been spawned, but very infrequently. Being a surface fish, accustomed to open areas, a high temperature is indicated, about 85°. The male drives the female into a patch of floating plants, where they assume a head-to-tail position. Tiny amber-colored eggs are laid, a few at a time. The adults do not eat the eggs, but would probably raise havoc with the fry once they hatched, so there is no point in leaving the parents in the same tank.

The Marbled Hatchetfish, *Carnegiella strigata*. The color differences between the three fish are temporary. Photo by G. J. M. Timmerman.

Chanda buruensis, the East Indian Glassfish, comes not only from the island of Buru, for which it is named, but also from other parts of the Malay Archipelago. It has a very transparent body and attains a length of about 2 inches at maturity. The fins are pink and the body has an amber tint. The female is considerably heavier in body than her mate. We do not see this fish anywhere near as often as its cousin, the *C. ranga,* which is described next.

A pair of East Indian Glassfish, *Chanda buruensis.* The female, the heavier of the two, is the uppermost fish. Photo by G. J. M. Timmerman.

The *Chanda* (also called *Ambassis*) species are native to brackish and even salt water as well as fresh water. It should be given water which is a bit hard (10° to 15° of hardness) and has some salt added. One tablespoonful of salt to each gallon is about right. Breeding temperature should be 80°, and the breeders should be conditioned with generous feedings of living foods. This fish is strictly carnivorous and shows little interest in foods which are not moving. The tank should be large, 15 to 20 gallons in capacity. There should be floating plants provided. The male coaxes the female under the floating vegetation, where she finally sidles up to him and they both do a backward somersault together, releasing the eggs into the plants. These eggs are very tiny, as are the fry when they hatch in less than a day. Infusoria are necessary for these fish at first, but once they begin to grow to the point where they can take larger food, growth is rapid.

Chanda ranga, the Glassfish or Glass Perch, is seen much oftener than the above species. It is a slightly shorter, deeper-bodied fish. A male with the sun shining on him is a thing of real beauty. The body looks like amber-colored glass, and the tip of the first dorsal fin, which is high and pointed, is black. The second dorsal and anal fins, which are usually spread to their utmost, are edged with gleaming, icy blue.

Everything that has been said about keeping and breeding *C. buruensis* also applies to this fish. The habitat is limited to India and Burma. When kept away from other fishes in their own tank, this species often spawns without any other attention, and babies are found swimming

A trio of *Carnegiella strigata*, the Marbled Hatchetfish. Photo by Harald Schultz.

Snakehead, *Channa* species.

The Glassfish, *Chanda ranga*. The male has soft dorsal fin and anal fin edged with light blue. Photo by Rudolf Zukal.

The Burmese Glassfish, *Chanda baculis*. Photo by Dr. Herbert R. Axelrod.

A pair of Glassfish. The female has the heavier body of the two. Notice the light edge of the anal fin of the smaller male. Photo by G. J. M. Timmerman.

around with their parents, who if well fed will pay them no heed. Not an easy fish to raise, however, because of their constant need for living foods of the proper sizes.

Channa asiatica, the Snakehead, can scarcely be classified as an aquarium fish, although it has been kept in aquaria and even bred on occasion. It occurs in southeastern Asia, where it grows to more than a foot in length and is often sold as a food fish. It has a round, ophidian head and elongated body with a long dorsal and anal fin. There is a dark eye-spot at the tail base, and the sides are light brown to olive green, with a row of dark diamond-shaped markings along the back. The sides are also peppered with silvery dots. The large mouth is armed with efficient teeth, which are used without hesitation on anything which might look like food—which is to say, anything. The male is considerably larger than the female and a bit more brightly colored.

Spawning takes place at a temperature of 80°, and of course the largest kind of aquarium must be used. The eggs float in masses at the surface and hatch in 72 hours. For the first week or so, the fry may seem to be in trouble; they will often be found belly-up at the surface, but this seems to be a natural buoyancy which is overcome in time. The young grow with amazing rapidity, and the only problem encountered is that of keeping their terrific appetites satisfied. If you like your fish big and nasty, this is the fish for you!

170

Cheirodon axelrodi, the Cardinal Tetra, is by far the most beautiful and popular imported aquarium fish ever to have reached the market. Its introduction to the American aquarist was due to the pioneering efforts of one of the world's foremost collectors of aquarium fishes, Mr. Fred Cochu of Paramount Aquarium. The fish was first described by Dr. Leonard P. Schultz in the *Tropical Fish Hobbyist* magazine where he placed it in the genus *Cheirodon* rather than the genus *Hyphessobrycon*, even though external similarity caused other ichthyologists to differ in their generic placement of this fish.

The first person to spawn the Cardinal Tetra was Dr. Cliff Emmens, author of a wonderful book *"How to Keep and Breed Aquarium*

The Snakehead, *Channa asiatica.* Photo by Sam Dunton.

Fishes." Dr. Emmens suggests that the fish breeds in a manner very similar to the Neon Tetra, though it requires water a little more acid. Aquarists all over the world differ in their reports of the necessary pH value of the water with statements which range from a pH of 4.5 to 6.8. They all agree that soft water is necessary.

The Cardinal Tetra scatters adhesive eggs all about bushy plants. They do not eat their spawn immediately though care should be exercised to keep this danger at a minimum. Sex is difficult to distinguish in young fish and only the apparent fullness of a female is any sure sign of sex. Slim females are easily mistaken for males.

The young should be fed infusoria for at least one full week, followed by newly hatched brine shrimp. They grow very rapidly.

The upper fish is a Cardinal Tetra, *Cheirodon axelrodi*, while the lower fish is the similarly well-known Neon Tetra, *Hyphessobrycon innesi*. The similarity between them is superficial, for they are quite different with respect to physical characters. Photo by Arend van den Nieuwenhuizen.

A pair of Cardinal Tetras. The larger upper fish is the female. Photo by Stanislav Frank.

The Beautiful-scaled Characin, *Copeina callolepis*. These fish are jumpers, so they should be kept in covered tanks only. Males have much larger fins than the females.
Photo by Dr. Herbert R. Axelrod.

Copeina callolepis, the Beautiful-scaled Characin, is one of three popular aquarium fishes in this genus, each of which appears in a different section because each has a distinctly different method of spawning. This fish is elongated in form, with large scales. The sides are light tan in color, and each scale has a black area which is edged with red. The male may be distinguished by his long, pointed dorsal fin which bears a large black spot. The female's dorsal fin is smaller, and has several smaller spots.

Spawning is performed in the usual characin manner at a temperature of 78°, the eggs being laid in bunches of bushy plants, which should be provided for them. The aquarium should be at least 10 gallons in size and must be covered, as this fish is an accomplished jumper. Spawnings are small in number, averaging about 50 eggs, which hatch in 24 hours. The young must be well supplied with infusoria at first, as their appetites are large and their mouths small. Once they are large enough to take brine shrimp, growth is fairly rapid.

Copeina eigenmanni, the Redlined Pencilfish, is a relatively recent addition to the American market. Males are differentiated from females by their longer and more pointed fins. Males also have a lightening mark in their dorsals and this mark seems to develop before their fins become elongated.

Spawning is typical as the pair spray adhesive eggs about the aquarium in a haphazard manner. The eggs hatch in about two days at 80°F. They require quite a bit of conditioning before they spawn and their favorite food is newly hatched brine shrimp and *Daphnia.*

This is probably the most beautiful aquarium species in the genus *Copeina.*

CATFISH. *Corydoras æneus,* the Bronze Catfish, brings us into the interesting Catfish group. Because they are always reputed to be efficient scavengers, which indeed they are, catfish are sometimes subjected to abuse. They are placed into the dirtiest tanks with the mistaken notion that this is what they prefer. Don't depend on your catfish to clean up your dirty tanks; they will help if there is a filter in the tank by stirring up the sediment so that the filter will suck it in, but don't expect them to *eat* it!

C. æneus is probably the best-known of the genus, and it naturally follows that it is the one most often bred. It attains a length of 3 inches, and the chunky body is covered on the sides with a double row of scales which are so large that they might be called plates. These plates are of a greenish bronze color. The underslung mouth is provided with a double pair of barbels, or whiskers; these are sensitive aids to the taste as well as the sensory organs, and permit the fish to find his way about and locate food even in complete darkness. There is some calcium needed for normal growth, and therefore we should give our catfish water of at least 10 degrees of hardness. *C. æneus* comes from Venezuela and Trinidad, and many books tell us that sex may be distinguished by the more pointed dorsal fin of the male; this is not always so. We have seen some females with slightly pointed dorsals, as well as males with blunt ones. Here is a better way: look down at the fish from the surface; it will be seen that some are considerably wider than

The Bronze Catfish, *Corydoras aeneus*, is the common catfish known to aquarists. It is easily bred, though it is so inexpensive that most breeders do not bother.

the others; these of course are the females. Separate them from the males and give them a clean tank with plenty of food. Gravel is not necessary on the bottom; it only makes the food more difficult for the fish to get at. Feed generously with live foods, preferably worms. When the female is well rounded, put her with a male, preferably two if you have them, into a tank of at least 15 gallons capacity. A bare tank is better; it makes it easier for the fish to find each other. Add about $\frac{1}{4}$ fresh water and bring the temperature up to 80°. There should then be a great amount of activity. Finally the female will carefully clean a small area, usually on the glass sides, until she is satisfied. Shortly afterward, one of the males will roll over on his side on the bottom. The female then attaches herself to a point near his vent, shortly thereafter releasing 5 or 6 eggs into a pocket which she forms by folding her ventral fins together. She releases the male and then swims to the spot previously cleaned, touches this spot with her mouth and then pushes the eggs against this same spot. This process is repeated until the female's eggs are spent. Eggs will be seen all over the glass sides. These eggs hatch in 72 hours, and the young begin to swim in 5 days. Microworms are a good food at this point, but a paste made of finely ground prepared food mixed with water so that it will sink is an acceptable substitute. Feed often, and just generously enough not to foul the

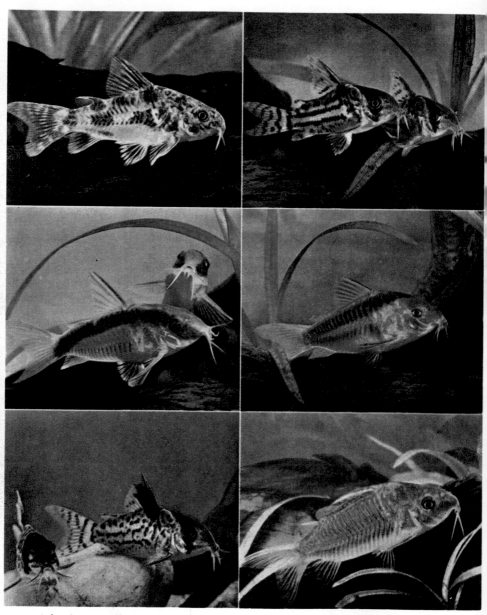

Left column, top to bottom:
Corydoras paleatus;
Corydoras arcuatus;
Corydoras punctatus punctatus;

Right column, top to bottom:
Corydoras schwartzi;
Corydoras myersi;
Brochis coeruleus;

Photos by Burkhard Kahl.

Left column, top to bottom:
Corydoras julii;
Corydoras aeneus;
Corydoras hastatus;

Right column, top to bottom:
Corydoras melanistius melanistius;
Corydoras schultzei;
Corydoras pygmaeus;

Photos by Burkhard Kahl.

water. Remove the parent fish after spawning. The young grow rather slowly, but a tankful of them is a pretty sight.

An albino strain is available.

Corydoras hastatus, the Dwarf or Pygmy Catfish, comes from the Amazon Basin. It is the smallest member of the family, measuring a bare 1½ inches when fully grown. It is olive to light brown in color, and has a dark horizontal stripe, ending in an arrow-shaped mark at the tail base. The females, when ripe, are considerably plumper than the males. This fish spends more time off the bottom than the rest of the *Corydoras* species, and is very popular among European aquarists.

Corydoras hastatus, the Dwarf or Pygmy Catfish. Photo by G.J.M. Timmerman.

Breeding this little fish is not very difficult, but we have seen no reports on how it is done. Probably the procedure is similar to the above, but is best accomplished in the dawn's early light, or even at night. Temperature should be about 80°, and the tank need not be a very large one. 8 to 10 gallons is about right. If you have a long tank, all the better. The young should be provided with a hiding place; a layer of pebbles covering part of the bottom is enough refuge. When the fish, which may number several pairs, begin spawning, a small number of eggs will be found clinging to the glass sides. They are surprisingly large for such a small fish, and are produced over a period of several days to a week. The parents need not be removed; they will not touch them if well fed. In 3 days the young hatch, and again it is surprising how large they are. Newly-hatched brine shrimp are taken at once, and raising them is easy. When there are no more new eggs to be found, remove the parents and separate them to give them a rest and a chance to fill up once again.

Corydoras rabauti a newcomer (confused with *C. myersi*) is from the Rio Javari, which empties into the Amazon Basin. This fish resembles the *C. aeneus* in shape and size, but is a pinkish tan in color, with a dark, almost black stripe running from the top of the head to the caudal base. Requirements and spawning are exactly as described for the *C. aeneus*, but the youngsters deserve description: the head half of the body is red, and the rear part of the body to the tail base is green. All the fins are red. The sight of a school of these is startling after seeing the comparatively drab colors of the parents. These colors persist until the fish are about

Corydoras myersi is sometimes mistaken for other 'skunk' catfishes because of the distinguishing stripe down its back. It has incorrectly been called *Corydoras rabauti*. Photo by G.J.M. Timmerman.

$\frac{1}{2}$ inch long, when they gradually fade and the stripe appears. We once had the interesting experience of watching this fish spawn in the home of Fred Corwin, of Roselle, N.J., who presented us with a few youngsters when they could be moved. This gave us the opportunity of observing the unusual color phase of this very pretty little fish.

Corydoras paleatus, the Peppered Corydoras, has a wide range between southern Brazil and northern Argentina. It is one of the largest member's of the family and is usually in fairly good supply. Three inches is given as the maximum size, but we have seen them a bit larger. The body has a marbled design of dark brown markings on a lighter background, and the dorsal and tail fins are adorned with rows of dots. Care and breeding are exactly as for *C. aeneus.*

An albino strain has appeared and is being bred by commercial interests in Europe, the U.S.A. and the Far East.

Copeina species. Note the large fins of this fish.

Copeina eigenmanni, the Redlined Pencilfish. Upper fish is the male. Photo by Dr. Herbert R. Axelrod.

The Sailfin Characin, *Crenuchus spilurus*, from South America. Photo by Dr. Karl Knaack.

An albino *Corydoras paleatus*. This strain is popular in Europe, having been bred in the aquarium successfully. Photo by Stanislav Frank.

Corynopoma riisei is popularly known as the Swordtail Characin. It is a silvery, peaceful fish which attains 3 inches in length, and the male can be distinguished not only by the larger dorsal and anal fins and prolonged rays of his tail in the lower lobe, but also by a peculiar elongation of the gill-plates. There is a long protuberance reaching half-way toward the tail, ending in an odd, paddle-like point. Exactly how this protuberance is used has been the source of much conjecture for a long time.

Spawning this fish is quite easy; water conditions do not seem very important, as long as extremes are avoided. A 20-gallon aquarium is about the right size, and heat should be brought to 80°. If well conditioned, the male will soon begin his interesting courtship. After a lively chase, he circles the female, dancing like a male guppy, and finally ejects a lump of sperm in her direction. During this dance, the projections from his gill-plates are extended at right angles; how they are used in courtship is not known, but the female somehow is able to get this sperm mass into her body, where it mingles with the eggs. Later the eggs are placed on a plant leaf or in a thicket without any further attention from the male, whose job is already done. The eggs hatch in 24 to 32 hours, and the fry swim 2 days later. They are easily raised but should get infusoria until they begin to grow.

Another strange thing about this fish is that the female is able to retain spawn after the first mating and produce fertile eggs at a later time without further assistance from the male.

Creagrutus beni comes from the Rio Beni in South America, for which it is named. It is peaceful and attains 3 inches in length. The sides are olive green toward the back, shading gradually to a white belly. There is a dark lateral stripe which begins halfway down the body and extends to the tail base. The dorsal and anal fin are pinkish in color, with a spot on the dorsal; there is another spot on the side, just behind the gill-cover. Sexes are very difficult to distinguish; the only clue is the slightly heavier body of the female.

Given a 20-gallon aquarium and a temperature of 80°, this fish will occasionally breed. The male does a little dance around the female, in a manner similar to the *Corynopoma riisei* male, and the female also has the power to absorb the sperm into her body. Eggs are hung in plant thickets and hatch in about 24 hours. The fry spend most of the time near the bottom and are difficult to find. Some finely powdered prepared food, which is first sprinkled into a jar of water and then stirred or shaken in to cause it to sink, should be fed in addition to the usual first feedings of infusoria.

A female (lower fish) and a male *Crenuchus spilurus*. Photo by G.J.M. Timmerman.

Crenuchus spilurus comes from the Amazon Basin and Guyana. It is one of the larger characins, the male as large as 4 inches, and the female an inch shorter. The mouth is large, and they should not be trusted with smaller fishes; actually, they are quite shy but are better kept by themselves. This is a rather attractive fish, and the males have large dorsal and anal fins peppered with red reticulations. There is a large black spot at the tail base.

This species does not spawn readily, and conditions must be to their liking; one requirement is plenty of space, at least 15 gallons. Another is that they be accustomed to their surroundings; condition them in their own aquarium by separating them with a glass partition. When the female becomes well rounded and the male wants to get through the glass, the time has come. The best temperature is 78°. Spawning usually does not take place at once, but be patient. A bushy clump of

Corynopoma riisei, the Swordtail Characin. The male fish (right) has much larger fins than the female. Photo by Rudolf Zukal.

A pair of spawning Giant Danios, *Danio malabaricus*. Photo by Rudolf Zukal.

plants should be provided upon which they will deposit tiny pink eggs. The usual egg-hunt, common to most characins, is not practiced, and the eggs are quite safe until they hatch three days after spawning time. The fry must have infusoria at first, followed by the larger foods.

This is a fish which takes a long time to become mature. For this reason we do not see many specimens which are tank-raised.

Ctenobrycon spilurus comes from South America, and is commonly known as the Silver Tetra. It is a large, silvery fish with small scales; there is a black spot on the sides just behind the gill-plate, and another at the base of the tail. Females are distinguished by their fuller bodies, and are slightly bigger than their mates. Maximum size is $3\frac{1}{2}$ inches.

Many large tetras, this one included, prefer a diet which contains a good percentage of vegetable matter. This should be provided in the form of an occaisional feeding of boiled spinach. In the summer months, if a good source of Duckweed can be found, you will find that this fish is very fond of this food. Be careful not to introduce fish enemies with the food, or the fry will be in for trouble.

For a fish of this relatively large size, a good-sized breeding tank should be provided. One of 20 gallons capacity is not too big. The usual tetra set-up is used, with a clump of bushy plants on one side.

This is the Silver Tetra. It is known for its odd shape, monotonous color, and insatiable appetite for aquarium plants. It is a fast swimmer and eats its food in swallows and gulps. It is not a peaceful fish and it does not make a desirable member of a community aquarium, but it is so easy to spawn that there is always an oversupply of them.

These plants should not be too closely bunched, however, to give the pair room to swim among them. At a temperature of 75°, the pair will usually begin chasing each other in and out of the plants as soon as they have become accustomed to their new surroundings. Spawnings are usually large, and after a few days of infusoria feeding will consume great amounts of brine shrimp or sifted daphnia. Growth is very rapid. Of course, the parents should be removed as soon as they have spawned.

Danio malabaricus is native to the west coast of India and the island of Ceylon. It is a large species, but of a peaceful temperament despite its size of 6 inches. The sides are bright blue and the upper part shows two pinkish horizontal lines. There is a third line under this, which is broken toward the anterior part of the body. The belly is suffused with bright pink, as are the ventral and anal fins and part of the lower caudal lobe. The dorsal fin is also pink in color. The female is a bit larger than her mate, but the colors are not quite so bright.

This species is very prolific, and directions for spawning them are exactly as for the *Brachydanio* species. The fry grow quickly and soon outgrow their quarters.

The author (HRA) swam with these so-called Giant Danios in Ceylon where they are found in shallow (6 feet or less), fast-moving, crystal clear streams.

So easy are these fish to breed, that importations are almost unknown.

Gymnocorymbus ternetzi is known by several popular names: Black Tetra, Blackamoor, Petticoatfish, and in German, *Trauermantelsalmler*, or Mourning Cloak Tetra. It comes from Paraguay and the Guaporé Basin, and is said to attain 3 inches in length, although we have never seen any quite that big. Larger specimens are likely to be somewhat aggressive toward smaller fishes, and for this reason we do not recommend them wholeheartedly as community fish.

This fish has only two colors, silver and black. There are three vertical bands: one passes through the eye, the second descends from the back three-quarters way down the side just behind the gill-cover, and the third, which is fainter, starts at the first dorsal rays and passes almost down to the ventral fins. In younger specimens, the after half of the body is a solid black as far as the caudal base. The dorsal and anal fins are included by these black markings. The tail is colorless. As the fish gets older, the vertical bands remain distinct, but the black fades to a dark grey. Males are considerably smaller than the females and much more slender.

A large tank should be given these fish for spawning, one of at least 20 gallons. The best temperature is 80°, and water hardness is not very

A trio of long-finned strain of the Black Tetra, *Gymnocorumbus ternetzi*, originally developed in Europe. These fish were brought back from Czechoslovakia and photographed by the author. Photo by Dr. Herbert R. Axelrod.

Helostoma temmincki, the Kissing Gourami. It is fairly difficult to identify the sexes except during the breeding stage. Photo by Hans Joachim Richter.

important, as long as it is not too high. A generous amount of bushy plants should be provided, and the sexes should be separately conditioned with large amounts of live foods. It is suggested that enough live daphnia be provided that some can be seen swimming in the tank at all times. When the female is bulging with eggs, place her in the breeding tank and add the male a day later. Spawning should follow soon afterwards, and the number of eggs produced will often be surprising. Parents should be removed when they begin to hunt for eggs. Incubation takes from 36 to 48 hours, and the fry begin to swim 2 days later. Frequent feedings of brine shrimp should then be begun.

The author (HRA) discovered a long-finned, tank-raised variety of this fish in Czechoslovakia. He nicknamed it "G.T.O." and bred millions of them. This variety is now a standard aquarium fish. It was originally bred in Poland.

Helostoma temminckii, the Kissing Gourami, has been known to attain a length of 12 inches in its natural habitat. It gets its name from the strange behavior of a pair of fish during an encounter. Puckering up their thick, rubbery lips they will push against each other with what imaginatively may be called a kiss. This act does not seem to have a sexual significance; it has not been observed to be a prelude to spawning. They just seem to do it because they like to. Older specimens are much less apt to kiss than younger ones.

The fish we know as *H. temminckii* nowadays is a golden color variety of the original species and has been called *H. rudolfi*. The entire body is a light pink in color and would be classed as an albinistic form if it were not for the fact that the pupil of the eye is black and not pink as it would be in a true albino. Fins and tail are short, and it is an impossibility to sex them accurately until they have attained a size of 5 inches or more. At this time the females develop a heavier body, which can be distinguished by looking down on them. These larger fish should not be kept in the company of other fishes which are smaller than they are; they may show a tendency to bully the others. As is the case with most of the anabantids, they are native to sluggish streams, swamp ponds and lakes. They come from Java, Borneo, Sumatra, Malaysia and Thailand.

Once having attained breeding size, this fish is very prolific. For this reason, the largest aquarium available should be provided for them. Water hardness is not important, as long as extremes are avoided. The pair should be well fed; here the problem arises as to what foods to offer them. One of the best is chopped up garden worms; salmon eggs are also eaten eagerly. Their appetite is enormous, and proper conditioning demands that it be well satisfied. It is best to keep a pair separated while conditioning them until the female is bulging with roe. If the male gets

The Kissing Gouramis in this photo are doing just that. It is difficult to spawn them in the home tank. In Florida they are bred in large concrete vats of 100 to 500 gallons.

too rough with her, the female is not yet ready, and they should be separated again. When things go well, the male encircles the female in a nuptial embrace. The large, lighter-than-water eggs float up to the surface to form clusters. There may be a thousand eggs or more, and the parents should be removed as soon as the female is spent. Start a heavy culture of brine shrimp when the young hatch, which takes place in three days. Before they become free-swimming, they spend most of their time belly-up at the surface, which is no cause for alarm. When they right themselves and begin to swim, their appetites must be appeased at once. Besides feeding brine shrimp, a few small pinches of finely powdered prepared food may also be spread on the surface. Your only problem from here on is to provide enough food to keep their bellies swelled without overfeeding and fouling the water.

80° to 85° is the proper temperature for spawning the adults and raising the young.

Hemigrammus armstrongi, the Golden Tetra, comes from Guyana. It is small, being fully grown at 1½ inches; the color is a gleaming gold, which looks as if it had just been polished. Fins are colorless, but there are a pair of red spots on the upper and lower portions of the caudal base. The only sexual distinction is a slightly deeper body in the females.

These should be given a well-planted aquarium, which need not be large. Five gallons is sufficient. When the aquarium is sparsely planted, they are very much inclined to be timid and too scared to give any

191

A school of Golden Tetras, *Hemigrammus armstrongi*, in a large display tank. Photo by Dr. Herbert R. Axelrod.

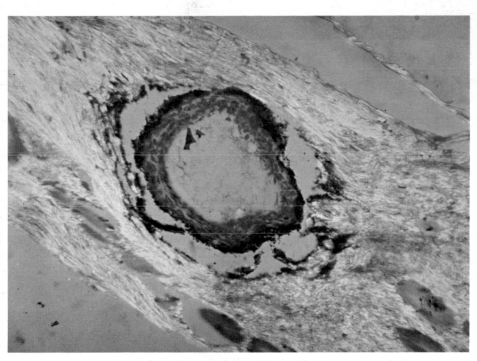

An encysted parasite from *Hemigrammus armstrongi*. The cyst is surrounded externally by a layer of guanin, a highly reflective material present in the skin of most fishes. Photomicrograph by Ginsburger.

A pair of very healthy Buenos Aires Tetras, *Hemigrammus caudovittatus*. Note the stunning breeding coloration of these fish. Photo by Rudolf Zukal.

attention to the business of propagation. However, when they become accustomed to their surroundings, breeding will take place if they are properly conditioned. Water should be about neutral and fairly soft, and the temperature 78° to 80°. Eggs hatch in 36 hours, and the fry are rather small; therefore, food for the first week should consist of infusoria.

Golden Tetras which are raised in captivity are silver in color and never develop the golden hue of their parents. The reason for this is a parasite which becomes embedded in the fish's skin. After becoming embedded, the parasite forms a cyst or case around itself which is golden, metallic yellow. Since the parasite never leaves its fish host it probably originates as a bird parasite requiring a passage through the bird's digestive system in order for the cyst to mature. The parasite is host specific, that is, it only (almost) attacks *Hemigrammus armstrongi*.

Hemigrammus caudovittatus is known as the Buenos Aires Tetra, for the very good reason that it comes from the region of Buenos Aires, Argentina. It is one of the largest of the genus; measuring 4 inches when fully grown. The body color is silvery, and all the fins with the exception of the pectorals are bright red. There is a horizontal streak which begins three-quarters of the way down the body and passes completely through the center of the tail. .This is crossed by a black vertical bar almost at the caudal base and is surrounded by four yellow dots. Males are slimmer and·slightly smaller than their mates.

A trio of Buenos Aires Tetras.

Large specimens of this fish are apt to be just a bit too rough on their smaller neighbors, and should be kept only in the company of large fishes which are able to take care of themselves. One of their favorite tricks is to nip off the long, filamentous ventral fins of angelfishes and gouramis. Females when ready to breed are also likely to develop a "chip on their shoulder" attitude, even toward their mates. For this reason it is preferable to keep the sexes separated when conditioning them for spawning. The breeding tank should be a large one; 20 gallons is good. Planting should be heavy for best results. The female is often the aggressor and should be watched at first. Once spawning has begun, all will go well. Remove the pair as soon as they have finished, or many eggs will be eaten. At a temperature of 78°, the eggs will hatch in from 2 to 2½ days, and the fry will begin to swim 2 days later. Brine shrimp may be fed at once.

Hemigrammus nanus is commonly known as the Silver-tipped Tetra, and comes from southeastern Brazil. It is a silvery fish with a black horizontal stripe running from three-quarters of the way back on the fish all the way through the center rays of the tail. The only other decorations are silvery white tips on all the fins. The male is considerably more slender than its mate, which is the only way of determining sex.

Breeding this little fish, which attains a size of only 1½ inches, is not the difficult task it was once considered to be; like some of its cousins, it demands soft water, that is, water of 5° of hardness or less. Being small, it does not require a large breeding tank; 10 gallons is sufficient. Bushy plants such as *Myriophyllum* are needed, or a substitute such as Spanish Moss. Breeders must be well conditioned on live foods such as daphnia, and the water temperature may range from 78° to 80°. Fry are quite small and need infusoria for the first stages of growth.

Hemigrammus ocellifer is the popular Head-and-tail Light Tetra, which attains a length of 2 inches and comes from Guyana and the Amazon Basin. This is a peaceful fish and also one of the easier members of the family to spawn. There is a faint spot on the shoulder, and a deep black spot at the caudal base, which is topped by a glowing, reddish-yellow color. This is the so-called "tail-light." The top of the eye also glows with a deep red, forming a "head-light." Males have a thin white line which passes through the anal fin. This line is absent in the female.

German breeders recommend a unique and very successful way of propagating this attractive fish. Breeding temperature should be about 80° in a tank of about 5 gallons capacity. The bottom is covered with clean pebbles, as for spawning the *Brachydanio* species. Collect about 2 gallons of rain water in an enameled or glass container and stir in

The Head-and-tail Light Tetra, *Hemigrammus ocellifer*. The male (left) leading the female to the well-planted part of the tank.

The male ready to place his body parallel to that of the female.

Upon collision of their bodies, simultaneous expulsion of eggs and sperm occurs. Photo series by Rudolf Zukal.

Hemigrammus nanus, the Silver-tipped Tetra, The upper, thinner, fish is the male. Photo by Dr. Herbert R. Axelrod.

Sexing Garnet Tetras, *Hemigrammus pulcher*, is not easy. Males and females resemble each other except that mature females have deeper bodies.

about a handful of whitewash. Allow the water to stand for several days until it is perfectly clear and then siphon it off. This is the water to use; if the breeders are properly conditioned, they will oblige by spawning almost at once. A couple of bushy plants will catch some of the eggs, but being semi-adhesive, many will fall through the pebbles where the parents cannot get at them. When the parents are finished spawning, remove them and shade the tank for three days; at the end of this time the fry may be seen hanging on the glass and plants, and they soon begin to swim; at this time, feed infusoria for a short time and follow with fine crustacea such as brine shrimp, small *Daphnia* or *Bosminae*.

Hemigrammus pulcher is known to some American aquarists as the Pretty Tetra. The Germans call it *"Karfunkelsalmler,"* the Garnet Tetra. It comes from the Peruvian Amazon and is a heavier-bodied fish than most of the tetra family. Maximum length is 2 inches, and the body is silvery bluish in color. There is a black dot on the side behind the gill-covers and a large black area extends from behind the abdomen to the lower part of the caudal base. This is topped by a dark red spot which looks as if a garnet had been set in. Thus the German name. The only distinction between the sexes is the heavier body of the female.

This fish is not by any means as easy to breed as some of the other members of the family, but the task is not an impossible one. A 10-gallon tank should be used, and the pair spawns in the usual characin manner on bushy plants. However, the fish seem to mature slowly and results may be had only with the use of older specimens. These should be conditioned until the male shows brilliant colors and the female is almost bursting with spawn. Sometimes it is better to use 2 males. Spawnings are usually large, and generous feedings of infusoria followed by brine shrimp are recommended. The usual temperature of 80° also holds good here.

Hemigrammus rhodostomus is known as the Rummy-nosed Tetra. The reason for this inelegant appellation is the fact that the fish has a bright red coloring across the entire front of the head. Coming from the region around Pará, Brazil, it is a small fish, the females attaining a length of 2 inches and the males a half inch less. Besides being smaller, the male is also more slender. The sides are bluish and there is a narrow horizontal stripe which widens toward the tail, forming a black area which narrows again as it extends through the center rays. The tail is white in color, and carries a black bar through each lobe. When the fish are in good condition, there is a distinct green spot on the forehead.

Breeding this little beauty is an achievement which so far has eluded many an experienced aquarist. It has been done, however, and it seems that we may follow in the footsteps of the successful few. Like many another so-called problem fish, time may prove that it was not such a difficult job after all when the rules are followed. A tank of 10 gallons capacity may be used. The water should be extremely soft, no more than 1 or 2 degrees, and slightly acid, about 6.8 pH. Temperature should be a bit lower than that usually used, about 76°. The tank should be heavily planted with bushy plants. *Nitella* has been used with success. The breeders seem to do best when fed large quantities of *Daphnia*. Watch the female closely and look for eggs when she suddenly becomes slimmer. Remove the breeders to prevent them from eating the precious little yellow eggs which will hatch in 24 hours. The addition of methylene blue (5%) in the amount of 2 drops per gallon will tend to reduce the incidence of fungus. When the fry begin to swim, feed them with brine shrimp. Don't be discouraged if spawnings are small; remember that it is an accomplishment to get spawnings at all.

A very similar looking species, also from South America, is *Petitella georgiae*.

Hemigrammus unilineatus is the popular Featherfin. It comes from Trinidad and Guyana and attains a length of 2 inches for the female,

Axelrodia riesei, the Ruby Tetra was discovered in Colombia by the author (HRA) and Mr. William Riese. Photo by Dr. Herbert R. Axelrod.

The Featherfin Tetra, *Hemigrammus unilineatus*. Sexing this species is not difficult. Photo by Dr. Herbert R. Axelrod.

The Rummy-nosed Tetra, *Hemigrammus rhodostomus*. Note the striking resemblance of this fish to the False Rummy-nosed Tetra shown below. Photo by Dr. Herbert R. Axelrod.

The False Rummy-nosed Tetra, *Petitella georgiae*. Photo by Stanislav Frank.

A pair of Featherfins, *Hemigrammus unilineatus.*

and slightly smaller for the male. His much more slender form is also an easy means of identifying him. The sides are silvery, with light pink fins and tail. The dorsal fin has a black streak, edged in front and tipped with white. A similar marking adorns the anal fin.

A mature, well-conditioned pair will usually give little difficulty when put out to spawn. A 10-gallon tank may be used, but a larger one will give better results because spawns are often well over 1000 fry and two weeks later, the female is again bulging with eggs and ready to spawn once more! Conditioning is easy with generous feedings of *Daphnia.* The best breeding temperature is 76°, and the tank should be densely planted with bushy plants at one end. Water conditions are not critical, as long as the water is not too hard and somewhere around neutral. Put the pair into the breeding tank during the evening and check the aquarium frequently the following morning. When the female has become depleted, remove the pair. A light held behind the tank so that it shines through the bushy plants will show plainly whether or not the spawning has been successful. Hatching takes place in 24 to 36 hours, and the youngsters begin to swim in 3 days from this time. They have huge appetites, and devour generous quantities of newly hatched brine shrimp or sifted *Daphnia.* Growth is rapid, and they will soon outgrow their living quarters.

Hyphessobrycon callistus is known as the Jewel Tetra, and also as *H. serpae* and *H. minor.* These are not separate species, but color variations. Their range is wide, from Guyana to the Rio Paraguay in Brazil.

Size does not exceed 1½ inches, and this fish should not be kept with thread-finned fishes, as it is apt to nip at filamentous appendages. Otherwise, it may be considered peaceful. The body color is red, in varying shades. There is a large black spot behind the gill plate, which is absent in some of the color varieties. The fins, all but the dorsal, are also red, and the dorsal of the male is completely black. The female's dorsal fin has a small white area at the base which serves as an indication of sex in addition to her heavier body.

This fish must be carefully conditioned before spawning, preferably with live *Daphnia*. It is best to have a number of breeders from which to make a selection; some females cannot always be induced to fill up with eggs. A 15-gallon tank may be used; the water should be both soft and close to neutral. The ideal temperature is between 75° to 78°. A thicket of bushy plants or their substitutes should be provided. If they are not

A pair of Serpae Tetras. These fish are technically known as *Hyphessobrycon callistus*. They are an aquarium hybrid and do not exist in this red color in nature.

Megalamphodus sweglesi, Swegles' Tetra, bears a noticeable resemblance to the *Hyphessobrycon* species in these pages. Photo by Karl Knaack.

One of the several types of fishes commonly called Serpae Tetra by hobbyists. Photo by Rudolf Zukal.

This is another aquarium strain of the systematically complicated *Callistus* tetras. Photo by Dr. Stanislav Frank.

A pair of magnificent looking tetras, presumably *Hyphessobrycon callistus*, the Callistus Tetra. Photo by Stanislav Frank.

This is *Hyphessobrycon serpae*. It doesn't look too much like the fish aquarists call the Serpae Tetra. It is a silver fish.

removed at once after spawning the parents will eat the eggs. Incubation period is from 2 to 2½ days, and the fry grow very slowly. They should be given infusoria at first, followed by fine *Daphnia* or newly hatched brine shrimp. This fish is somewhat sensitive to changes of water and should be moved as little as possible.

Hyphessobrycon flammeus, the Flame Tetra, Red Tetra, or the Tetra from Rio. As the latter name indicates, it comes from the neighborhood of Rio de Janeiro. This pretty little fish, whose length does not exceed 2 inches, is an old favorite the world over and was probably one of the first characins to be bred by aquarists. In a well-planted aquarium, the fish will show its full colors, which are not at all evident in the bare tanks of pet shops. The after part of the body, behind the belly region, is a bright red, as are the fins. The fore part of the body is light golden, and two black streaks adorn the sides. The dorsal fin is edged with black anteriorly, and the ventral fins are black-tipped. The anal fin is the sure guide to sex distinction: that of the male is squarer and prominently edged with black, while the female's is more concave and shows scarcely any black edging.

This is a good fish for those who have never before spawned any of the tetras. It is one of the easiest of the family to breed. The water should be nearly neutral, temperature 76° to 78°. Being a small fish, they will oblige by spawning in a tank of 5 gallons capacity if nothing larger is available. The tank should be well stocked with bushy plants or an artificial spawning medium. Spawning is in the usual tetra fashion, the male chasing the female repeatedly into the thickets where about 10 eggs are deposited each time. Some breeders use 2 males for a female. Fry hatch in 72 hours and should be provided with infusoria for a week before the first feedings of finely screened live foods.

Hemigrammus gracilis is the very popular Glow-light Tetra, which comes from Guyana and the lower Amazon. It is a small, peaceful fish which reaches 1½ inches in length. The sides are a greenish color, divided by a horizontal stripe of fiery, glowing red. The upper part of the eye also shows this color. The dorsal fin is pink, and the anal as well as the ventral fins are tipped with white. The male of this species is much more slender than the female.

Actually, getting a good pair to spawn is not very difficult. Feed them well, preferably with live *Daphnia,* until the female is loaded with eggs. Then provide them with a 5-gallon tank of clean, soft, slightly acid water. Put in a few clumps only of spawning grass. The breeders will often spawn right out in the open, and the eggs will fall to the bottom. The spawning is unusual: the pair will swim close together and

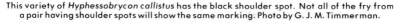

This variety of *Hyphessobrycon callistus* has the black shoulder spot. Not all of the fry from a pair having shoulder spots will show the same marking. Photo by G. J. M. Timmerman.

An aquarium fish identified as the Serpae Tetra. The shoulder spot is not developed at all. Photo by Dr. Karl Knaack.

Hyphessobrycon flammeus, the Flame Tetra. The two characteristic shoulder streaks are recognizable. Photo by Rudolf Zukal.

A very attractive specimen of a Tetra from Rio as the Flame Tetra is also sometimes called. Photo by Klaus Paysan.

Hyphessobrycon heterorhabdus, the Flag Tetra. The upper fish is the female. Photo by Rudolf Zukal.

up and over, dropping the eggs as they go. Sometimes they will be seen doing this in the community aquarium, providing the other fishes with a feast. When spawning is over and the parents have been removed, shade the tank until the fry have become free-swimming; the eggs and very young fry have been found to be a bit sensitive to light. The usual first feeding of infusoria, followed by small crustacean foods, is also recommended.

Hyphessobrycon herbertaxelrodi, the Black Neon, comes from South America. It is very peaceful and makes a very interesting and beautiful addition to the community aquarium. It spawns in a typical manner and the breeders usually require soft, acid water.

A pair of Black Neons, *Hyphessobrycon herbertaxelrodi.* Photo by Rudolf Zukal.

Hyphessobrycon heterorhabdus has been referred to erroneously as *Hyphessobrycon ulreyi.* It resembles this latter fish closely, but is by far the commoner of the two in aquaria. The German aquarists call this one the Flag Tetra, because the horizontal stripes resemble the red, white and black of the old German flag.

Unfortunately we must still depend on imported specimens for almost all the stock available today; this is not one of the "easy" ones. As there is no way of telling the age of a wild fish, the only thing that can be

A beautiful pair of Glowline Tetras as these are sometimes called. The male *Hyphessobrycon heterorhabdus* is the lower fish.

recommended is that full-sized, 2-inch specimens be used. Condition them until the female is distended with eggs, and then try your luck.

This peaceful fish comes from the Amazon basin. The body is silvery, with a three-colored horizontal stripe which extends from the gill-cover to the caudal base. The upper part of the line is bright red, as is the top part of the eye. The middle of the line is a pale gold, and the lower part is black. Males can be distinguished from females by a greater fullness in the anal fin, as well as their more slender body. A 10-gallon aquarium is best, with the usual thicket of plants provided. The water should be soft and slightly acid, and the aquarium should either be in a partly shaded location or shaded with a piece of cardboard toward the light. Remove the parents when the loss of plumpness in the female indicates that they have spawned. The best spawning temperature is 76°. Incubation period is very short: 22 to 26 hours. The usual procedure for first feedings is followed.

Hyphessobrycon (Paracheirodon) innesi is the famous Neon Tetra. This fish created a furore in aquatic circles after its introduction, not only because of its spectacular colors, but because of the difficulty encountered in breeding it. We have since learned a few things which make the task a much easier one.

This fish occurs far up the Amazon River in Peru, Colombia and in the Rio Purus, Brazil. These waters seem to be lacking in mineral content to an unusual degree, and are made up mostly of rain water. The fish is small, attaining a size of only 1½ inches. The back is olive green, and a stripe of brilliant greenish blue runs upward from the upper part of the eye to a point on the back halfway between the dorsal fin and the tail. The belly is white; between it and the caudal base the entire area is bright red. Fins are colorless.

A pair of Glowlight Tetras, on their way to the next spawning site. Notice some of the eggs laid a few moments earlier are still suspended in the water. Photo by Rudolf Zukal.

Hemigrammus gracilis, the Glowlight Tetra. The female is the upper fish. Photo by Rudolf Zukal.

A male (upper) and a female Black Neon, *Hyphessobrycon herbertaxelrodi*. Photo by Dr. Herbert R. Axelrod.

Neon Tetra afflicted with Neon Disease. Compare this with the color photograph and note the difference in the shading of the red part of the body. Photo by Chvojka Milan.

Breeding this lovely fish was at first considered to be a virtual impossibility; not long ago several discoveries were made which have simplified spawning them. One is that our little friend is *very* finicky where water is concerned. Although the Neon Tetra will live quite well in hard as well as soft water, the water which is provided for spawning must be very soft, no more than 3 degrees of hardness, as well as definitely acid, pH 6.5. Besides, the water has to be clean, which means that the tank must also be clean. Use an all-glass tank of about 2 gallons capacity; these aquaria are easy to make perfectly clean. However, a metal frame aquarium, scrubbed with steel wool and hot water, can be made to serve the purpose. A slightly larger size, 3 to 5 gallons, is also preferable. Well-filtered rain water, aged a week or longer, might be found to meet the specifications. If a greater acid content is required dry out some oak or elm bark, and cut it up into small chips. Bring some distilled water to a boil and throw in about a handful of these chips. Let the brew stand until it cools and settles, after which it may be bottled for future use. This solution will be found to be strongly acid and may be added to the water a little at a time until the desired acidity is reached.

Now comes the job of cleaning the plants. The usual clump of bushy plants is required, and they may be cleaned of all impurities by dipping them for 5 minutes in a solution of 1 tablespoonful of powdered alum to 1 quart of distilled water. The plants are then rinsed under the tap and placed in the tank. The temperature is brought to 74°, and the tank is ready for occupancy.

As for the breeders, we come to another discovery which has been made in recent years. The Neon Tetra, in spite of being a rather hardy fish, is sometimes the victim of a devastating disease which is caused by a sporozoan parasite, *Plistophora*. Neon disease is characterized by a wasting of the tissues. One of the first symptoms is a lightening of the red area of the body.

Sexes of adults are not too difficult to distinguish. Even half-grown male specimens will show a perfectly straight blue line, and the females, a slightly bent one. Condition them until the female is well rounded, and place them in the breeding tank. Do not feed them while they are in the breeding tank; remember, it must be kept clean. If there is no spawning in two days, take them out, feed them well for a few more days, then try again. Sooner or later, your fish will spawn. When this takes place, remove them and then keep the tank in complete darkness by covering it for 24 hours, and then shading the tank from direct light until the fry are free-swimming. At this point it is best to feed with newly hatched brine shrimp, which will contaminate the tank less than any other food.

A similar fish is known as *Hyphessobrycon simulans*.

Hyphessobrycon pulchripinnis is known as the Lemon Tetra. It comes from the Amazon basin and attains 1¾ inches in length. Here we have

A pair of Lemon Tetras, *Hyphessobrycon pulchripinnis*.

215

Hyphessobrycon (*Paracheirodon*) *innesi*, the Neon Tetra. The upper fish is a male. Photo by Stanislav Frank.

Hyphessobrycon simulans is popularly called Schwartz's Neon in the honor of its discoverer, H.W. Schwartz. It resembles to a great degree the true Neon Tetra. Photo by Hilmar Hansen.

Black-lined Tetras, *Hyphessobrycon scholzei*. Photo by Dr. Herbert R. Axelrod.

another fish which, like the Red Tetra, does not look attractive when it is not in a favorable environment. The fins have a lemon-yellow edge in front, from which the fish gets its name. The anal fin has a black area behind the yellow edge, extending along the fin's lower margin. The tail is without color. A pleasing contrast to the yellow in the fins is the bright red of the upper part of the eye. Disposition is peaceful, and the fish always has a lively, perky carriage. Males may be distinguished by their more slender lines and a bit more color in the fins.

Spawning is not very difficult, and the procedure described for *H. flammeus* may be followed, with the exception that a slightly higher temperature be given them, about 80°. Hatching takes place in 24 hours.

Hyphessobrycon rosaceus, the Rosy Tetra, comes from Guyana and the lower Amazon basin. It gets to be almost 2 inches in length and is one of the more attractive members of the tetra family. The body is a deep rosy pink, and the ventral and anal fins, as well as the upper and lower margins of the tail, are edged with bright red. The first rays of the anal and dorsal fins are tipped with white, and the upper half of the dorsal fin is deep black. Sexes are very easy to distinguish: the male has a long, high dorsal fin, and the first rays of the anal fin are elongated as well.

A trio of Rosy Tetras, *Hyphessobrycon rosaceus*

The Black-lined Tetra, *Hyphessobrycon scholzei*. Female fish to the rear of the male. Photo by Rudolf Zukal.

A 20-gallon tank should be provided for spawning. The usual spawning vegetation should be provided, and the pair should be well conditioned. Spawning will take place at a temperature of 80°, and the fry hatch in 72 hours. After a week of infusoria, they should be large enough to take brine shrimp or sifted *Daphnia*.

Hyphessobrycon scholzei comes from the Amazon basin and is popularly known as the Black-lined Tetra. This active fish is usually peaceful, but should not be kept with thread-finned fishes, which it might nip. The sides are silvery in color, and there is a prominent black stripe which runs the length of the body and ends as a triangular spot at the caudal base. Males are considerably slimmer than the females.

This is among the easiest of the tetra family to breed. It is a good fish to start with, being hardy as well as prolific. The usual tetra set-up should be provided, with at least a 10-gallon tank. Make sure the female is heavily laden with eggs; if she is not ready to spawn, the male may nip her frequently. Eggs hatch in 2 to 3 days at a temperature of about 78°; fry begin to swim 2 to 3 days later. Spawnings are generally large, and fry should be generously fed.

Hyphessobrycon peruvianus, the Loreto Tetra. Photo by Stanislav Frank.

Hyphessobrycon pulchripinnis, the Lemon Tetra. Photo by Stanislav Frank.

Hyphessobrycon rosaceus, the Rosy Tetra. The male is the fish on the left. Photo by Dr. Karl Knaack.

Hyphessobrycon rubrostigma, the Bleeding Heart Tetra. Photo by Stanislav Frank.

Melanotaenia maccullochi, the Australian Rainbow Fish, is one of the few aquarium fishes to come from "down under." It is one of the popular favorites, however, and has much to recommend it. The length attained is close to 5 inches. There are 7 reddish horizontal lines, interspersed with greenish to yellowish. The anal fin is red, and the double dorsal fins are mostly greenish. There is a red spot on the gill-covers, encircled with golden yellow. The tail is brownish red. When in the midst of spawning, the male develops a bright, canary-yellow streak from the forehead all along the back. He is otherwise distinguished by his brighter colors and more slender proportions.

The spawning aquarium should be large and heavily planted. Eggs are scattered among the plants, usually in the early morning hours. Parents are removed after spawning, and the incubation period for the eggs varies from 10 to 12 days at a spawning temperature of 78°. Fry must be fed generously with infusoria the moment they begin to swim in order to satisfy their terrific appetites. Their growth is rapid, and they are soon large enough for fine crustaceans. They spawn readily in outdoor ponds in Florida.

The Australian Rainbow Fish, *Melanotaenia maccullochi.*

This is another Australian Rainbow Fish, *Melanotaenia nigrans*.

Melanotaenia nigrans is also known as the Australian Rainbow Fish, but is so seldom seen that there is not much chance for confusion. It is a smaller fish, which reaches a length of 4 inches and despite its size is peaceful. Body color is green, with large, red-edged scales giving a reticulated effect. There is only one horizontal line. Fins are yellow with red dots.

This attractive fish has been pushed into the background by its larger cousin. Care and spawning exactly as for *M. maccullochi*.

Moenkhausia oligolepis is known as the Glass Tetra. It ranges from the Brazilian Amazon to Guyana and is a fish which does not enjoy a great deal of popularity. In the first place, it has no bright colors: the entire body is a lead gray, the large scales edged with black. The only spot of color is the bright red eye, and a black area which extends from the tail base through half the caudal fin. Another drawback is its size, 4 inches, and still another is that it enjoys a vegetable diet which extends to the plants in the aquarium.

Spawning this fish requires roomy quarters. An aquarium of about 30-gallons is about right. There should be abundant spawning plants, and

An unidentified species of Australian Rainbow Fish of the genus *Nematocentrus*. This genus is closely related to *Melanotaenia*.

Australian Rainbow Fish, *Melanotaenia maccullochi*. The male (upper fish) becomes more colorful during breeding time than the female. Photo by G.J.M. Timmerman.

The Emperor Tetra, *Nematobrycon palmeri*, a very beautiful aquarium fish first imported from Colombia. Photo by Rudolf Zukal.

A pair of Glass Tetras, *Moenkhausia oligolepis*, sometimes called Mirror Tetras because their scales shine like a mirror. The male is to the right. Photo by G. J. M. Timmerman.

the parents should be well fed for about 2 weeks previously with live foods and if available, some Duckweed, of which they are very fond. Spawning temperature need not be very high, 75° being about right. There is usually a great number of eggs, and copious amounts of infusoria should be prepared for the time when the hatched fry become free-swimming. The eggs hatch in 72 hours, and the fry begin to swim 2 days later. Feedings may be augmented by very fine prepared food.

Moenkhausia pittieri has the popular name "Diamond Tetra." The body does not exceed 2½ inches. The scales are small, and with lighting from above and in front, give off an iridescent sparkle. The male is easily recognized by his higher dorsal fin and much larger anal fin. The range of this fish is Venezuela.

Breeding quarters should be roomy, but need not be as large as for *M. oligolepis*. Otherwise, spawning procedure is similar. The fry, however, seem to be a bit touchy, and changes in temperature should be avoided.

Nannostomus anomalus is known as the Golden Pencilfish. It comes from the Amazon and Rio Negro basins. The pencilfishes are so named because of their long, slender bodies and pointed snouts. They have much to recommend them, being colorful as well as peaceful.

This species has a dark horizontal line which runs the length of the body, bordered above with gold. The tips of the ventral, anal and caudal fins are white. Males are easily distinguished by a diffuse deep red mark on the dorsal, anal and caudal fins. This species is inclined to be slightly shy when in company with other fish species.

Breeding this pretty fish is not very difficult. A well-conditioned pair is placed in a 5 to 10-gallon tank. The water should be neutral to slightly acid, and soft, not more than 8 DH. Temperature should be 80°, and there should be the usual bundle of bushy plants, on which the pair will spawn. Eggs are not very adhesive, and a bed of glass marbles or glass rods on the bottom will save some which would otherwise be eaten. Partial shading is recommended, as the fry are somewhat sensitive to light until free-swimming.

Nannostomus marginatus is sometimes called the One-lined Pencilfish. In this species, there is a wide black band above and below a golden stripe. This is the smallest of the genus, and probably the most popular. Besides the horizontal stripes, all the fins except the pectorals and the tail are red, edged with black. The females are fuller in body and have much less color in the anal fin. Length does not exceed 1½ inches.

A pair of Diamond Tetras, *Moenkhausia pittieri*. The fish on the right is the male.

Glass Tetras, *Moenkhausia oligolepis*. The black edges of each scale create the net-like pattern on the body. Photo by Rudolf Zukal.

Nannostomus anomalus, the Golden Pencilfish. Photo by Rudolf Zukal.

Moenkhausia pittieri, the Diamond Tetra. The male (upper fish) has a considerably larger fin.
Photo by Dr. Karl Knaack.

This is a pair of Golden Pencilfish, *Nannostomus anomalus*. The lower fish is a male. Though this photograph doesn't show it too well, the male has more red in the dorsal, anal, and tail fins. Photo by G. J. M. Timmerman.

A pair of One-lined Pencilfish, *Nannostomus marginatus*. The one line refers to the golden stripe which runs from the snout through the top of the eye to the base of the tail. The fish on the left is the female. Photo by Rudolf Zukal.

Propagating this lovely little fish requires a good deal of preparation. A 5-gallon aquarium is half-filled with clean, aged water which is soft and neutral to a little acid. A layer of glass marbles, pebbles or a bed of glass rods should be used, as this species is an egg-eater and the eggs are almost non-adhesive. A bundle of plants such as Anacharis is placed at one end. The pair will spawn on this, but most of the eggs will roll off the plants, to lodge on the bottom. Breeding temperature should be about 76°. Spawnings as a rule are not very large. A spawn of 50 eggs is considered very good. The fry tend to stay near the bottom at first and in order to get food to them, they may be fed at first with the finest-grained prepared food. This is eaten greedily. Finely sifted *Daphnia* or newly hatched brine shrimp may be added as growth progresses.

Nannostomus trifasciatus is known as the Three-lined Pencilfish. It comes from the Amazon, near the mouth of the Rio Negro. This beautiful member of the family bears three horizontal golden stripes. These stripes are bordered with brownish black. There are bright red patches on the dorsal, ventral and anal fins, as well as in the upper and lower portions of the tail.

This species spawns like the *N. anomalus*, but it requires very soft water.

Three-lined Pencilfish, *Nannostomus trifasciatus*. These are apparently both females. Photo by G. J. M. Timmerman.

One-lined Pencilfish, *Nannostomus marginatus*. The female, to the right, is visibly full of eggs. Photo by Stanislav Frank.

A diseased One-lined Pencilfish. The beautiful coloration of a once-healthy fish is now all gone, particularly the red and gold colors. Photo by Stanislav Frank.

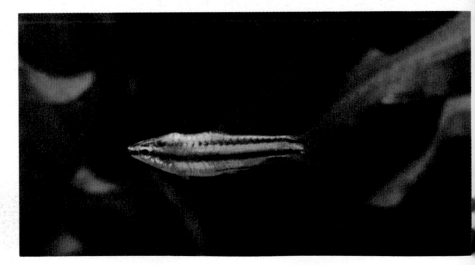

Three-lined Pencilfish, *Nannostomus trifasciatus*. Photo by G.J.M. Timmerman.

Nannostomus beckfordi, Beckford's Pencilfish. This species resembles to a very great degree the Golden Pencilfish, *Nannostomus anomalus*. Photo by Stanislav Frank.

Neolebias ansorgei is a tetra species from Africa. Male fish is to the left.

Neolebias ansorgei comes from Western Africa, in the region of the Niger basin. This fish is seldom seen, which is a pity. It has a dark blue body, white belly and blood-red fins. It never exceeds 2 inches in length. While it is peaceful enough in the company of other fishes, it is inclined to be a bit shy under these conditions and is best kept with its own kind.

A 5-gallon aquarium is sufficient for spawning these fish. Bushy plants or their substitutes should occupy half the aquarium, and the water should be soft and have a temperature of 82°. Spawning takes place in the plant thickets, and the eggs may take as long as 4 days to hatch and the fry 2 days to become free-swimming. The usual fry menu of infusoria, followed by newly hatched brine shrimp and *Daphnia*, is recommended.

Pantodon buchholzi is called the Butterfly Fish and comes from western Africa. Its large, spreading pectoral fins label it as a jumper, and it should never be kept in an uncovered aquarium. The body is tan,

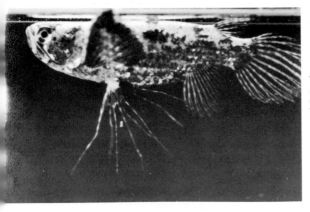

The Butterfly Fish, *Pantodon buchholzi*. Not a very common aquarium fish, though it has its followers. The fish illustrated is a female.

mottled with brown. Males may be distinguished by their slightly larger "wing-spread" and lighter bodies.

The greatest difficulty encountered with this interesting fish is feeding it properly. In its natural environment, it catches floating insects or makes prodigious leaps after flying ones. Judging from the size of the mouth, a good-sized beetle could easily be accommodated in this way. It must be hand-fed with pieces of earthworm, small fish, swatted flies, beetles or grasshoppers. When these are not available, substitute raw slices of beef, clams, oysters or shrimp.

On the few occasions when it has spawned in captivity, it is reported to have laid masses of buoyant eggs among floating plants. At a temperature of 75°, these eggs hatch after 7 days. A suggested manner of feeding the young would be to catch some live *Daphnia* in a net and allow them to remain there for a few minutes until partly dried. The buoyancy of the partly dried shells will cause the *Daphnia* to flounder around on top, unable to sink.

Phenacogrammus interruptus, the Congo Tetra, is one of several beautiful large tetras which come to us from the Stanley Pool region of the Congo River. A tankful of these beauties is a sight to make even a hardened aquarist gasp. They are fairly large, the female attaining 3 inches in length, while her mate exceeds these dimensions slightly. The sides, which are covered with large scales, are a shimmering violet, which reflect all the colors of the rainbow. The fins have a reddish color with deep violet edgings. The male has a much longer dorsal fin than his mate, and the tip has a frayed appearance. The middle rays of its tail fin also are elongated, and have this frayed appearance.

Spawning this lovely fish is not an easy task, and certain requirements must be considered. In the first place, this is a fish which needs a good amount of room. The largest tanks available should be provided, and a 20-gallon aquarium is considered minimum. The proper water conditions must also be given them. Soft, acid water is what is needed. Dr. Meder, one of the great German authorities, uses a solution of tannic acid in water of no more than 6 degrees of hardness. One tenth of a grain is used for every 10 liters of water. This water must be left standing for at least 2 days after mixing, or the fish will suffer. Another popular method of acidifying water is to filter it through peat moss until it shows an amber tint. A heaping teaspoonful of non-iodized salt for every 10 liters of water is also recommended. The recommended spawning temperature is 76°, and the usual spawning set-up for large tetra species, a mass of fine-leaved plants at one end of the large aquarium, is used. Parents are removed after spawning activities have ceased. Eggs hatch in 6 days. The fry are able to take newly hatched brine shrimp at once.

Neolebias ansorgei. Photo by G.J.M. Timmerman.

Phenacogrammus interruptus, the Congo Tetra. Photo by Dr. Herbert R. Axelrod.

Pantodon buchholzi, the Butterfly Fish. This fish should only be maintained in a covered tank. Photo by Dr. Herbert R. Axelrod.

Note the wing-like pectoral fins of the Butterfly fish, which enable it to skim the surface of the water in search for live food. Photo by Dr. Herbert R. Axelrod.

A magnificent pair of Congo Tetras, *Phenacogrammus interruptus*. The male is the upper fish, and he has long fin rays. The caudal extension breaks off from time to time. Photo by Rudolf Zukal.

Pristella riddlei comes from the Orinoco Basin, eastern Venezuela and Guyana. This small tetra is one of the old favorites. It is full-grown at 2 inches. The back is brown to olive green, and there is a faint horizontal stripe. The dorsal, ventral and anal fins are whitish. Each has a centrally situated large black spot. The tail is a bright pink. Males may be distinguished from females by their much more slender bodies. Maturity is not attained until it is past its first year.

A 5-gallon aquarium is filled with rain water which has been allowed to stand for a week. To this is added a small amount of potassium permanganate, enough to stain the water a light pink. A bundle of fine-leaved plants is placed at one end, and the water raised to 80°. They spawn like the other small tetras. They should be removed when spawning activities cease. Eggs are sensitive to bright light and should be shaded for three days, after which time the fry will have emerged and may be seen hanging everywhere in the aquarium. The young are sensitive to variations in temperature. They will be able to consume newly hatched brine shrimp as soon as they begin to swim. Growth seems to slow down considerably between the age of 3 and 9 months, after which it again resumes.

There is an albino strain of this fish. This is much lighter in color, having a yellowish tint. It appears to be easier to breed, which may be the reason for their great abundance on the aquarium market.

Pseudocorynopoma doriae, the Dragonfin, comes from the La Plata basin in Brazil. The male is distinguished by his large dorsal and anal fins, which in older speciments have elongated first rays. The body is silvery, except for a faint horizontal line. These fish are peaceful, but their tank should be kept covered. They are good jumpers. Full size attained is $3\frac{1}{2}$ inches.

A large breeding tank is required, but the water level should be low, about 8 inches. Eggs are released in clumps of finely-leaved plants, but are not very adhesive; for this reason it is advisable to provide a layer of marbles. Males perform a very elaborate courtship dance before the female of their choice before they are accepted and the pair dashes off into the plants. The eggs hatch in about 48 hours. Parents should of

A pair of *Pristella riddlei* with normal pigmentation. The male is the lower fish. Photo by G. J. M. Timmerman.

A male Rosy Barb, *Puntius conchonius*, displaying to a female (upper fish). In non-spawning condition, the reddish coloration is scarcely perceptible. Photo by Hans Joachim Richter.

Dragonfins (*Pseudocorynopoma doriae*) are peaceful fishes and should not be included with other fish species that nip fins. Photo by Gunter Senftt.

course be removed when their spawning activities are over. Fry will be seen swimming near the bottom in 2 to 3 days, and the first feedings should be with infusoria.

We now come to the *Puntius* species, popularly referred to as the "barbs." "*Puntius*" is really not the correct general name for all these fishes. Some belong to the genera *Capoeta* or *Barbodes*. Some authors place all of these fishes into the genus *Barbus*, but *Barbus* is a coldwater, European fish and in no way could include African and Asian tropicals. The correct generic classification may be found at the beginning of this chapter. The species listed here all spawn in the same manner, so it may be less repetitious to give general instructions here which will cover them and list the deviations, if any, under the individual species.

One thing we need not worry about with the *Puntius* species is the water characteristics. Any clean water which is not abnormally hard or soft will do nicely. Of course, the water should be aged.

Feeding barbs is no problem; their appetites are excellent, and they are usually the first to rush for any food which is offered and the last to leave it. The presence of a few barbs in a community tank is usually a good insurance against food being left to decay on the bottom. They will find it as readily as catfishes usually entrusted to this job. Of course, the individuals selected for spawning should be pampered a bit and given a preponderance of live foods. Worms, mosquito or glass larvae, *Daphnia*, and brine shrimp are taken eagerly. Fry should have a few days of infusoria to start them off, after which they are ready for sifted *Daphnia* or newly hatched brine shrimp.

The *Puntius* species are peaceful, as a rule. They are very active, and there is one thing which they *may* do: thread-finned fishes such as the angelfish and some of the gouramis should not be kept with them. Sooner or later these long, stringy ventral fins are going to look good to eat. This is not viciousness on their part; it's just hunger! This appetite of theirs might also be the cause of some of their slower, more dignified tankmates being short-changed at the dinner-table.

The best temperature for spawning is from 78° to 80°. Tank sizes range from a 3-gallon aquarium which would be enough for *P. gelius* to the really large aquarium of 50 gallons or so needed for the big fellows like *B. everetti, P. filamentosus* and *B. lateristriga.*

Spawning usually is not fraught with much difficulty, except for such rarities as Butterfly Barbs, *C. hulstaerti,* from Zaire (Congo) which require a pH of about 4.5 to stay alive!

Sexes should be separated while conditioning is in progress, to prevent them from spawning before you are ready. Some aquarists leave the sexes together and, when they are looking for a spawning pair, choose a female which is well loaded with eggs and a likely-looking male. The trouble with this system is that the male might have emptied himself of sperm a half hour before with another female! A well-conditioned pair may very well begin to spawn a short time after they have been put into the breeding tank. Usually they will oblige the next morning. As with some tetras, there should be a clump of fine-leaved plants at one end of the tank. It is not necessary to have gravel on the bottom; the plants may be weighed down with a small stone or a piece of glass rod. Spanish moss may be used instead of the plants as a spawning medium, but it should be soaked overnight before use and then well washed.

Pseudocorynopoma doriae, the Dragonfin. Note the fringed tip of the dorsal fin of the male (upper fish). Photo by Dr. Herbert R. Axelrod.

Pristella riddlei. It is very easy to distinguish the sexes during breeding time. Photo by Stanislav Frank.

Capoeta hulstaerti, the Butterfly Barb. Two males are pictured here. Photo by Dr. Herbert R. Axelrod.

The spawning act begins with a wild chase all over the tank with the male in pursuit. The female comes to an occasional stop. The male nudges her into the nearest thicket, where he quivers beside her usually wrapping his tail over her back behind her dorsal fin in the process. After a few seconds, she swims away, to be chased again. After a few false starts like this, the female will begin to drop 4 or 5 eggs on such occasions, which are immediately fertilized by the male. When all is over, an egg-hunt begins unless the parents are removed at once. Hatching takes place for some species in 24 hours, up to 48 hours for others. Fry are easy to raise; the best way to start them is on infusoria, but some success may be had using a finely powdered commercially prepared food. This should be shaken up in a jar of water before feeding, in order to saturate it and make it sink to the bottom where the youngsters will look for it. Growth is rapid, and the size of the food should be increased as the fish grow. The rule of thumb to be applied here: the size of the food should be no larger than the eye of the fish.

Once your barbs are growing, it is important that they are not crowded. Spawnings are apt to be large, and there must be enough room for all.

Capoeta arulius was introduced to the American market by Mr. Henry Huber of Staten Island, New York when he brought some fish back from Germany in 1955. Mr. Vanderpoel of Miami, Florida also shared

A pair of mature *Capoeta arulius*. Upper fish is the male.

A female *Barbodes binotatus*, the Spotted Barb.

in the propagation of these species initially. *Capoeta arulius* was first described by Jerdon in 1849, from specimens discovered in Travancore, India.

Mature specimens may get a little large for an aquarium barb, sometimes reaching five inches in length. As the males mature their color becomes more intense and the rays in their dorsal fins become elongated.

Breeding is typical with the pair scattering eggs all about the aquarium over bushy plants. This type of breeding has been referred to as "goldfish style."

The breeders eat their eggs as soon as they complete their spawning unless they are properly fed with tubifex and *Daphnia* during their spawning sequel. Eggs hatch in 36 to 48 hours after spawning, depending upon the temperature of the water.

These fish are very fond of plants and algae and unless some small amounts of algae or cooked spinach are made available, they will nibble the soft plants down to the stems.

Barbodes binotatus, the Spotted Barb, occurs in the East Indies, Malaysia and Thailand. Being large and not particularly colorful, we do not often see this species. It attains a length of 7 inches and has silvery blue sides with an indistinct horizontal stripe which ends in a spot at the tail base. There is another dark spot at the base of the dorsal fin.

A large aquarium of at least 30 gallons capacity should be used.

On account of the longer fins of the male (lower fish), *Capoeta arulius* is also called Longfin Barb. Photo by Rudolf Zukal.

Barbodes callipterus, the Clipper Barb from West Africa. Photo by Dr. Herbert R. Axelrod.

Capoeta chola, the Swamp Barb. A specimen collected and photographed by Dr. Herbert R. Axelrod in Sri Lanka (formerly Ceylon).

Capoeta callipterus; these fish were collected by the author in the Cameroons. The female (upper fish) is much heavier and larger than the male. Photo by Dr. Herbert R. Axelrod.

Barbodes callipterus comes from Cameroon and the Niger River in Africa. It attains 3 inches in length, and is peaceful as a member of the community aquarium. Many barbs from Africa have proven difficult to spawn, and some have so far defied all efforts in this direction. This is one of the difficult ones. They spawn like the others, but the difficulty seems to be in getting them into the proper condition. A medium-sized tank, in the neighborhood of 15 gallons, is sufficient.

The sides are a golden yellow, and the tail is a light red, which sometimes turns to orange. A black spot appears at the front of the dorsal fin. Males have a slightly deeper color, and are more slender.

Capoeta chola, the Swamp Barb, comes from India and Burma. It is often confused with the Rosy Barb, *P. conchonius*, but can be distinguished by the presence of a small pair of barbels or whiskers, which are absent in the other species. Another means of identification is a large purplish spot on the gill-plate. It spawns like the others, but, being a bit large (4 inches), a 20-gallon aquarium is recommended.

Puntius conchonius, the Rosy Barb, comes from India. This is one of the most popular members of this family and gets to be $3\frac{1}{2}$ inches in length. The female is silvery at all times, but the male undergoes quite a transformation when ready to spawn. The entire body becomes a deep, rosy red. The tail also becomes red, and the remainder of the fins a dusky black. There is a single black spot on the body, near the tail base.

This is one of the most easily spawned of all the barb family, and sometimes produces a staggering number of eggs. For this reason, give them a large tank if possible. Otherwise, the general instructions may be followed with success.

Puntius cumingi, Cuming's Barb, comes from Ceylon. It is one of the so-called "dwarf barbs," seldom attaining a length of 2 inches. Scales are large in comparison with overall size. The sides are adorned with two large black spots, the first behind and above the pectoral fin and the other near the tail base. The female's fins are colorless, but the dorsal and ventral fins of the male are a deep pink. This peaceful little fish makes a pretty addition to the community aquarium.

It spawns like the other barbs. Being small, a 5-gallon aquarium is sufficient.

A pair of Rosy Barbs, *Puntius conchonius*, from India. The male, to the right, is brilliant red in contrast to the silvery female.

Barbodes dunckeri, Duncker's Barb, comes from Malaysia. It is one of the larger members of this genus, with a maximum length of 5 inches. This fish is seldom kept by aquarists, for the simple reason that it is not attractive enough to warrant the amount of space it requires. It has a yellowish silvery color, with a dark spot below the dorsal fin. Females are slightly larger and heavier-bodied.

The Clown Barb, *Barbodes everetti*. Photo by Pinter.

Puntius cumingi, Cuming's Barb, is not too colorful even during breeding time. Photo by Klaus Paysan.

It is quite obvious why *Puntius filamentosus* is also known popularly as the Black-spot Barb. Shown is a pair spawning in the typical barb fashion. Photo by Rudolf Zukal.

A pair of Cuming's Barb, *Puntius cumingi*; the male is the lower fish. Photo by G. J. M. Timmerman.

A female *Barbodes dunckeri*. Photo by G. J. M. Timmerman.

A pair of Clown Barbs. The male is to the right. Photo by G. J. M. Timmerman.

It spawns like the other barbs, but does not seem to respond to pre-spawning conditioning as readily as most of the others.

Barbodes everetti, the Clown Barb, is native to Malaysia and Borneo. This 5-inch barb is one of the most popular of the larger species, as well as one of the most colorful. The fins are a bright red and the body a brownish pink. There are two wedge-shaped vertical bars, one just behind the head and the other halfway between the dorsal fin and the tail fin. A dark area occurs at the dorsal fin base, and a large round spot beneath it. There is a narrow horizontal line which extends from this spot to the caudal base. The male is slimmer and more brightly colored than the female.

This beautiful barb will spawn readily if given plenty of food and large quarters. An outdoor pool in the summer or a salvaged refrigerator liner are good substitutes for a suitable aquarium when spawning the large barbs.

A pair of young *Puntius filamentosus*. The male is the fish to the left. As the fish get older their appearance changes. Photo by G. J. M. Timmerman.

Puntius gelius, the Golden Dwarf Barb, is a small-sized species and which will not require a very large aquarium. Photo by G. J. M. Timmerman.

The T-Barb, *Barbodes lateristriga*. This species can grow fairly large even in captivity. Photo by Dr. Herbert R. Axelrod.

A pair of Checkered Barbs, *Capoeta oligolepis*, in pre-spawning display. Photo by Rudolph Zukal.

Within seconds of the time this photo was taken, this pair of Checkered Barbs spawned. The eggs were violently scattered and most of them were caught on the fine leaves of the plant nearby. Photo by Rudolf Zukal.

Puntius filamentosus is another of the larger barbs which come from Sri Lanka, Burma and India. Wild specimens are reported to attain a length of 7 inches, but we have never seen them any larger than 5. Body color is golden, with an indistinct dark area below the dorsal fin, and a large black spot a short distance from the caudal base. The upper and lower last rays of the tail are a bright pink, tipped with black. The dorsal fin is also pink. Mature males develop elongated dorsal rays, which give the fin a ragged appearance. Another sign of sexual maturity in the males is the appearance of nuptial tubercles on the face. These resemble pimples and are not a sign of poor health, as might be suspected.

It spawns prolifically in the usual barb fashion when given plenty of space, as for *B. everetti*.

Puntius gelius comes from India and is sometimes called the Golden Dwarf Barb. It is truly a dwarf, seldom exceeding 1½ inches length. For a barb, it is unusually slender; the sides are greenish gold, becoming olive green on the back and silvery on the belly. The sides are sprinkled with irregular black spots, and the fins are colorless. Males are slimmer, with deeper colors.

Spawns easily and does not require a large aquarium. Eggs are deposited in the usual barb fashion, but this fish has a voracious appetite for its own eggs, and a dense planting plus a layer of marbles or pebbles on the bottom is recommended.

A pair of Golden Dwarf Barbs, *Puntius gelius*. The male is the lower fish. Photo by G. J. M. Timmerman.

Barbodes fasciatus, the Striped Barb, is a very attractive species from Sumatra and Borneo. Photo by G.J.M. Timmerman.

Barbodes hexazona, the Six-banded Tiger Barb, is one of a confusing group of very attractive barbs which are often incorrectly called *"Barbus sumatranus."* *B. hexazona* is distinguished by having *six* vertical bars which are deep black in color. The ventral and dorsal fins are orange-red at the base, as is the anal fin of the male; females may be distinguished by a lack of color in this fin. This barb is native to Sumatra, and is of medium size, attaining a length of $2\frac{1}{2}$ inches. It is peaceful and active. Breeds like the other barbs; a 10-gallon aquarium is sufficient in size.

Barbodes lateristriga, the T-Barb, is a large member of the family that is found in Java, Borneo, Sumatra, Malaysia and Thailand. Wild specimens grow up to 8 inches long, but those in captivity rarely exceed 5. The sides are silvery, and there is a horizontal black stripe along the latter half of the body. This extends into a vertical bar in the middle, forming a letter "T" lying on its side. There is another vertical bar just behind the head.

Directions for spawning the other large barbs apply to this one, but spawning is not easy; on the rare occasions when it *does* spawn, it is usually very prolific.

Barbodes hexazona, the Six-banded Barb. Photo by Dr. Herbert R. Axelrod.

Capoeta semifasciolatus, the Half-banded Barb. Photo by Rudolf Zukal.

Puntius nigrofasciatus, the Black Ruby Barb. Notice the very attractive reddish coloration of the male, lower fish. Photo by Rudolf Zukal.

A pair of T-Barbs. The female is to the left. Photo by G.J.M. Timmerman.

A pair of Black Ruby Barbs. The male, to the left, is fully blushed with red. These *Puntius nigrofasciatus* are extremely beautiful when in full bleeding color. Photo by Rudolf Zukal.

Puntius nigrofasciatus, the Black Ruby or Purple-headed Barb, comes from Sri Lanka (Ceylon). It attains the size of $2\frac{1}{2}$ inches and when in color is one of the most strikingly beautiful of all the barbs. Unfortunately, the colors are not permanent. When seen in a dealer's bare tanks, it seems like a gray fish with four darker vertical bars. When put into a planted aquarium which it finds to its liking, however, a change takes place, especially in the male. The lighter portions of the body become a deep, ruby red. The bars become a deep black. All fins are colorless, with the exception of the male's dorsal fin, which is purple

Breeds like the other barbs; a 15-gallon tank is just about right. The temperature should be near 80°.

Capoeta oligolepis comes from Sumatra, as do so many other members of the genus. This pretty, 2-inch barb is known as the Checkered or Iridescent Barb. The male's dorsal, anal and ventral fins are red, edged with black. The caudal fin is also red, without the edging. The large, silvery scales are suffused with pink, and there is a double row of black spots on the sides, which alternate in position, giving a checkerboard pattern. The female's body is yellowish, and her only other adornment is the same checkerboard pattern on the sides.

These Checkered Barbs are very attractive. The male is the larger fish (uppermost). *Capoeta oligolepis* are also called Iridescent Barbs. Photo by G. J. M. Timmerman.

Capoeta tetrazona, the Tiger Barb. The fish in the foreground is the female. The dorsal fin of the male is edged with bright red. Photo by Hans Joachim Richter.

Barbodes pentazona, the Five-banded Barb. The fish on the left is the female. Photo by Rudolf Zukal.

A pair of albino Tiger Barbs. The fish lack black pigments on the body, including the eyes, which are red instead of black. Photo by Hugo Walters.

This species spawns readily, and a 10-gallon aquarium is sufficiently large. The fry should be fed generously with infusoria for the first days.

Capoeta partipentazona is native to Malaysia and Thailand. It attains a size of 2 inches, and is another in the group of small, banded barbs which is sometimes incorrectly known under the name *"Barbus sumatranus."* This species is distinguished by the fact that there are only three bands which cross the body completely; the other two pass through the dorsal edge and end a short distance below. The dorsal fin of the male is bright red, and there is only a slight suggestion of this color in the female.

Spawns like the other barbs, but is not as prolific.

Barbodes pentazona is another of the banded barbs. It is native to Malaysia and Borneo. It attains a length of 2 inches. This one is not as likely to be confused with the other banded barbs: the bands are not as wide, and are blue rather than black. The sides are coppery to red, and the belly is yellow. The fins are red at the base, with the exception of the pectorals, which are pink in the male and colorless in the female.

Breeding is not difficult and follows the pattern described for the others.

This is a pair of the rare *Capoeta partipentazona*. They are identical with *C. tetrazona* except that their second band is incomplete. Photo by G.J.M. Timmerman.

Barbodes pentazona, the Five-banded Barb. The male fish is to the right. Photo by Rudolf Zukal.

A pair of Half-banded Barbs, *Capoeta semifasciolatus.* The upper fish is the female. Photo by G. J. M. Timmerman.

A pair of H-Barbs, a variety of the Tiger Barb. The horizontal bar is absent in the regular *Capoeta tetrazona*. Photo by Herbert R. Axelrod.

A pair of Golden Barbs. For the present this popular fish is considered as a color variety of the Half-banded Barb. Photo by Rudolf Zukal.

Capoeta semifasciolatus is one of the few aquarium fishes which is native to China. It is small and peaceful, attaining a size of $2\frac{1}{2}$ inches, but not very colorful. The sides are a greenish gold with a series of narrow vertical bands which extend halfway down the sides. The fins are reddish-brown. Females are heavier in the body and have slightly less color. There is a golden fish with irregular black markings on the sides, and red fins, which was at first marketed as"*Barbus schuberti*,"after the late Thomas Schubert, a Camden, N.J. breeder who was the first to breed and distribute this attractive fish. This was later claimed to be a color variety of *C. semifasciolatus.*

Spawns like the other species. A 10-gallon aquarium is sufficient.

A pair of Golden Half-banded Barbs, *Capoeta semifasciolatus.* This fish is sometimes called "*Barbus schuberti*" because Tom Schubert was supposed to be the first one to breed the fish. The female is the upper fish. They are very simple to spawn. Photo by G. J. M. Timmerman.

A magnificent pair of *Puntius stoliczkai*. The male is to the right.

Puntius stoliczkai, Stoliczka's Barb, is native to Burma and Thailand. This fish looks like a small edition of *P. ticto*, with which it is often confused. The body is slightly deeper and assumes a rosy tint when the fish is ready to spawn, which *P. ticto* does not. Otherwise, *P. stoliczkai* has the same red-edged dorsal fin and the sides have the same two spots in the same places one behind the gill-plate and the other a short distance from the caudal base.

It should not be kept with thread-finned fishes; its willingness to nip these long fins is usually too great. Otherwise, it will usually get along quite well with its neighbors in a community aquarium.

This species breeds like the other barbs. Being prolific, a 20-gallon aquarium is not too big to use.

Puntius terio comes from India and attains a length of 4 inches. It is called the One-spot Barb for the obvious reason that it has only one spot on the sides, located above the last rays of the anal fin. The male of this species becomes deep orange at breeding time.

This species will usually spawn readily in a tank of 20-gallon capacity.

Puntius stoliczkai, Stoliczka's Barb. The dorsal fin of the male (left) is edged with bright red. Photo by Rudolf Zukal.

A pair of One-spot Barbs, *Puntius terio*. The male is the lower fish. Photo by G.J.M. Timmerman.

Capoeta tetrazona, the Sumatran or Tiger Barb, comes from Sumatra and Borneo. This another of the banded barbs, and is the one usually sold as "*Barbus sumatranus*."

Both fish are easily spawned by following the general directions for the genus. It is the most popular aquarium barb. An albino strain is established.

Puntius ticto comes from southern India and Sri Lanka (Ceylon), and is sometimes called the Two-spot Barb. It attains a length of 4 inches, and is generally peaceful when kept with other fishes of its size, but unfortunately it also will trim the long filamentous fins of the thread-finned fishes.

The color is silvery, with two black spots on the sides, one above the pectoral fin and the other a short distance from the tail. The dorsal fin of the male has a wide red edge which is absent in the female. All other fins are colorless.

Breeds readily, and an aquarium of at least 20 gallons should be provided.

Capoeta titteya, the Cherry Barb, is native to Sri Lanka (Ceylon). No chance of confusing this little 2-inch beauty with any of the others; it does not resemble any of them. There is a black horizontal stripe which runs from the chin to the tail base. The back is brown; the lower area and head of the male are deep cherry red. His fins are bright red. The

The Tiger Barb, *Capoeta tetrazona*, the most popular of all aquarium barbs. When in good condition they are extremely beautiful. They breed easily, but there must be a lot of room or they will be seen gasping for air at the top of the water. Photo by Rudolf Zukal.

The Two-spot Barb, *Puntius ticto*. The fish to the right is the female. Photo by Gunter Senfft.

The Cherry Barb, *Capoeta titteya*. The lower, more colorful fish is the male. Photo by Rudolf Zukal.

Puntius vittatus is another species of barb from India and Sri Lanka (Ceylon). Photo by Dr. Herbert R. Axelrod.

The Red-tailed Shark, *Labeo bicolor*, is a popular aquarium fish imported in large numbers from Thailand. Although individual spawnings have been reported locally, large scale spawning for commercial purpose is still not successful. Photo by Rudolf Zukal..

Labeo erythrurus, the Red-fin Shark, is another well-known Labeo found in many pet shops. Photo by Karl Knaack.

Rasbora daniconius spawning on the sand (above) and among the fine leaved plants (below). A large number of eggs are produced but many of them will be eaten unless the parents are removed soon after spawning. Photos by Rudolf Zukal.

Rasbora einthoveni, the Brilliant Rasbora. Photo by Dr. Herbert R. Axelrod.

Rasbora dorsiocellata does not show much color except for the single black spot on the dorsal fin. Photo by Klaus Paysan.

A pair of *Rasbora einthoveni*, male to the right. Photo by G.J.M. Timmerman.

layer of marbles or a bed of glass rods is a precaution which would save many eggs from being eaten. Fry hatch in 36 to 40 hours and are easily raised by the usual feeding methods.

Rasbora einthovenii is a smaller fish than the above, attaining 4 inches in length. Otherwise it is greatly similar to the above species, with the exception that the horizontal stripe is green and bordered with gold only on the upper edge.

Spawning as for the previous species.

Rasbora elegans, the Yellow Rasbora, is another large species, which attains a length of 5 inches. It comes to us from Malaysia, Sumatra and Borneo. There is a dark spot in the middle of the body, and a smaller one at the caudal base—this one is ringed with gold. A narrow, indistinct horizontal line connects the two spots. The anal fin of the male is yellow.

This fish spawns like the barbs, and an aquarium of 20 gallons capacity should be provided.

Rasbora maculata, the Spotted or Dwarf Rasbora, comes from Malaysia and is the smallest member of the family, growing to a length of only 1 inch. This is one of the most beautiful of all aquarium fishes, but its beauty will remain hidden unless proper conditions are provided.

Rasbora elegans, the Yellow Rasbora from Singapore. The male is the fish to the left. Photo by G.J.M. Timmerman.

The tiny Dwarf Rasbora or Spotted Rasbora, *Rasbora maculata*. The upper fish is the male. Photo by G. J. M. Timmerman.

Rasbora maculata may be a very small species, but it is a very colorful fish when in good condition. Photo by Klaus Paysan.

The Yellow Rasbora, *Rasbora elegans*. The male (upper fish) has deeper color than the female. Photo by Dr. Herbert R. Axelrod.

Rasbora pauciperforata, the Red-line Rasbora. Photo by Stanislav Frank.

Rasbora kallochroma, the Big-spot Rasbora. The lower fish is the female. The position of the body spots is distinctly different from that of *R. maculata*.

Body color is wine-red, with a violet iridescence. There are three large dark blue spots on the sides, ringed with a brilliant red. The first spot occurs directly behind the gill-cover, the second at the base of the anal fin and the third at the base of the caudal. The belly is yellow and the fins are red. Females are slightly paler in color and have more rounded bodies.

Requirements for spawning this fish may sound exacting, but the results obtained are well worth the extra trouble. In the first place, living quarters should not be too small; although 5 gallons is sufficient, 10 gallons is not too large. The water should have two qualities: it should be soft as well as acid. Three degrees of hardness is right, and the acidity should be in the neighborhood of 6.5 pH. Any deviation should be lower, not higher. Allowing peat moss to stand in clean rain-water for several days will get somewhere near the desired quality of water. A heater should be installed which will hold the temperature at 82 to 84°. Needless to say, these are not optimum conditions for the general run of fishes, and R. *maculata* should have its own quarters.

When first they become acclimated to a well-planted tank, the full beauty of this lovely fish becomes apparent. Soon the males begin to "feel their oats" and lively chases begin. Now is the time to select a well-rounded female and a lively male, if you wish to let them spawn. A smaller tank, say 2 or 3 gallons, may be used for this purpose. Provide a layer of glass marbles or glass rods on the bottom, as the eggs are not very adhesive. A clump of bushy plants should be weighed down to rest

A pair of *Rasbora meinkeni*. The male is the fish to the right. Photo by G.J.M. Timmerman.

Rasbora trilineata, the Scissor-tailed Rasbora, is probably the most commonly spawned of all *Rasbora* species. Photo by G. J. M. Timmerman

on these. Heavy paper should be pasted on three of the sides, and the tank placed so that a little morning sunlight falls into the open side. This little sunlight is important; it seems to stimulate spawning activity. As soon as things are to their liking, driving will start. Most of the spawning is confined to the darker portions of the aquarium, some in the plants, and some in the open portions. When driving has stopped, the parents are removed and the tank is then shaded completely. The fry hatch in 15 to 18 hours and become free-swimming two days later. The tank may then be uncovered, and feeding with infusoria is begun at once. Once past the earliest stages of growth, they increase in size rapidly.

Rasbora meinkeni, Meinken's Rasbora, is native to Sumatra. This fish attains a length of 3 inches and is not very strikingly colored. Body color is yellowish, and a green stripe runs from the gill-cover to the caudal base. There is a short dark line at the base of the anal fin. Females are fuller in the body, the only indication of sex.

The same general instructions for breeding the barbs also are applicable to this fish.

Rasbora trilineata, the Scissor-tailed Rasbora, comes from Borneo, Sumatra and Thailand; it is reputed to reach a length of 8 inches in its native land, but we have never seen them any longer than 5 inches. It is a slender, silvery fish, with a dark horizontal stripe. The real attrction is in the pattern of the tail: each lobe has a dark area in the center, with a margin of white on each side. The male is smaller and considerably more slender than his mate.

This Rasbora is easily spawned, and a 15-gallon aquarium set up as for the barbs will do nicely. Spawns in the fine leaved plants like the barbs.

Rasbora trilineata, the Scissor-tailed Rasbora. The upper fish is the female. Photo by Stanislav Frank.

Rasbora caudimaculatus, the Giant Scissor-tailed Rasbora. Photo by Dr. Herbert R. Axelrod.

A wild *Rasbora argyrotaenia* collected in a small pond outside Djakarta, Indonesia. Photo by Dr. Herbert R. Axelrod.

A male *Telmatherina ladigesi*, the Celebes Rainbow Fish. Photo by Hilmar Hansen at the Berlin Aquarium.

A pair of *Telmatherina ladigesi*, the Celebes Rainbow Fish. The male, lower fish, has longer fin rays. Photo by Chvojka Milan.

Telmatherina ladigesi, the Celebes Rainbowfish, is native to the island of Celebes, as the name indicates. No danger of getting these beauties mixed up with any other species; they have two separate dorsal fins, the first very small and the second dorsal and anal fins large and bright yellow. In the male, the first dorsal and anal rays are black and greatly elongated. The tail is also yellow, with a black streak in the upper and lower lobes. The body is light yellow with a bright blue horizontal line.

These fish should be kept in a well-planted aquarium which gets a good amount of sunlight, and the water should be slightly alkaline, pH 7.6.

A spacious aquarium is required, about 15 gallons. Some table salt added to the water, a teaspoonful for each gallon, is beneficial. At a temperature of 80°, eggs are deposited in the finely leaved plants, usually one at a time. If the parents are well fed, there is little danger that the spawn will be eaten, but the parents should be removed after a few days. Eggs hatch in 8 to 12 days, and the fry begin swimming (and eating) at once. A week of infusoria, followed by brine shrimp or sifted *Daphnia*, gives them a good start.

Thayeria obliquua is an attractive characin from the Amazon basin. It attains $3\frac{1}{2}$ inches in length, and makes an attractive addition to the community aquarium. It has a brownish back, and a silvery belly. A wide black stripe runs to the lower tip of the forked caudal fin.

Spawns easily at a temperature of 80° in a manner similar to the tetras. A tank of about 15 gallons is about right. One slightly different characteristic is that they will usually come together below the plants and swim straight upward, releasing the eggs while in a vertical position. The fry are very small. They hatch in 20 hours and begin swimming in 4 days. An extra week or two on infusoria may be required until they are large enough to take the larger foods.

Thayeria sanctaemariae comes from the same district in the Amazon; it is very similar in appearance to *T.obliquua,* the only distinction being that they are an inch smaller in size and the elongation of the lower caudal lobe is not as pronounced. Females of this and the above species have a heavier body than the males.

The Blackline Thayeria, *Thayeria boehlkei*, was, it seems, the fish which aquarists have been led to believe was *Thayeria obliquu* Eigenmann. The rare fellow is the real *obliquua*. As far as is known, all *Thayeria* breed and are to be maintained in the same manner.

Two species of Penguin Fish (also called Hockeysticks). The upper fish is *Thayeria obliquua;* the lower fish is *Thayeria boehlkei.* Photo by Dr. S. Frank, Prague, Czechoslovakia.

A pair of Blackline Penguins, *Thayeria boehlkei*. The lower fish seems to be heavier than the upper fish indicating she may be a female. Photograph by John Morgan.

A pair of *Thayeria obliquua*. This very beautiful fish was brought into the aquarium trade in 1960 under an "assumed" name. What we once called *Thayeria obliquua* (see photo facing page) is now *T. boehlkei*. Photo of the first fish imported into the U.S. by Dr. Herbert R. Axelrod.

A White Cloud Mountain Minnow, *Tanichthys albonubes*.

Tanichthys albonubes, the White Cloud Mountain Fish, is one of the few aquarium fishes which come from Canton, China. To be sure, it is not a tropical fish in the sense that it requires tropical water. It can easily be maintained in unheated aquaria where the temperature gets as low as 45°F. or as high as 85°F. They are the ideal fish for the beginning aquarist as it is quite a job to kill them by mistakes. For food they will take anything small enough to ingest: *Daphnia,* tubifex worms, dried food, brine shrimp, and any kind of mash that is offered.

Though their main attraction may be their hardiness, they are, without any doubt, the simplest egglaying fish to breed. As egg scatterers, they merely spray their eggs among fine grasses (they prefer *Nitella*) and ignore them from then on. As the young hatch they may be left in with parents for if the breeders are even moderately fed they will not eat their young, nor the young of any other fish for that matter.

The fry should be given infusoria for a week and then finely powdered dried food or newly hatched brine shrimp. You can raise babies and parents together without any trouble.

If you are ever called upon to present an aquarium to someone who knows nothing about tropical fishes, don't give him guppies, give him White Cloud Mountain Fish.

To the left is the usual, wild form of White Cloud Mountain Fish, *Tanichthys albonubes.* To the right is the long-finned variety which first appeared in a strain produced by Edward Sollory in Canada. After Sollory was ill and allowed the strain to disappear, it took ten years before another long-finned strain made its appearance in eastern Europe (1972).

FIRST GROUP

B. THE EGG HANGERS

Aphyosemion australe. The Lyretail
    bivittatum. The Red Lyretail
    calliurum. The Blue Calliurum
    cognatum
Aplocheilichthys flavipinnis. The Yellow-finned Panchax
    macrophthalmus. The Lamp-eye
    myersi
    schoelleri
Aplocheilus blocki. The Dwarf or Green Panchax
    dayi. The Ceylon Killifish
    lineatus. The Panchax Lineatus
    panchax. The Blue Panchax
Epiplatys annulatus. Clown Killie
    dageti. The Fire-mouth Panchax
    fasciolatus. The Banded Panchax
    longiventralis
    sexfasciatus. The Six-barred Panchax
Fundulus chrysotus. The Golden-ear
    dispar. The Star-head Top Minnow
    notti
    heteroclitus. The Zebra or Common Killie
    sciadicus. The Plains Top Minnow
Leptolucania ommata. The Swamp Killie
Lucania goodei. The Blue-fin Top Minnow
Pachypanchax playfairi. The Playfair's Panchax
Rasbora heteromorpha. The Harlequin or Rasbora
Rivulus cylindraceus. The Brown Rivulus
    dorni. Dorn's Rivulus
    harti. Hart's Rivulus
    ocellatus. The Ocellated Rivulus
    santensis
    strigatus. The Herringbone Rivulus
    tenuis. The Slender Rivulus
    urophthalmus. The Golden or Green Rivulus
    xanthonotus. The Yellowback Rivulus
Valencia hispanica. The Spanish Tooth Carp

The Lyretails, *Aphyosemion australe*, are probably the most commonly bred of the genus. As a result many color varieties have appeared, each with more or less red and orange, and with more or fewer red spots.

A male Lyretail with regenerated tips on his tail. Compare this fish with the male on the facing page. More details on all rivulins can be found in Col. Jorgen Scheel's book RIVULINS OF THE OLD WORLD, from which this photo has been taken.

A male hybrid *Aphyosemion australe*, the result of a crossing between *A. australe* and another species of lyretail. This hybrid is not fertile. Photo by Col. Jorgen Scheel.

An aquarium strain of the Lyretail, *Aphyosemion australe*. Note the predominance of orange and the slender filaments of the tail in this male. Photo by Hilmar Hansen.

This fish group, which we have chosen to call the "Egg Hangers," is distinguished from the first group by the fact that the eggs are hung from plants, usually near the top. These eggs are laid singly as a rule, and are attached to the spawning medium by a fine, sticky thread. A pleasant contrast to the first group is that these fish are not as a rule apt to eat their own eggs.This is not to say that they will not make a fine distinction between their own fry and other swimming food, however. Most of this group may be left with their eggs until hatching time, but should be removed as soon as the fry begin to put in an appearance.

It will be found that most of these fishes have a comparatively long incubation period. Because of this, the fry are able to swim as soon as they have left their egg-shells and are immediately on the prowl for food. The yolk-sacs are used up while the fry are still in the shell, and they are literally "born hungry."

Eggs are usually not all released in one spawning; a female will release up to 10 or 12 eggs in one day and on the following day may repeat the performance; the next day, she may not have any ripe eggs, and take a "vacation." Sometimes a healthy female will continue to lay eggs every day until she has accounted for 150 to 200 eggs. These eggs will begin to hatch when the incubation period for the first ones has ended, after which they will continue hatching. This results in a hodge-podge of growing fry of assorted sizes. These must be sorted and separated to prevent the smaller ones from being eaten by their bigger brothers and sisters. This accounts for the fact that few breeders want to bother with them and that prices are always high, in spite of the fact that they are almost all very easy to breed.

Water for these fishes should be soft, not more than 10 DH, and on the acid side, 6.5 to 6.7. They are native to swampy regions where rains feed the pools and there is a great deal of dead vegetation in the water. The type of water found in some swamps may conform perfectly with what is needed here. Look for water with a brownish tinge which is clear and clean, and test it; chances are that it will be very close to ideal. Unlike the egg scattering species, these are fishes which are not quite as active and do not need as large accommodations for successful spawning.

Water which is naturally acid as well as soft harbors very few fungus spores, thus even an egg which is sterile will not show a fuzzy white growth of fungus which spreads to other eggs and ruins them. This fungus is the greatest enemy which the incubating eggs have, but it may be controlled by adding enough 5% aqueous methylene blue to tint the water a light blue.

A male Lyretail chasing the female towards the bushes. Note the eggs laid earlier hanging on the plants.

With their bodies held in an S-curve and accompanied by quivering, a single egg is laid and fertilized.

The pair leaving the bushes in search of the next possible spawning site. The eggs are fairly large and can be picked up by hand individually. Photos by Rudolf Zukal.

A male Red Lyretail, *Aphyosemion bivittatum*. Photo by Col. Jorgen Scheel.

Two very beautiful Red Lyretail males. These are hybrids and are, unfortunately, sterile. Photo by Col. Jorgen Scheel.

A male Blue Calliurum, *Aphyosemion calliurum*. This species is very variable, and different color strains are known even in the wild state. Photo by Col. Jorgen Scheel.

Aphyosemion cognatum, male. This is a strain developed under aquarium conditions and may possibly not exist in the wild. Photo by Col. Jorgen J. Scheel.

Coming as they do from well-shaded pools, many of these fishes tend to show a preference for the shadier parts of the aquarium if the light is bright. It is therefore better to give them a tank location which is not too bright, as well as a well-planted tank. When spawning is desired, a bare tank with a small bundle of fine-leaved plants such as *Riccia, Utricularia,* or *Nitella,* may be used. Most aquarists when spawning these fishes have dispensed with the use of plants in favor of a much handier gadget, the "spawning mop." This consists of about 20 threads of nylon yarn, such as is used for knitting, cut into 6-inch lengths and tied together in the middle, with a small cork attached to make it float. Some prefer green yarn, which should be boiled before using to remove excess dye, but we have always had as much success with white-yarn.

There are two courses of action to take after spawning has taken place: one is to allow the eggs to accumulate for a week or so and then to remove the mop, eggs and all, to a hatching container; the other is to remove the mop each day and shake out all the excess water and then remove the eggs one by one. It will be found that this can be done most easily with the finger-tips. The eggs have a hard shell and a bit of pressure does them no harm. Tweezers may also be used, but here we must be careful not to apply pressure directly to the egg, but to close the tips behind the egg and then lift it away. When plants are used as a spawning medium, a bit of the plant may be removed with the egg.

Now the question arises, what to do with the eggs? We have found that the perfect hatching containers are the small dishes designed to hold a small amount of leftovers in the refrigerator. Some of these are made of plastic and others of glass. Some are clear and some are tinted. The best ones for our purpose are the tinted glass ones. Glass is easier to clean with boiling hot water, and if it is tinted there will be less light getting through to the eggs, which in some cases are somewhat light-sensitive. The glass covers which are provided with these containers should be kept on. This prevents evaporation of the water and keeps out bacteria and fungus spores; it also prevents sudden changes in temperature. Do not keep too many eggs in one container; containers are inexpensive and do not take up much room. Crowding eggs is as bad as crowding fish. 20 to 30 is plenty in a one pint dish. Every day, especially for the first few days, the dish should be held over a light. If any eggs have turned a milky white, they should be removed at once. The best and easiest way to do this is with an ordinary eye-dropper.

The fry should be removed as soon as they have hatched because of their immediate need for food. Here again the eye-dropper may be put into use; with a little practice, you will soon become adept at sucking in the elusive little fellows. A large container should now be provided. It may contain anything from a few quarts to 2 or 3 gallons. The water should match that from which the fry are taken, in temperature as well as chemically. Not much infusoria feeding is required; the fry's mouths are big and they are able to swallow newly hatched brine shrimp and the smaller sizes of *Daphnia*. Growth is rapid.

Aphyosemion australe, the Lyretail, comes from the Cape Lopez region of Africa and attains a length of 2 inches. This beautiful cyprinodont is a perennial favorite. The male has a virtual monopoly of the colors: body is chocolate brown, shading to a yellow in the belly. Pectoral and ventral fins are a bright orange. There are a great many irregular dots and short streaks of deep red in the body. The anal fin is orange at the base with a purple edge and white tip, and the dorsal is greenish yellow, spotted with red and topped with violet, again with a white tip. The tail is lyre-shaped, the center rays blue dotted with red and bordered with purple. The upper rays are yellow and the lower orange, both tipped with white. The female has a lighter brown body, and round fins. Her only other coloring is a few scattered red spots.

General spawning instructions cover this fish, and it is a ready breeder. One good male can easily take care of 2 or even 3 females. A spawning aquarium of 1 to 3 gallons is sufficient, and a temperature of 75° seems to be ideal. Incubation period is 12 to 16 days, and the eggs should be kept in a darkened location.

A pair of *Aphyosemion bivittatum*. The upper fish, the male, has longer fin rays. Photo by G. J. M. Timmerman.

The Lamp-eye, *Aplocheilichthys macrophthalmus*. These are two males; red dots are present on their tails which are missing in females. Photo by Dr. Karl Knaack.

Aplocheilichthys schoelleri, a pretty representative of the genus from Egypt. The male is the lower fish. Photo by Dr. Herbert R. Axelrod.

Aplocheilichthys flavipinnis, the Yellow-finned Panchax. The fish to the right is a young female. Photo by Klaus Paysan.

Aplocheilichthys katangae, the Katanga Lamp-eye. This fish is native to Katanga district of the Congo. Photo by Dr. Herbert R. Axelrod.

A yellow color variety of this fish has been developed. It lacks the intense color contrasts of the common variety, however, and it is safe to say that it will not supplant it in popularity.

Aphyòsemion bivittatum, the Red Lyretail, is another popular member of the family. It gets to be 2½ inches long. It occurs in West Africa.

As with this entire group, the male again has a virtual monopoly of the colors. Both sexes are characterized by two dark brown stripes which run the length of the body. The upper one runs from the tip of the snout to the upper part of the tail base, and the lower one from the chin along the lower part of the body to the lower part of the tail base. The dorsal, anal and tail fins of the male are large and have long tips and are covered with red spots. There are also some golden flecks on the sides. The female's only color besides the two stripes is a light sprinkling of red spots.

This attractive fish has the same requirements as *A. australe* and breeds in the same maner.

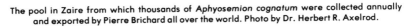

The pool in Zaire from which thousands of *Aphyosemion cognatum* were collected annually and exported by Pierre Brichard all over the world. Photo by Dr. Herbert R. Axelrod.

A pair of *Aphyosemion cognatum*. The male is the fish to the left. He is distinctly more colorful than the female. Photo by Chvojka Milan.

Aphyosemion cognatum comes from Zaire. Like most of the others, the size attained is about 2 inches; colors are few but effective. The entire body is reddish, suffused with blue. The gill-covers are blue, and carmine dots cover the body. These dots extend into the dorsal, anal and caudal fins, which in turn are edged with purple. The female is a bit lighter in color and is also dotted, but she lacks the edgings on the fins.

Breeds readily, and has the same requirements as the others.

The author collected thousands from a single pool close to Kinshasa, Zaire (which used to be Leopoldville, Belgian Congo).

All *Aphyosemion* breed more or less alike. For a very complete discussion of all *Aphyosemion* read Col. Jorgen Scheel's magnificent book RIVULINS OF THE OLD WORLD. It is a masterpiece.

Aphyosemion calliurum, the Blue Calliurum, comes from Liberia to Luanda, Africa. Size attained is 2 inches. The male is dark blue with a lighter back. The sides are decorated with rows of deep red dots which are crossed with vertical bars toward the tail. The dorsal fin is purplish blue and edged with yellow. The anal is also blue, with a purple edge. The tail fin is lyre-shaped. Its center portion is blue with red dots, and there is a red stripe with yellow edging above and below. The female is lighter in color and there are small red dots on her body and tail, which is round.

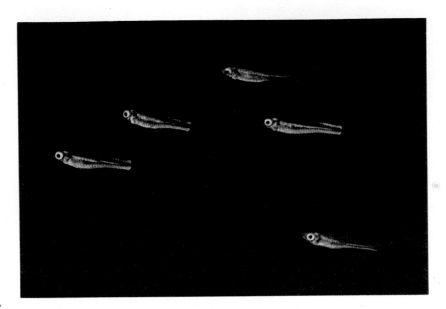

A small school of Myer's Lamp-eyes, *Aplocheilichthys myersi*. Photo by Mervin F. Roberts.

Aplocheilus blocki, the Dwarf or Green Panchax. This particular strain has red dots on the sides of the body and on the tail. Photo by Col. Jorgen J. Scheel.

A pair of African Lamp-eyes, *Aplocheilichthys pumilus*. Photo by Dr. Herbert R. Axelrod.

Aplocheilus blocki strain which lacks the red dots. This is an adult male. Photo by Col. Jorgen J. Scheel.

Aplocheilichthys flavipinnis, the Yellow-finned Panchax, comes from Nigeria. Length attained is only 1½ inches. This little fish and other members of the genus must be given the proper surroundings to be properly appreciated. The background should be dark, the aquarium well planted (it need not be a large one), and the light should come down from above. This fish comes from a region near the coast where there is sometimes an infiltration of sea water, therefore the addition of a teaspoonful of non-iodized table salt per gallon will be found beneficial. It travels in schools, and a small group will be happier than a single pair. It spawns readily in water which is slightly acid (pH 6.8), at a temperature of about 75°. Water hardness should not exceed 6 degrees.

When given proper feedings with a preponderance of live foods, it shows little inclination to eat its own fry or eggs, and the fry will be seen swimming near the surface unmolested. In order to give them their proper share of food, however, they should be given their own quarters. The youngsters can be removed with a spoon and a little patience. Immerse the spoon without getting any water into it, and work the tip near the little fish when he is near the surface. Gently lower the spoon so that the water and fish flow into it; a little practice and you are an expert. If you prefer to allow the eggs to hatch separately, the "spawning-mops" mentioned for use in breeding the *Aphyosemion* species will also be found useful here; these eggs cannot be handled as roughly, however, and it is best to allow them to accumulate. Incubation period is a bit shorter than for *Aphyosemion* species: 8 to 10 days. Leave the mop in the breeding tank for a week, and if it shows a good number of eggs, which are suprisingly large for such a small fish, remove the mop to the nursery tank. A second mop is then put in with breeders, to be removed after the second week and replaced by a third mop. By the time the third mop is removed, the first is again ready for use. A bit of patience is required in raising the fry. They grow rather slowly; for this reason, the commercial supply is usually limited and prices high.

The color of *A. flavipinnis* is greenish, shading to brown on the back and white on the belly. The dorsal and anal fins are trimmed with blue, and the males have reddish ventral fins, which are clear in the females.

Aplocheilichthys macrophthalmus, the Lamp-eye, comes from the vicinity of Lagos, Nigeria. Maximum size is 1½ inches. This little beauty is characterized by its large eyes which, in a properly lighted tank, reflect a bright blue glow. Two blue horizontal stripes, especially prominent in the male, run the length of the body. In addition, the male has a tail fin of light green which is edged with blue and peppered with red dots. The red dots are missing in the female.

Care and breeding as for *A. flavipinnis.*

Aplocheilichthys myersi is from Zaire. It attains a length of 1 inch and was first introduced to aquarists in 1955. The male carries two horizontal gold stripes, and the sides are gleaming blue; the difference here is that he has elongated rays in both the dorsal and anal fins. The last ray of the dorsal fin is especially long. An aquarist had a number of these fish in a 10-gallon aquarium with no plants and a box-type inside filter. He kept finding fry, but could find no eggs in the tank until he discovered that the top of the filter had come loose and the fish were swimming inside and spawning in the filter wool, where he found a a large number of eggs.

Normally the care and breeding is the same as for *A. flavipinnis*.

Aplocheilichthys schoelleri comes from Egypt. Maximum size attained is 1½ inches. The body is blue, with a fine black edge to the scales. The dorsal fin is blue, as is the tail fin; males have a red edge on the tail fin, and the ventral and anal fins are yellow. These fins are light blue in the females.

Throughout the edges of the rivers of Africa, tiny, colorless fishes may be found, floating slowly on the surface of the water waiting for some hapless insect to get close enough to be snapped up. No one has identified these fishes with any certainty. Photo by Mervin F. Roberts.

This is a difficult fish to keep, and care as well as breeding is similar to that of *A. flavipinnis*.

Aplocheilus blocki, the Dwarf Panchax, comes from India and Sri Lanka. Length attained is 2 inches. This is one of the old stand-by favorites among European aquarists which for some reason has not attained as great a popularity in the U.S.A. Body color is green, with a bright green spot on the gill-cover. Five rows of dark stripes adorn

The Ceylon Killifish, *Aplocheilus dayi*. Photo by Dr. Herbert R. Axelrod.

Aplocheilus lineatus, the Panchax Lineatus. This is the male fish. Photo by Hilmar Hansen.

Aplocheilus lineatus, female. The vertical bars are very distinct in the females. Photo by Col. Jorgen J. Scheel.

A pair of Panchax Lineatus photographed just immediately before spawning in the planted area of the tank.

the sides, and these are alternated with rows of red dots, which also pepper the fins. The fins are yellow, and the red dots are absent in the female, who has the further distinction of having a dark patch at the base of the dorsal.

This fish spawns in a manner greatly similar to that of *Aphyosemion australe*. The difference is that most of the spawning is done at or near the surface, attaching the eggs singly to floating plants or spawning-mops. Incubation period is 10 to 14 days, and well-fed parents are not very likely to make a meal of their offspring, so the technique of using spawning-mops described for the *Aplocheilichthys* species may also be used here. Fry grow rapidly but need infusoria for the first few days.

Aplocheilus lineatus is native to India and Sri Lanka and reaches $3\frac{1}{2}$ inches in size. This is the so-called *"Panchax lineatus"* which is popular and often available to aquarists here. The male is a light purple in color, and the body is lined horizontally with rows of yellow dots. There is a sprinkling of red dots which extend into the fins. The female is green in color and is easily distinguished by a dark area at the base of the dorsal fin, as well as a series of vertical bars on the sides. Both sexes have a red edge on the dorsal and anal fins and on the upper and lower part of the tail.

It must be remembered in connection with these pike-like fishes that they are predatory in nature but will not molest anything which they cannot swallow. They are not particularly fond of prepared foods, and will eat them only when very hungry. All living foods are eagerly consumed, and in the absence of these, bits of fish, shrimp, or beef are acceptable substitutes.

A pair of *Aplocheilus lineatus*, one of the best known of this group. The male is the upper fish. Note the characteristic mouth. Photo by G. J. M. Timmerman.

Like other members of the genus, *A. lineatus* spawns readily near the surface. A 5-gallon aquarium is sufficiently large and should be kept covered at all times, or they will surely be found on the floor some day; this goes for all of this family and is a good rule to follow with *all* fishes. *A. lineatus* eggs and fry are large, and the fry can be started on brine shrimp at once.

Aplocheilus panchax, the Blue Panchax, has a wide range which includes India, Burma, Malaysia and Thailand. This accounts for the fact that there is some variability as to colors in this fish. It attains a length of 3 inches. The male is usually bluish in color with a black lower lip. The tail is yellow with green edges and has a black border which in some specimens completely encircles the tail fin. The dorsal fin is black at the base and tipped with blue; the anal fin is yellow, edged with orange. The female is lighter in body color, and with the exception of a black patch at the dorsal base, her fins are colorless.

Care and breeding as for the other members of the genus.

Lucania goodei, the Blue-fin, is from Florida. It attains a length of 2 inches and is one of the most beautiful American fishes; in spite of this, it is seldom seen. The male has an olive-green body with a zigzag black line running from the mouth through the eye to the tail base. The dorsal and anal fins are large and colored a bright, shimmering blue. In contrast, the tail is pink. Females have no color in the fins.

It must be remembered that this fish is accustomed to somewhat lower temperatures than its cousins from distant climes. A proper spawning temperature for this species would be about 70° and not the usual 10° higher recommended for most "tropical" species. It is therefore not feasible to keep them with other fishes, although they are of a very peaceful nature. Slightly alkaline water (pH 7.2) is best for them, with a hardness of about 10 degrees. A few eggs are laid daily among bushy plants. These may be removed each day and placed in a cool, dark spot where they hatch in about a week. They may also be left in the breeding tank where the parents will not molest them if fed properly. After a few days of infusoria, the fry will thrive on brine shrimp, later graduating to the larger foods.

Epiplatys dageti, the Fire-mouth Panchax, comes from the African West coast and attains a length of 2½ inches. The species of *Epiplatys* are very similar in habits and appearance to the *Aplocheilus,* and what has already been said for them also applies here. *E. dageti* is one of the popular favorites; the body color of the male is a chocolate brown, shading to greenish toward the belly. There is a series of black vertical bars which begins toward the middle of the body and continues to the tail base. Red dots are sprinkled on the sides and continue into the

The Blue Panchax, *Aplocheilus panchax*. This is a widely distributed species, and numerous color varieties have been described from different areas of its range. Photo by Hilmar Hansen.

The Clown Killie, *Epiplatys annulatus*. Both males and females of this species are very attractive fishes. Photo by Dr. Karl Knaack.

Two male Fire-mouth Panchax, *Epiplatys dageti*. For a considerable length of time, Fire-mouths have been designated as *Epiplatys chaperi*, but ichthyologists have established that Fire-mouths are more correctly designated as *E. dageti*. Photo by Jorgen Scheel.

The true *Epiplatys chaperi*, as shown below, is a very rare fish and has probably never been available to hobbyists in commercial quantities. Photo by Col. Jorgen Scheel from his book RIVULINS OF THE OLD WORLD.

dorsal and tail fins. The anal and tail fins are edged with black and the outstanding feature of the whole fish is a bright red chin. The female is lighter in color and her only other markings are some vertical bars.

Like the *Aplocheilus* species, eggs are hung among plants near the surface, a few each day. Incubation period is 12 to 15 days; eggs are seldom eaten and may be left with the parents, but fry should be removed as soon as they are seen at the surface, lest they be confused with other food. If it is desired to remove the eggs for separate hatching, they are quite hard to the touch and may be removed with the fingers. Water which is soft and slightly acid is best.

A pair of Fire-mouth Panchax. The male is the upper fish. Photo by G. J. M. Timmerman.

E. dageti has an unusual characteristic: there is a great preponderance of females among the young. This may be a form of protection provided by Mother Nature; the males are eager spawners, and one male can easily fertilize the output of a "harem" of three females. When provided with a lone mate, he is apt to drive her too hard and then give vent to his frustration by tearing her fins if she is not separated from him for a time. It is therefore advisable to provide each male with at least two females. *Epiplatys dageti* for a long time was known in aquarium literature as *Epiplatys chaperi*.

Epiplatys fasciolatus, the Banded Panchax, attains a size of $3\frac{1}{2}$ inches and comes from the Sierra Leone region of Africa. The body color of the male is olive green with bright green dots forming a series of vertical bars. The dorsal, ventral and tail fins are edged with maroon. The female is lighter in color and shows faint vertical bars.

Care and breeding as for *E. dageti.*

Epiplatys longiventralis comes from Southern Nigeria to the Cameroons and attains a length of $2\frac{1}{2}$ inches. The male of this seldom-seen species is brown on the back, blending to greenish on the sides and a yellow belly. There are irregular dark bands on the sides and a sprinkling of red dots, which are not always plainly visible. Fins are bluish yellow in color. The female lacks the fin color and red dots.

Care and spawning as for *E. dageti.*

Epiplatys sexfasciatus, the Six-barred Panchax, comes from West Africa, attains a length of 4 inches, and looks a great deal like the preceding species. The difference is that the body color is more brown and the females have six vertical bars across the lower half of the body. The males also show these bars at times, but more faintly.

Care and breeding as for *E. dageti.*

Fundulus chrysotus, the Golden-ear, occurs along the Atlantic coast from South Carolina to Texas. Length is 3 inches; this attractive fish deserves a better place in the aquaria of hobbyists. It is a popular species abroad. Body color is green with a golden spot on the gill-plate and yellow fins. The body and fins are sprinkled with small red dots, among which are bright green dots.

There is a color variety of this fish which is even more attractive; besides the red and green dots, the body is covered with irregular black flecks.

Although it does quite well in totally fresh water, this fish is often taken from water which is at least slightly brackish. Therefore, the addition of a teaspoonful of salt per gallon is a definite benefit. Temperature should not be too high, 70 to 72° is perfect. Eggs are hung among plant thickets and are not likely to be molested. Hatching takes place in 8 to 12 days, depending on temperature. Fry are large and are able to take brine shrimp at once.

Fundulus dispar, the Star-head, occurs in the middle western and southern states of the U.S.A. Unlike *F. chrysotus,* this fish is very apt to be vicious toward other species, and this trait does not have any great beauty to offset it, so it is usually ruled out as an aquarium fish. Length attained is $2\frac{1}{2}$ inches. The most prominent marking is a golden star which appears at the top of the head; there is a dark bar which passes from the forehead through the eye to the lower part of the gill-plate.

Epiplatys sexfasciatus, female. Photo by Col. Jorgen J. Scheel.

Epilatys longiventralis (a male illustrated here) is a lesser known species that resembles the well-known *E. sexfasciatus*. Notice the greater number of bars across the body. There are other differences besides color pattern such as scale and fin counts, chromosome number, etc. Photo by Col. Jorgen Scheel.

Epiplatys fasciolatus, the Banded Panchax. This species has been a favorite for almost a half century. Different varieties are known both in nature and under aquarium conditions. Photo by Col. Jorgen Scheel.

Fundulus chrysotus, the Golden Ear. The male, lower fish, is very colorful, having more red dots than the female. Photo by Dr. Herbert R. Axelrod.

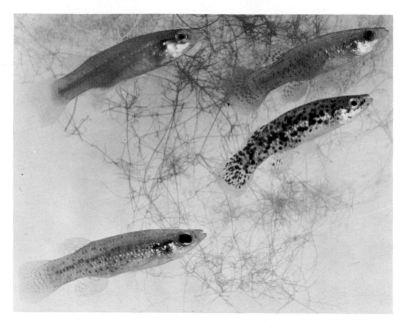

The most colorful fish in this group of *Fundulus chrysotus* is a male. Photo by Mervin F. Roberts.

A pair of *Epiplatys sexfasciatus*. The male fish is to the right. Photo by Gene Wolfsheimer.

The male is bluish, shading to green on the sides and a light yellow in the belly. There are a considerable number of dark brown dots and about 10 narrow vertical bars in the after half of the body. The female is lighter in color, but has 9 horizontal narrow stripes running the length of her body. Care and breeding as for *F. chrysotus*.

Fundulus notti is a close relative of the preceding species. It is more brownish in color and the fins are a brownish red. Care and breeding as for *F. chrysotus*.

Leptolucania ommata, the Swamp Killie, is found in swamp waters from Georgia to Florida. It gets as big as 1½ inches. The male is smaller than his mate and his sides are a yellowish brown. A dark stripe runs through the middle of his body. At the base of the tail there is a dark round spot which is ringed with gold. The after half of the body shows up to 8 vertical bars. The dorsal fin is yellow, tipped with blue and the anal is of the same color, edged with black. The female is lighter in color and lacks the vertical bars; she shows an extra ocellated spot on her side, just above her vent.

Care and breeding as for *F. chrysotus;* a 2-gallon aquarium is large enough here, however, where a 10-gallon one would be right for *F. chrysotus*.

Pachypanchax playfairi, Playfair's Panchax, comes from the Seychelles and Zanzibar. It will sometimes attain 4 inches in length, but the

A male *Fundulus notti*. Photo courtesy of the New York Zoological Society.

Leptolucania ommata, the Swamp Killie. The male, to the left, has a series of vertical bars which are lacking in the female. Photo by Gene Wolfsheimer.

Lucania goodei, the Blue-fin Top Minnow. This is a male with adult coloration. Females lack color in the fins. Photo by Aaron Norman.

Playfair's Panchax, *Pachypanchax playfairi*. The upper fish is the male. Males are more colorful than females, but the latter has a black bar on the fin base. Photo by Rudolf Zukal.

It is unusual for Playfair's Panchax to spawn on the bottom of the aquarium, but that's just what they are doing here. Note the black marking on the base of the female's dorsal fin. Photo by Rudolf Zukal.

usual maximum is nearer 3 inches. A close examination of this fish will show an unusual characteristic: the scales along the back stand out from the body, which is normal for this species but would be an indication of dropsy in any other. This fish has an undeserved reputation for viciousness; the only indication of this we have ever seen was with males which had depleted their females and wanted to keep on spawning. This is common with almost all males of the panchax family, who should be provided with 2 or 3 females each.

The body color of the male is tan; there are 5 rows of red dots on the sides, with an irregular sprinkling of blue dots among them. Fins are orange. The female is darker and a bit smaller, with colorless fins except for a dark spot at the base of the dorsal.

This hardy and prolific fish breeds like *Epiplatys dageti.*

A pair of *Pachypanchax playfairi*. The fish to the right is a male. The scales of the male seem to be extended from the skin. This is typical. Photo by G.J.M. Timmerman.

Rasbora heteromorpha, the Harlequin or Rasbora, attains a length of 2 inches and comes from Malaysia. We have separated this fish from the group which included the other *Rasbora* species because of its different manner of breeding. Its great popularity is richly deserved, being one of the most peaceful as well as one of the most beautiful of all aquarium fishes. The fore part of the body is silvery, changing to deep red in the after part. Covering most of the red area is a large, velvety-black triangle. The dorsal fin is red, edged with white, as is the tail. The first rays of the anal fin are also red. When the sun is playing upon it,

A trio of *Rasbora heteromorpha*. The fish to the right is a female; the other two are males. That the fish are from Malaysia is evidenced by the deep red color in their dorsal fins. Photo by G.J.M. Timmerman.

there is a beautiful overcast of violet. Both sexes share these colors; females are not easy to recognise, except when they are ready for spawning. Otherwise, their body is a bit more full, and the triangle not quite as clearly defined underneath as in the males.

Many aquarists regard them as an impossibility to breed rather than a challenge; however, anyone with the ability to breed Neon Tetras may find that this fish is easier. As with Neons, we must begin by getting a number of these fish accustomed to water like that in their native haunts. Here we find them in overgrown places where the water is very soft and strongly acid. For our purpose, a hardness of 1 or 2 degrees and a pH value of 6.3 or 6.4 will do nicely. A tank of 5 gallons, planted with wide-leaved plants like *Cryptocoryne willisii* and placed in a location which is not too sunny, completes the picture. As for fish, the best method of being sure of a good pair is to raise a number of them to breeding size. Feed them well on a good proportion of live foods and get them gradually accustomed to the water values specified above. Changing them from a hard, alkaline water to one which is soft and acid too suddenly may cause them a permanent injury or even kill them. Temperature should be maintained at 76 to 78°. Once things are as they should be, it will be noticed that the males are beginning to show an interest in the females, and courtships begin to take place. It is then time to separate the sexes until the females become swelled with eggs. Place a ripe female with the most colorful and active male, and things will soon begin to happen. The first stage is for the male to swim around

A pair of *Rasbora heteromorpha* spawning on the underside of a *Cryptocoryne* leaf. Many *Cryptocoryne* species are found in the same range as *Rasbora heteromorpha*. Photo by Rudolf Zukal.

A pair of *Rasbora h. espei*, probably from Thailand. They are much less colorful than the Malaysian species, *R. h. heteromorpha*. Photo by Rudolf Zukal.

The Golden Rivulus, *Rivulus urophthalmus*. The male is the fish at the left. Photo by Dr. Herbert R. Axelrod.

A pair of Brown Rivulus apparently in breeding condition. The female, lower fish, has a distinctive spot at the upper part of the tail base. Note the normal brown color of healthy fish. Photo by Stanislav Frank.

A comparison of the triangles of black on the sides of these two *Rasbora* species, *R. hetero-morpha* and *R. hengeli*, will immediately differentiate them. At the present time many new sources of *Rasbora* between Malaysia and Thailand are producing fishes which are slightly different in coloration. The fish from Malaysia look like the fish shown on the left; the fish on the right are from Thailand.

directly atop the female, making his presence felt by continually pushing her down. Next, the female begins to swim about under the broad leaves, assuming an upside-down position and rubbing the leaves with her belly. At first the male leaves her alone, but soon he swims under with her, and wraps his body around hers while in the upside-down position; she expels a few eggs which adhere to the leaf. This act is repeated over and over, sometimes using many leaves for the purpose; when completed, the parents are removed. Eggs hatch the following day, and when they begin to swim, the fry should be fed on infusoria. They are good eaters, and should be fed several times a day if possible. Once they are able to take brine shrimp and sifted *Daphnia*, feedings may be augmented with prepared dried foods, and growth is rapid.

Rivulus cylindraceus is native to the island of Cuba. Size is 2 inches. The male is slightly larger than his mate; body color is a chocolate brown, becoming greenish on the sides and yellow on the belly. There is a horizontal stripe of deep red along the entire body, as well as many red dots. The dorsal and tail fins are bright green, and the anal is golden. The female is greatly subdued in color, but has a marking all her own: at the upper base of the tail, there is a large black spot ringed with gold. Easily spawned, using the same set-up as for *Epiplatys chaperi*. Although somewhat sluggish in its movements, all *Rivulus* species are excellent jumpers, and a tank containing them should be covered at all times.

Rivulus dorni, Dorn's Rivulus, comes from the region of Rio de Janeiro. It attains a size of 2½ inches. The male is chocolate brown on the back, shading to lighter brown on the sides, and white on the belly. Each scale carries a tiny blue spot, and there are two larger spots at the tail base. A number of dark vertical bars adorn the sides. The fins are blue with dark brown bands and edges. The female has much less color.

This fish is not as easy to spawn, and sexes must be separated and conditioned for some time beforehand. Otherwise the same instructions as for breeding *Epiplatys chaperi* apply here.

Rivulus harti, Hart's Rivulus, comes from Trinidad and Venezuela and is the giant of the family, becoming 4 inches long. The male's back is brown, shading to green on the sides, which are covered with rows of red dots running the length of the body. The female is paler in color and has the usual "rivulus spot" at the upper part of the tail base which is evident even in young, half-grown specimens.

Spawning is typical, but, being a larger fish, somewhat larger accommodations should be provided.

Rivulus ocellatus, the Ocellated Rivulus, is native to the south eastern part of Brazil. It gets to be $2\frac{1}{2}$ inches long. The male is light brown on the sides, darker on the back and lighter on the belly. The sides are mottled irregularly and the fins are green; the dorsal, anal and tail fins have a black border, edged inside with yellow. The female is much lighter in color, and the "rivulus spot" at the upper tail base is much more distinct than the male's. Breeding as for the others.

Two males and a female *Rivulus cylindraceus*. Photo by Mervin F. Roberts.

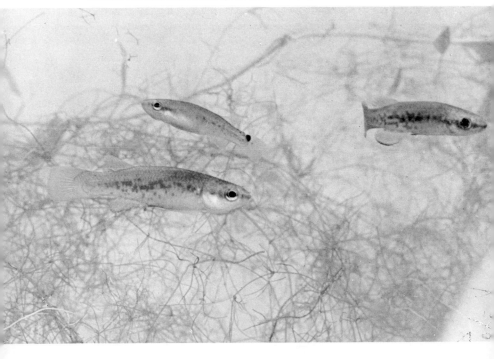

A pair of *Rivulus holmiae*, the Golden-tailed Rivulus. The male fish is easily identified by the colorful tail. The remaining photographs show the fish in different attitudes prior to spawning on the plants. Photos by Rudolf Zukal.

Rivulus strigatus is popularly called the Herringbone Rivulus on account of the chevron-like or herringbone pattern created by the arrangement of the red dots in the posterior half of the body. Photo by Dr. Karl Knaack.

A pair of *Rivulus strigatus*. The female (to the left) is lighter in color and mottled in appearance. Photo by Dr. Karl Knaack.

Rivulus compressus, the Blue Rivulus. This pair was collected from the Amazon and it is very unlikely to be found in pet shops. The male is the upper fish. Photo by Harald Schultz.

An unidentified *Rivulus* species. The female to the right has a very distinct caudal spot. Photo by Dr. Karl Knaack.

Rivulus ocellatus. Photo by G. J. M. Timmerman.

"rivulus spot." Some time ago, there was developed a strain of this fish with a golden yellow body, with the same pattern of red dots. This strain has become so popular that we scarcely ever see the original one.

Care and breeding as for the others.

Rivulus xanthonotus, the Yellowbacked Rivulus, is native to the Amazon Basin and attains a length of 3 inches. As the popular name indicates, the male has a bright yellow back, becoming lighter at the sides and gray on the belly. The sides are covered with red dots which extend into the greenish fins. The female has a "rivulus spot," with few red dots.

Care and breeding as for the others.

Almost all *Rivulus* spawn the same way.

Valencia hispanica is native to the southeastern portion of Spain. There is a considerable disparity in size between the sexes: the female attains a size of $3\frac{1}{4}$ inches, and the male an inch shorter. The male has a brown back, greenish sides, and a yellow belly. There is a large dark area just above the pectoral fins, and the latter half of the body has about a dozen dark vertical bars. Fins are reddish yellow. The female lacks the spot on the side, also the vertical bars, and her fins are colorless.

This fish spawns panchax-fashion, but the eggs should be promptly removed, lest they be eaten. Incubation period is 12 to 14 days.

FIRST GROUP

C. THE EGG BURYERS

Aphyosemion arnoldi. Arnold's Lyretail
    filamentosum
    gardneri
    sjoestedti. The Blue Gularis
    occidentalis. The Golden Pheasant
Cynolebias adloffi
    bellotti. The Argentine Pearl Fish
    nigripinnis
Nothobranchius guentheri. Guenther's Nothobranch
    orthonotus
    rachovi
Pterolebias peruensis. The Peruvian Longfin
Rachovia brevis

    We have here a group of fishes with perhaps the most unusual breeding habits of all. Mother Nature has really gone overboard to provide these beauties with a set of instincts which enables them to survive in places where there is water only during the rainy months.

Dr. Herbert Axelrod and Dr. Carvalho collecting *Cynolebias whitei* in Porto Alegre, Brazil. The water holes in the area are temporary and they disappear during summer.

Aphyosemion gardneri. Photo by Hilmar Hansen.

Aphyosemion filamentosum. Photo by Jorgen J. Scheel.

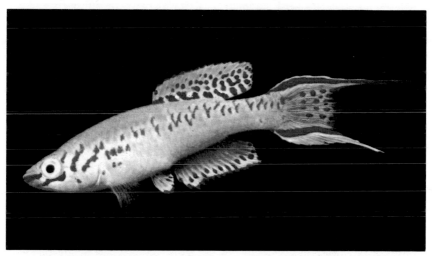

Aphyosemion arnoldi. Photo by Col. Jorgen J. Scheel.

Aphyosemion sjoestedti, the Blue Gularis. Photo by Dr. Herbert R. Axelrod.

These are the so-called "annual" fishes. They occur in parts of South America and Africa where there is a sharp contrast between the rainy and dry seasons. Streams and ponds are sizeable in the wet months but undergo a sharp change when the rains cease. In the ensuing hot, dry months which follow they shrink to a point where there is nothing left but a bed of dried, caked mud which is covered with countless bodies of dead, decomposing small fish. When the rains come later on, tiny fry seem to come out of nowhere and the water is soon swarming with fish life again. Aided by the rich infusoria culture produced by the decayed, dried-out plants, and also the bodies of their parents, these tiny fry grow at an amazing rate and are soon able to begin reproducing again. At about this time, the rains have stopped and things are getting crowded with the constantly diminishing water volume. Cruel, relentless death soon follows either from a lack of oxygen in the small pools where the last survivors are ultimately crowded or from desiccation when the last of the water evaporates. However, by this time thousands of eggs have already been produced, fertilized and buried in the mud. These eggs lie dormant through the dry season, like seeds through the winter. When the rains begin again, the shells of the eggs quickly deteriorate and release the fry.

Needless to say, these fishes, if we wish to breed them, confront us with a set of conditions which are difficult to duplicate exactly in the aquarium. Added to this, there is a long period of incubation which is sure to tax all but the most patient; after all this bother and long waiting, the result is a fish which in its natural habitat is destined to lead a very short life and cannot be counted upon to improve on this short span by very long in captivity. Why does anyone bother to breed them, except that they present a challenge? A good, long look at any of the genera listed above will give the best answer there is: they are among the most beautiful of all aquarium fishes!

For a very complete review of all African annuals, read Scheel's *Rivulins of the Old World*.

Aphyosemion arnoldi, Arnold's Lyretail, comes from Nigeria and is 2 inches in length when fully grown. Colors are difficult to describe, especially as there seem to be two variations. Both color varieties have a bright blue body with irregular dots and streaks of carmine red. The difference in colors lies in the fins. One variety has an olive-green dorsal fin covered with carmine dots, and the anal as well as the caudal fins are predominantly orange. The other variety has predominantly blue fins. The tail has the same lyre shape as the *A. australe*. The females have round tails and very little color. The two color varieties do not seem to interbreed very readily, but it will probably be just a matter of time when we will see all sorts of variations in color of this lovely fish.

A properly conditioned pair of these fish, that is, a pair which has been separated and fed generously on live foods, will be found to be ready and even eager to spawn. Getting eggs is the simplest part; what to do with them afterwards is what counts. Let us first consider what to do for a breeding tank. One of 5 to 10 gallons capacity, but not smaller, is right. If you have one with a plate glass bottom, all the better; it will be easier to find eggs. This tank is filled to a depth of 4 to 5 inches with soft, aged water to which has been added a heaping teaspoonful of salt for every 3 gallons. Temperature should be 73° to 76°. We now come to the problem of what to use on the bottom for a spawning medium. German breeders use a 1-inch layer of *Fontinalis*, or Willow-moss, for the purpose, which is perfect if available. If not, a bed of Spanish moss or fluffy nylon knitting wool may be used. Some floating plants should also be added to cut down the light. Further shading is also recommended by fastening dark green or black paper about half-way down the sides and back of the tank, leaving the front open. To prevent the fish from getting down under the bottom plants where the eggs are, several glass rods should be used to weigh them down.

All is now in readiness for the fish to be added. They will soon begin spawning, readily accepting the bottom as a substitute for the mud into which they would normally bury their eggs. They usually pick the dark corners of the tank for their operations, and this is where most of the eggs will be found. In the evening of a day when spawning has been observed, the floating plants are first removed, then the glass rods, and then the bottom plants. These are shaken as they are lifted out, to release the non-adhesive eggs which have not fallen through. If it is difficult to see the eggs, remove the dark paper.

We must now consider what to do with the eggs; a series of clean glass jars is prepared by adding water to about a depth of 1 inch. This water is important, as the eggs will spend a long time in it. It has been found that there is very little bacterial life in water which is acid as well as clean, so we must prepare some clean, aged rain water by adding peat moss and letting it stand until a pH value of 5.8 to 6 is attained. This is the proper water for the jars, unless you find some spring water of the same values. The eggs are picked up with a thin glass tube, using it like a dip-tube. When transferring the eggs to a jar, hold the tube into the water and do no release the water from the breeding tank; merely allow the eggs to roll in of their own weight. The fish are waiting patiently in a dark corner while

A male Golden Pheasant, *Aphyosemion occidentalis*. Photo by Hans Joachim Richter.

A pair of Golden Pheasants diving into the spawning grass. The female is the fish to the right. Photo by Hans Joachim Richter.

A pair of *Nothobranchius rachovi* shown in different attitudes prior to spawning. The less colorful fish is the female. Photo series by Hans Joachim Richter.

A pair of *Cynolebias adloffi*. This species is highly sexually dimorphic. The male fish has a barred pattern missing in the female, to the right. Photo by Harald Schultz.

A closer view of the male *Cynolebias adloffi*. In addition to the presence of black bars, the fins of the male are also different from those of the female. Photo by Dr. Karl Knaack.

A pair of Blue Gularis, *Aphyosemion sjoestedti*, in spawning condition. The male, to the left, is actively driving the female who is receptive of the attention.

The male slightly pinning down the female into spawning position.

While lying side by side, with their tails half-buried in the sand, eggs are laid and fertilized in the shallow excavation. Photos by Rudolf Zukal.

fish are very able jumpers. In a few days, things should be progressing; it is now time to hunt for the eggs. To do this, there should be a weak light placed at the side of the tank; the eggs are then brought up by gently stirring the sand with a glass rod; they are then picked up in a glass tube, as was described for *A. arnoldi*, and transferred to a small jar which contains water from the breeding tank, tinted a light blue by the addition of a drop of 5% methylene blue to hold down fungus. Like all the others in the genus, only a limited number of eggs are laid each day. This does not mean that eggs must be gathered daily, but the greedy parents are not above eating any eggs they might stir up while spawning, so it is best not to wait too long between egg-hunts. Hatching jars should be stored in complete darkness and should be taken out only once in a while in a weak light to remove those eggs which have turned white.

Now comes the bad news: these eggs do not hatch until a period of at least 4 mouths has passed. This period may be prolonged to as much as 6 months. If, at the end of this time the fry are seen wriggling inside the shell, they can be released by frequent changes of water. Once they are out, feeding with brine shrimp and fine *Daphnia* should begin at once; their appetites are enormous, and they grow unbelievably fast.

Cynolebias adloffi is fully grown at 2 inches and comes from the Santa Catarina region of Brazil. This genus is a representative of the true annual fishes and the pools they inhabit dry out completely in a normal summer. The male is a bright blue, with a dark bar running through the eye. A series of dark, narrow bars, 9 to 12 in number, runs vertically on the body. The fins are dark blue, with almost black margins. The female bears little resemblance to her mate; she is a light, dirty brown and the vertical bars are barely visible.

This fish spawns like the *Aphyosemion arnoldi*, and a similar set-up may be used. The eggs are gathered in the same manner, but instead of putting them in a small jar for incubation purposes, they should be put between two layers, ½-inch thick, of boiled peat moss in a covered dish. This peat moss is allowed to drain, but should not be more than moist. The dish being covered, the peat moss will not become completely dry. The eggs are stored in a place which is completely dark and has a fairly constant temperature of 75° to 78°. After 6 weeks, the eggs should be closely examined. If the eyes are visible, the time has come to let them hatch. Place them in a shallow aquarium of the same water the parents had. If the eggs do not hatch within 1 or 2 days, try frequent changes of water. Allowing them to hatch too soon causes many of them to have defective swim-bladders, as a result of

The Argentine Pearl Fish, *Cynolebias bellotti*. This is a male fish. Females of this species are not blue but mottled brown in color. Photo by Hilmar Hansen.

A male *Cynolebias nigripinnis* diving into the bottom followed by two females. Photo by Rudolf Zukal.

A male, left, and a female *Nothobranchius guentheri*. Typical of the group, the male is very colorful. Photo by Rudolf Zukal.

The male pinning the female on the sand with his dorsal fin wrapped around her body. For serious breeding of annual fishes it is best to use a soft spawning material instead of plain sand. Photo by Rudolf Zukal.

which they slide around on the bottom on their bellies. These fish are usually healthy otherwise and will often live a long time in spite of this malady. If a spawning turns out to be healthy, make a note of the length of the incubation period; it is a handy bit of information for future spawnings. Fry require generous feedings and grow rapidly.

Cynolebias bellotti, the Argentine Pearl Fish, is native to the region around Buenos Aires, Argentina. Maximum size is 3 inches. The male is green in color, and the entire body, as well as the fins, is covered with fairly large, white spots. The dorsal and anal fins are deep blue, becoming deeper at the edges. The tail is green with a red border. The female could not possibly be mistaken for a male, but might be believed to be a different species: body color is a much lighter green, with a series of irregular vertical brown markings. The fins are a yellowish olive, veined with brown markings.

These fish breed like the preceding species; all the *Cynolebias* group, it should be mentioned, will not take dried foods readily; they should be fed on as great a variety of living foods as possible.

A young male (smaller fish) and an older male Argentine Pearl Fish. Photo by G.J.M. Timmerman.

A pair of *Cynolebias nigripinnis*. The male is the lower fish. Photo by Rudolf Zukal.

Cynolebias nigripinnis comes from the same region as *C. bellotti*. Maximum size is 2 inches. The body and fins of the male are blue-black, sprinkled all over with dots of shimmering blue. These dots are closely grouped on the gill-plates, and form a line on the upper edge of the dorsal fin. The female is smaller than her mate by a good half inch. Her body is a light brown, marbled with reddish irregular markings. Her fins are very light, veined with reddish streaks.

Spawns like the others.

Nothobranchius guentheri, Günther's Nothobranch, comes from the east coast of Africa and Zanzibar. It attains a size of 3 inches. The male is blue and has a golden edge on his anal fin. The tail is bright red with a brown edge. The dorsal and anal fins are a yellowish green with red markings, and the rest of the fins are bright blue with a white edge. The female is green, with colourless fins.

Breeding procedure is similar to that for *Cynolebias adloffi*.

Nothobranchius orthonotus comes from the east coast of Africa and attains a length of 3 inches. The male's body varies from green to blue, and is dotted irregularly with red. The fins are red with darker margins. The female is green with a sparse sprinkling of red dots.

Care and spawning are also similar to *C. adloffi*.

Nothobranchius rachovi, Rachow's Nothobranch, has a maximum size of only 2 inches and comes from Portuguese East Africa. The

A male Peruvian Longfin preventing the female from leaving the bottom. Photo by Horst Abel.

A male *Pterolebias peruensis*, the Peruvian Longfin. Photo by Stanislav Frank.

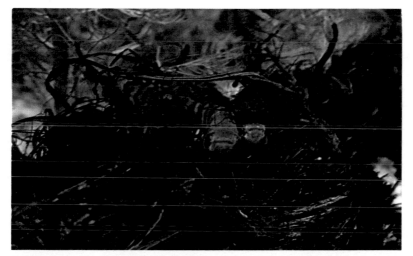

A pair of Peruvian Longfins almost buried in the spawning material where the eggs are dropped. Photo by Horst Abel.

A pair of *Rachovia brevis*. This is a poorly known species from Colombia. The upper fish is the male. Photo by Dr. Herbert R. Axelrod.

Rhodeus amarus, an aquarium coldwater fish suitable for keeping with goldfish. Photo by Dr. Herbert R. Axelrod.

The Bitterling is a very popular fish in Europe, probably mostly because of its unusual breeding habits. Photo by Klaus Paysan.

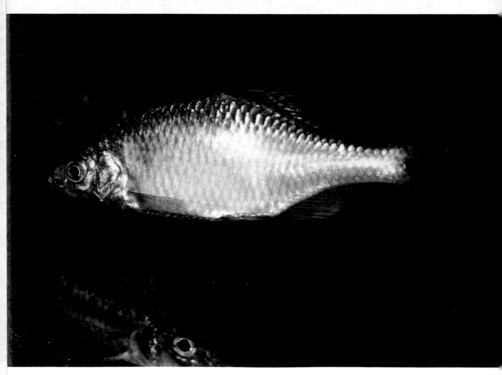

A female Bitterling on the verge of inserting her ovipositor into the siphon of a fresh-water mussel. Photo by Laurence E. Perkins.

Rhodeus sericeus, the Bitterling, attains a length of 3 inches and occurs in many sections of central and southern Europe. As with many fishes from the temperate regions, they are brilliantly beautiful when spawning and at other times just silvery with an indistinct horizontal stripe in the latter half of the body. At spawning time, this stripe becomes a bright blue, and the belly and anal fin of the male are bright red. The outer half of the tail is yellow, and the dorsal fin yellow with green markings. The female shows the horizontal stripe,. but her only other color is a faint pink maidenly blush.

The natural spawning period for this fish is between the months of April and June. When the female is plump with eggs and the male in full color, they should be given a well-planted aquarium of about 10 gallons capacity, with aged water and a temperature of about 70°. Several freshwater mussels are laid on the bottom, where they will soon dig in. When she is ready to lay eggs, the female develops a long pink tube which dangles down; this tube is about 2 inches long and looks like a worm hanging from her body. She selects one of the mussels and very gently inserts this tube between its valves. This ticklish operation completed, she sends down as many as 40 eggs; the male stands by, and when the tube is removed, ejects his sperm near the opening. This is inhaled by the mussel with the stream of water which constantly passes through its gills and reaches the eggs in this manner. The eggs remain in the mussel for a period of 4 to 5 weeks, protected and aerated constantly by their host, and causing it no harm nor inconvenience whatsoever. After this time the young emerge, and after a few days on infusoria, they grow nicely on brine shrimp and larger foods.

If you look closely at this pair of Bitterlings, you can see the extended ovipositor of the female (fish to the left). Photo by G. J. M. Timmerman.

SECOND GROUP

A. THE EGG ANCHORERS

Aequidens curviceps
    maroni. The Keyhole Cichlid
    portalegrensis. The Black Acara
    pulcher. The Blue Acara
Astronotus ocellatus. The Oscar
Cichlasoma aureum. The Golden Cichlid
    bimaculatum. The Two-spotted Cichlid
    cyanoguttatum. The Texas Cichlid
    facetum. The Chanchito
    meeki. The Firemouth
    nigrofasciatum. The Convict Cichlid
    octofasciatum. The Jack Dempsey
    severum. The Banded Cichlid
    spectabile
    spilurum. The Blue Convict Cichlid
    tetracanthus
    urophthalmus
Crenicichla dorsocellata. The Two-spotted Pike Cichlid
    lepidota. The Pike Cichlid
    saxatilis. The Ring-tailed Pike Cichlid
Dormitator latifrons. The Broad-headed Sleeper
    maculatus. The Spotted Sleeper
Elassoma evergladei. The Pygmy Sunfish
Geophagus brasiliensis. The Pearl Cichlid
Hemichromis bimaculatus. The Jewel Fish
    bimaculatus II. The Red Jewel Fish
Julidochromis marlieri. Marlier's Julie
    ornatus. The Julie
Lamprologus brichardi. The Lyretail Cichlid
Loricaria parva. The Whiptail
Mogurnda mogurnda. The Purple-striped Gudgeon
Monocirrhus polyacanthus. The Leaf Fish
Nanochromis nudiceps. The Congo Dwarf Cichlid
Pterophyllum scalare. The Angelfish
Pyrrhulina vittata. Banded Pyrrhulina
Steatocranus casuarius. The Lionhead Cichlid
Symphysodon aequifasciata axelrodi. The Brown or Common Discus

Aequidens portalegrensis, the Black Acara is also known as the Port Cichlid. Photo by Hilmar Hansen.

Aequidens maroni, the Keyhole Cichlid. Photo by Wolfgang Bechtle.

A Keyhole Cichlid watching a clutch of eggs laid on the log. Photo by Rudolf Zukal.

A pair of wild *Aequidens pulcher*, collected and photographed in Venezuela by Dr. Herbert R. Axelrod, in a posed tug of war.

A pair of *Aequidens curviceps* in breeding condition. Note the very prominent breeding tube of the female fish to the right. Photo by Rudolf Zukal.

In the breeding of this group of fishes the eggs, and in most cases, the fry receive parental attention. Definite spawning sites are sought out and prepared, and the eggs are kept under constant surveillance. This duty is at times shared by both parents and sometimes taken over by either parent. The sight of a well-mated pair of these fishes herding their young like a mother hen fussing with her chicks is one of the most charming spectacles which the aquarium hobby has to offer.

Unfortunately, all is not "beer and skittles" with these fishes. For one thing, they are a bit choosy when it comes to picking a mate; the advice that it is best to let at least a half-dozen grow up together when breeders are desired becomes doubly important here. When they become mature and ready to breed they will "pair off." When pairing is observed and the pairs are given their own quarters they will usually be found to be compatible and there is not much trouble. If, however, circumstances are such that only one pair is available, then it is best to separate them until the female is plump with spawn and the male signifies that he is also ready for spawning by his bright colors and aggressive manner. Put them together at a time when they can be observed. If there is no friction between them and the male does not snap at the female so viciously that her fins are torn, it can usually be assumed that all will go well. Sometimes things go well for a couple of days and suddenly for no apparent reason one or the other parent will decide that the eggs or fry should be eaten and proceeds to do so. A number of factors can cause this: one might be hunger; the female might be so busy with the eggs and young that she pays no attention to food and finally finds that the eggs are the only thing fit to eat. The usual reason for cannibalism is an undue amount of disturbance. This leaves the prospective breeder of these fishes with a decision to make, whether to play safe by taking the eggs away from the parents and incubating them by artificial means, or to leave the eggs with the parents and possibly get hours of pleasure afterwards, watching the parental behavior of these fascinating fishes. For the answer to this question, it is merely necessary to ask one's self which is wanted more, the youngsters or the pleasure of watching the family in operation, with the gamble that the youngsters might be eaten.

The female A. curviceps is about to drop the first egg as the male fish waits patiently alongside. Photo by Rudolf Zukal.

Eggs may easily be removed from the tank where they were laid, unless they were attached to the glass sides or the bottom. In this case, the parents must be removed. The eggs when left with the parents are constantly fanned with a gentle motion of the pectoral fins; this operation is duplicated mechanically by placing an aerator near the eggs and passing a gentle stream of air through it so that the water

The male *Aequidens curviceps* (?) follows the female in a tight circle, fertilizing the eggs as she lays them on the rock. It is amazing that she never lays one egg on top of another. Photo by Hans Joachim Richter.

is set in motion over the eggs. Do not make the mistake of placing the stone so near that the bubbles cling to the eggs; this will often kill them. The reason for recommending a gentle stream of air is that a stream which is too strong will pick up too much sediment and land it on the eggs; this is also harmful. The parent fishes keep the eggs clean by gently mouthing them at intervals, and artificial incubation does not duplicate this act. Most of this group are large enough when they begin to swim to be started on brine shrimp; individual instructions will be more explicit on this score.

Aequidens curviceps occurs in many parts of the Amazon River system and is fully grown at 3 inches. The male's sides are blue, shading to green in the region of the belly. There are three indistinct bars located on the upper part of the body. Tail and anal fin are yellow as is the after tip of the dorsal fin. The rest is blue with a red edge. Females are slightly lighter in color, and the dorsal and anal fins are less pointed than those of the male.

This fish breeds in the typical cichlid manner. When ready, a small tube begins to protrude from the vent of both sexes; when this is seen, action can be expected very shortly, and if they have not already been given a tank to themselves, one of at least 10 gallons capacity should be provided. As this species is a bit shy, the tank should be generously planted and a few rocks placed at various points. Temperature should approximate 76°, and the type of water does not seem to be very critical. The pair, after much searching, will select a site for spawning, which they clean off with meticulous care. This having been done to their satisfaction, the female then swims with her vent close to the surface of the spawning site; at first nothing happens, but soon she leaves behind her a row of eggs. The male follows close behind, spraying his milt upon them. This action is repeated until the spawning site contains row after row of eggs, often numbering several hundred. When spawning is finished, one or the other takes a position close to the eggs, fanning them with alternate motions of the pectoral fins and occasionally keeping them clean by mouthing each one; this is done so gently that the eggs are neither crushed nor torn from their position. Hatching takes place in 4 days, and the parents provide the helpless, squirming young with scooped-out depressions where they continue to be fanned. Soon they begin to swim, at first in short hops. This is where the parents become really vigilant, picking them up in the mouth and spitting them back as soon as they stray too far. Infusoria should be added to the water as soon as the young begin swimming, as well as the live foods with which the parents were provided all along. Sometimes one or the other parent wants to have all

The eggs are laid mostly in short rows or strings and in some instances singly. Photo by Rudolf Zukal.

The female *Aequidens curviceps* withdraws from the egg mass and waits close by as the male fertilizes the eggs. Photo by Rudolf Zukal.

A group of *Aequidens curviceps* fry being watched by the female parent. The fry have been earlier transferred to this shallow pit by the male from the egg site. Photo by Hans Joachim Richter.

As growth proceeds the fry swim about the parents watching near-by. At this stage the fry are still dependent on their yolk sacs for nutrition. Photo by Hans Joachim Richter.

A male *Aequidens curviceps* fanning the eggs. Dead eggs are removed and each egg is meticulously cleaned by careful mouthing. Photo by Rudolf Zukal.

the parental duties to itself and signifies this desire by making life miserable for the other. If this is the case, remove the attacked fish to other quarters; one parent with the young is enough. When the youngsters are able to swim about freely and take care of themselves, the parents are apt to eat them. At this time the young will do very well by themselves. After a few days of infusoria, they can cope with newly hatched brine shrimp and gradually other larger foods.

A. curviceps is well-known as a frequent egg-eater. If one wishes to be assured of a safe hatching of young, the instructions for artificial hatching described under the general notes for this group should be followed.

Aequidens maroni, the Keyhole Cichlid, comes from northern South America. Length attained is $3\frac{1}{2}$ inches, and it is one of the more timid species. To be comfortable, its aquarium should be heavily planted and provide numerous retreats. Strangely enough, it is seen more frequently when it knows it can hide if necessary than in a sparsely planted tank where it is uneasy. The body color is a pleasing brown, with a vertical black bar running through the eye across the cheek, and another black bar from the dorsal to the first anal rays; this bar has an odd shape, just like a keyhole. There are some lighter streaks, which are almost yellow; one runs from the eye up toward the dorsal fin, and there is a light area around the "keyhole" marking. Both sexes have pointed tips posteriorly on their dorsal and anal fins, but those on the male are a bit longer.

This is not one of the "easy" cichlids. Their innate timidity seems even to extend toward their behavior to each other. Much patient conditioning is often required, but the reward is generally worthwhile; there is usually a good demand for this attractive fish. Spawns like *A. curviceps*.

A group of young Keyhole Cichlids, *Aequidens maroni*. The popular name is supposed to designate a keyhole marking on the sides of the fish. The scientific name *maroni* was to designate the Maroni River in French Guiana. This fish was first described by Steindachner in 1882.

A male *Aequidens pulcher*, Blue Acara, taken from its natural habitat in South America. Photo by Dr. Herbert R. Axelrod.

A female Blue Acara fanning the eggs laid on top of a smooth rock. Photo by Rudolf Zukal.

A pair of brooding Blue Acaras surrounded by their fry. With the passage of time the instinct to protect the young will gradually wane, and the young fish will have to take care of themselves. Photo by Kassanyi Jeno.

A male Aequidens portalegrensis. Photo by G.J.M. Timmerman.

Close-up view of the ovipositor of Aequidens pulcher. Notice also the translucent egg about to drop out of the ovipositor. Photo by Kassanyi Jeno.

Jaw-locking confrontations are normal activities for *Aequidens pulcher* prior to spawning. Photo by Starby, Stockholm, Sweden.

Aequidens portalegrensis hails from central South America and is one of the big ones: maximum length 5 inches. This species is as easy to breed as the preceding is difficult. The sides are green, and each scale has a darker edge, giving the effect of a reticulated pattern. There is a broad black stripe horizontally from the gill-cover to the tail base, and there is a black bar vertically at this point. The dorsal fin is greenish, as is the upper part of the tail; the lower portion is blue and there is a pretty pattern of dots and streaks throughout. The anal fin is also blue with a similar pattern. The eye is golden and the front of the head is yellow to deep gold. There is a definite distinction between the sexes: the points on the dorsal and anal fins of the mature male are considerably longer.

This fish should be given room, being one of the large species. A 20-gallon tank suits it well. There is usually very little friction between sexes, and a well-conditioned pair will spawn and raise their family almost always without any trouble. Procedure as for *A. curviceps*.

Aequidens pulcher, the Blue Acara, is widely distributed over Panama, Colombia, Venezuela and Trinidad. Size attained is 6 inches. This is another of the large, easily-bred cichlids and is an old favorite.

Baby Oscars of the regular breed taken from the wild. Photo by Harald Schultz.

Oscars, *Astronotus ocellatus*, are very prolific and a pair can raise several hundreds of youngsters. Photo by E. A. Baumbach.

The fish above is an Oscar, *Astronotus ocellatus*, with the usual coloration. (Photo by Klaus Paysan.) The fish below was developed by a Thai by carefully inbreeding the red coloration and is known as the Red Oscar. Photo by Dr. Herbert R. Axelrod.

A pair of Oscars fiercely guarding their eggs.

There is less of the placid easy-going disposition of the preceding species here, however. The Blue Acara is likely to be more quarrelsome with some of its neighbors, especially the smaller ones. They should be kept to themselves or with other fishes as large as themselves. The body color is a bluish gray, spotted all over with small, bright blue dots. There are several indistinct vertical bars on the sides and a large black spot in the center. The head is attractively marked with bright blue streaks and the fins are spotted blue like the body. Males may be distinguished by the longer dorsal and anal fins.

Breeds like the others; members of a pair will often seem to be attacking each other viciously, locking jaws and dragging each other all over the tank. This act, however, is frequently one of the preludes to spawning. Like *A. portalegrensis,* they should also be given plenty of room.

Astronotus ocellatus, the Oscar or Peacock Cichlid, comes from eastern Venezuela, the Guianas, the Amazon Basin and Paraguay. This is one of the largest of aquarium fishes to be kept by home aquarists, attaining almost one foot in length. Do not expect to keep this fish properly if you do not have a very large aquarium of at least 50 gallons capacity. The basic color of the body and fins is a chocolate brown, with irregular lighter mottled markings on the sides. There is a black spot at the tail base which is ringed with gold. The male has some bright red markings on the gill-covers and near the belly region on the sides. The female is drably colored. Colors vary greatly in intensity, depending on the mood of the fish. A red variety has been produced and is readily available.

Its large size is exceeded only by the size of its appetite. Many aquarists feed their dead fishes to the Oscars; some pamper them by giving them live goldfish. Others feed them live grasshoppers, crickets, earthworms and such. Usually, everything is accepted with a rush to the surface which almost lands them on the floor and splashes water all over. In outdoor ponds in Florida they are usually conditioned on live crayfish.

They spawn like the other cichlids; again we emphasize that their tank must be a large one. Sometimes a male will treat his mate somewhat roughly. A glass partition between them for a few days usually calms him down. Spawns are usually tremendous, numbering close to a thousand eggs. Sometimes they exercise very good parental care, but eggs or fry are also frequently eaten, especially if there is much disturbance.

Cichlasoma aureum, the Golden Cichlid, is known from southern Mexico to Guatemala. Size attained is 6 inches; the male is distinguished by his deeper colors, as well as by his larger and more pointed anal and dorsal fins. The sides are deep brown to golden, with about 6 dark vertical bars. There is a large ocellated spot on the sides, and another at the tail base. Fins are yellowish, with a bit of red.

This fish spawns like the other cichlids; it is usually a good parent under the right conditions, and it is not as likely to eat eggs and fry as most of the others.

Cichlasoma bimaculatum, the Two-spotted Cichlid, is a bit large for the average aquarist, attaining a length of 8 inches. Trinidad, Venezuela, the Guianas and Brazil are given as its habitat. Besides its size, there is another trait which does not exactly endear it to the aquarist: it will uproot most of the plants in an aquarium in a very short time. This seems to be a characteristic of many of the larger cichlids. Colors are olive to brown, with a considerable number of dark

A female Texas Cichlid, *Cichlasoma cyanoguttatum* guarding her eggs. This is the only cichlid found in the United States. Photo by Dr. S. Frank.

Cichlasoma aureum, the Golden Cichlid. Photo by Dr. Robert J. Goldstein.

A pair of Jack Dempseys, *Cichlasoma octofasciatum,* guarding and fanning the newly laid eggs. Photo by Rudolf Zukal.

The young Jack Dempseys stay close to the parent fish for some time and may nibble the skin of the adult fish. Photo by Wolfgang Bechtle.

vertical bars. There are two spots, one at the center of the sides and the other at the tail base. A dark stripe runs from the gill plate to the center spot. Males, as usual, have slightly brighter colors and more pointed fins.

A male (to the right) and female Golden Cichlid, *Cichlasoma aureum.*

Spawns in a manner typical of other cichlids; of course, being a large fish, it requires a large tank: at least 20 gallons.

Cichlasoma cyanoguttatum, the Texas Cichlid, occurs in northern Mexico and southern Texas. Size attained is 10 inches. This is the only cichlid which occurs naturally in the United States. The overall coloring is grayish with indistinct vertical bars, a spot in the center of the body, and another smaller one at the caudal base. This fish's most attractive feature is the sprinkling of bright blue dots all over the body and fins. Unfortunately its behavior is typically cichlid-like and it cannot be trusted with smaller fishes. Females may be easily distinguished by their smaller, more rounded fins.

The Texas Cichlid needs plenty of room for spawning, being a large fish which may lay better than 1000 eggs at a sitting. Usual cichlid procedure is followed in every way. It is a very easy fish to spawn.

Cichlasoma octofasciatum, the Jack Dempsey, is another large, rough customer, as its popular name implies. Like the preceding species, the size attained is 8 inches. All the things said against the other species

The male Jack Dempsey, *Cichlasoma octofasciatum*, has pointed dorsal and ventral fins while the female (below) has such fins much shorter. Photos by G. J. M. Timmerman.

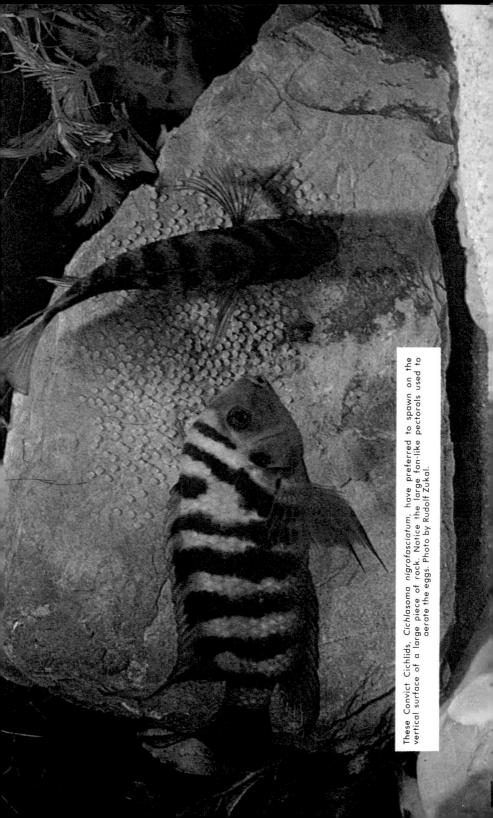

These Convict Cichlids, *Cichlasoma nigrofasciatum*, have preferred to spawn on the vertical surface of a large piece of rock. Notice the large fan-like pectorals used to aerate the eggs. Photo by Rudolf Zukal.

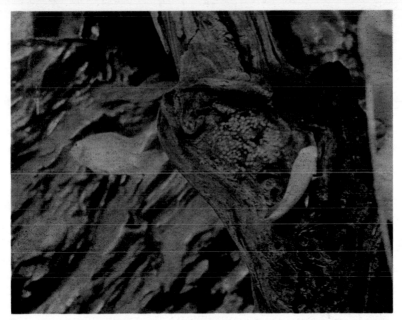

Shown above is a pair of albino Convict Cichlids. The eggs were laid on a piece of drift-wood while the pair below has chosen the inside wall of a flowerpot. Upper photo by Mervin F. Roberts, lower photo by Rudolf Zukal.

also apply to this one, but there is one saving grace: it is a very handsome fish. The sides are a deep brown, almost black. The entire body, including the head and the fins, is covered with brilliant spots, golden posteriorly and bright blue anteriorly. A large black spot adorns the sides and there is another at the caudal base. The dorsal fin has a large red edge, and the eyes are very pretty, with a red iris.

Again, a very large tank is needed; a well-conditioned pair will usually spawn readily and, ruffians though they are, will often make good parents. It seems to us that the most vicious cichlids in their behavior towards each other and other fishes are the most gentle and painstaking parents.

Cichlasoma facetum, the Chanchito or Chameleon Cichlid, comes from parts of Brazil, Uruguay and Argentina. Size attained is 10 inches, which makes it a monster, but an interesting one. This was one of the first cichlids known to aquarists, and all the old works contain pictures and descriptions of it. Ordinarily the color is brown with darker bars on the sides. The lighter colors can easily change to green, blue, or even reddish. The females have shorter fins and are slightly smaller than the males.

This species, besides being a bit large for the average aquarist, also has the further detriment of viciousness, being safe only with

The Chanchito, *Cichlasoma facetum*. This is a female fish. Photo by Gerhard Marcuse.

large fishes which are well able to take care of themselves. It has also a reputation for doing a great deal of digging and uprooting of plants. In other words, everything that can be said against any cichlid applies to this one.

Spawning is performed as for the other cichlids, and here is the one good thing which can be said about them: they make good parents. A large tank of at least 30 gallons should be used.

Cichlasoma meeki, the Firemouth Cichlid, comes from Yucatan. It attains a length of 5 inches and has a much more peaceful disposition that most give it credit for. The sides are bluish to slate-gray in color, with a black spot in the center. An indistinct, somewhat broken horizontal line extends to the gill-plate, and there is another black spot at the lower part of the gill-plate. The real attraction of this fish is an area of bright red which extends from inside the mouth over the lower lip, throat and belly. This red area becomes especially brilliant at spawning time. Again, the females may be distinguished by their shorter dorsal and anal fins and slightly smaller size.

A well-mated pair will produce many broods, which will often be cared for by the parents without mishap. There are no deviations from the standard cichlid procedure, and any tank of 15-gallon capacity or over may be used.

Cichlasoma nigrofasciatum, the Zebra or Convict Cichlid, has a range which includes Guatemala, Salvador, Costa Rica and Panama. Another though obviously inappropriate name which is sometimes applied to this species is "Congo Cichlid." It attains a length of 6 inches and is similar in disposition to its bigger cousin the Chanchito, which it also resembles in coloring. The sides are bluish in color with black bars. This fish is also easily confused with *C. facetum*. It is scrappy in disposition and inclined to uproot plants.

A well-mated pair will usually raise their families. Spawns like the other cichlids; the female is apt to be a bit scrappy at this time, and it is sometimes advisable to remove the male after his duties are completed.

Cichlasoma severum, the Banded Cichlid, comes from the Guianas, Rio Negro and the Amazon Basin. It is another large species, attaining a length of 6 inches. The body color is a yellowish green, the green becoming more accentuated around the head. There is a black spot in the last rays of the dorsal and anal fins; these two spots are connected with a bar, giving the appearance of a dumbbell standing on end. Fins are brown, and the males have a sprinkling of reddish dots forming horizontal lines on the sides. Another sexual difference is that the males have longer and more pointed anal and dorsal fins.

The female Firemouth Cichlid, *Cichlasoma meeki*, initiates the spawning process by laying several eggs as the male waits aside. Photo by Rudolf Zukal.

The male Firemouth Cichlid fertilizing the eggs. The male develops bright red coloration on its belly and chin. Photo by Rudolf Zukal.

A school of young Firemouth Cichlids, *Cichlasoma meeki*. At this early age the young fish show the fright pattern in their coloration.

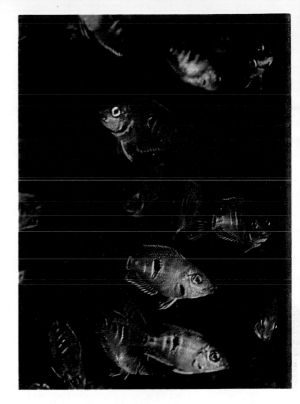

Below: a male Firemouth Cichlid tends his hundreds of babies. He mouths the fry from time to time to spit them into different nests he has prepared for their safety. Photos by Rudolf Zukal.

A normally colored male *Cichlasoma nigrofasciatum*, the Convict Cichlid. A pink variety, incorrectly called "Albino Convict Cichlid," has become very popular. Photo by G.J.M. Timmerman.

A pair of *Cichlasoma severum* locking jaws prior to spawning. Such activity is part of the courting behavior of this cichlid. Photo by Laurence E. Perkins.

A male Firemouth Cichlid, *Cichlasoma meeki*. Photo by G. J. M. Timmerman.

A pair of *Cichlasoma festivum*, male to the right.

The Banded Cichlid, *Cichlasoma severum*, with normal pigmentation. Photo by Aaron Norman.

A pair of Golden Severums, a color variety of *Cichlasoma severum*. The fish to the right is the male. Photo by Barbara Marlay.

The Blue Convict Cichlid, *Cichlasoma spilurum* is a willing spawner. It prefers caves or the side of rocks. Photo by Rudolf Zukal.

Cichlasoma festivum spawning. Photo by Rudolf Zukal.

This fish breeds in the standard cichlid manner, but getting them in the proper condition for doing so is a bit of a problem. Because of their large size, a considerable amount of live food is required before they get that healthy, well rounded appearance which presages spawning activity. In the summer months procure earthworms and small insects to satisfy their lusty appetites, but in the winter months this is not so easy. A large aquarium must be provided for them, 30 gallons and up. The youngsters are different in appearance from their parents: they are more compressed in body form, and instead of the single bar have 7 or 8 vertical black bars; they greatly resemble the young of *Symphysodon*, and have often been mistaken for them.

Cichlasoma spilurum, the Blue Convict Cichlid, is one of the most peaceful of the smaller cichlids. It has often been referred to as a cave spawner and for this reason may be the actual species from which the Golden Convict Cichlid derived. No one seems to know.

The male is distinguished from the female by lacking a dark spot on his dorsal. This spot is a continuation of the thickest mid-body bar which decorates the female with her "convict" markings.

Spawning is done on a rock or flat surface and usually on the underside. Of course the top inside wall of a flowerpot lying on its side is ideal. Both fish guard the nest and developing young. Spawns are large and very typical of South American cichlids.

Crenicichla dorsocellata, the Two-spotted Pike Cichlid, comes to us from the Amazon Basin and attains a length of 6 inches. Like the pike it has a long slender body. There is a further likeness to the pike in its large mouth and somewhat predatory habits. Don't place this fish together with smaller species. The body is a bluish green, and a prominent lateral line runs from the gill plate to the tail base, where it ends in an ocellus. There is another spot in the middle of the dorsal fin.

The members of this genus spawn like the other cichlids; they may differ in that the eggs are sometimes placed on the stalks and leaves of plants, as well as on the surface of a stone or the glass sides and they seldom uproot plants. A 20-gallon tank is the minimum which should be used, and the parents should be removed when the fry begin to swim. Males have more pointed and slightly larger fins.

Crenicichla lepidota is native to eastern Brazil and reaches 8 inches in length. This is the usual pike cichlid offered by dealers, and is one of the most attractive of the lot. Body color is a yellowish brown, with a lateral stripe running from the snout to the caudal base. Running from the back into the lateral line are a number of dark bars. There are flecks of orange and red dapplings here and there on the body, as well as on the fins. Males have more pointed fins than the females.

A male Pike Cichlid, *Crenicichla saxatilis*. Photo by G. J. M. Timmerman.

Crenicichla saxatilis, the Ring-tailed Pike Cichlid, has a wide range which includes Trinidad, Venezuela, the Amazon Basin, Paraguay and Uruguay. The largest of the three, it attains a size of 10 inches. The color is brown, with a black line extending from the upper lip through the gill plate. The remainder of the body and fins carries a few yellowish spots. There is an ocellus at the tail base, and a smaller one at the end of the center caudal rays.

Dormitator latifrons, the Broad-headed Sleeper, attains a length of 10 inches, although the ones we generally see are much smaller. It is native to the Pacific coast of Central America. This fish is not of the cichlid family, but belongs to the family *Gobiidae*, the gobies. These are fishes which inhabit brackish and even marine water, as well as fresh water. Their outstanding characteristic is a double dorsal fin, and they have been included here because their breeding habits are very similar to those of the other members of this group. The sleepers are not very popular as aquarium fishes; besides being large, they are inclined to be very sluggish, and spend most of their time hiding; there are no outstanding colors to recommend them either. The sides are light brown, covered with spots of a darker brown; there are some alternating light and dark stripes on the gill plate and a few red spots on the body. Females are lighter in color.

Crenicichla dorsocellata, the Two-spotted Pike Cichlid. This specimen was collected and photographed by Harald Schultz in South America.

Crenicichla lepidota is the usual Pike Cichlid species imported from South America by most dealers. The fish shown here was taken and photographed by Dr. Herbert R. Axelrod in Rio Aguaro, Venezuela.

In order to spawn this fish, we must remember that it is native to brackish waters, and a level tablespoon of salt per gallon should be added to its water. Eggs are laid on a flat surface and fanned. Parents should be removed as soon as the young begin to swim. Fry are small, and require infusoria feeding at first. Incubation period is 2 days; 76° is the best temperature. They are very difficult to spawn.

A Pike Cichlid devouring another cichlid fish, an *Aequidens*. The choice of tank mates for Pike Cichlids should be considered seriously on account of the voracious appetite of these fish. Photo by Dr. Herbert R. Axelrod.

Dormitator maculatus, the Spotted Sleeper. Photo by Laurence E. Perkins.

Eleotris pisonis is a common brackish water goby in the southern parts of the United States.

A pair of juvenile Spotted Sleepers. Photo by G.J.M. Timmerman.

Dormitator maculatus, the Spotted Sleeper, occurs along the Atlantic Coast of tropical America as far north as Florida. Size attained is 10 inches, but in the aquarium it is smaller. Body color is muddy brown. The anal fin of the male has some blue spots and stripes, and there is some blue in the area of the gill plates. Dorsals are spotted with brown. The females are lighter in color.

Spawning is similar to that for the preceding species. The fry are not hardy as a rule, and it is a task to get them through the first stages of growth. Of course, both species require a large aquarium.

A well-mated pair will take excellent care of many broods; spawning follows exactly the usual cichlid procedure, and plants are not usually disturbed much. We have seen them spawn in a 10-gallon aquarium, but a larger one is recommended.

Hemichromis bimaculatus, the Jewel Fish, attains a size of 4 inches and has a wide range in Africa which includes the three great rivers: the Nile, the Niger and the Congo. It is a great pity that this beautiful, easy-to-spawn fish does not have a more easy-going disposition, but the sad fact is that it is a fairly vicious proposition. The body color is greenish, with a large black spot in the center and at the tail base.

The Spotted Sleeper, *Dormitator maculatus*, except for some blue spots in some parts of the body and fins is predominantly brown in coloration. Photo by Stanislav Frank.

A pair of Jewel Cichlids, *Hemichromis bimaculatus*, spawning on top of a flat stone. The female is shown laying eggs as the male waits on the left side. Photo by Rudolf Zukal.

Shown above is a pair of Jewel Cichlids considered as a second color variety of *Hemichromis bimaculatus*. It is very popular in Europe because it is a very brightly colored fish. Photo by Hans Joachim Richter.

The sides are covered with large, brilliant green dots, and the dorsal fin is streaked and edged with red, and there are several blue lines. The tail is also edged with red, and there are several blue lines below this. At breeding time, the entire under part of the fish, from the lips almost to the tail, is a brilliant carmine red. The female may be as brilliantly colored as the male, and sometimes even more so.

Hemichromis bimaculatus II is a red color variety of the Jewel Fish. Due to selective breeding the red color of the wild fish has been intensified to such an extent that this variety is recognizable and given the designation (II) to differentiate it from the normal strain. This is not a scientific designation as this form cannot be found in nature. The basic color is red, the female being bright orange-red, whereas the male is a darker violet-red. The sides and fins are covered with bright bluish to greenish spots and there is a large black spot near the middle of the side and another on the corner of the operculum.

Breeding is the same as the normal Jewel Fish.

Julidochromis marlieri, Marlier's Julie comes from Lake Tanganyika, Africa. It reaches a size of about 4 inches, slightly larger than its close relative *Julidochromis ornatus.* The general aspect of this species is similar to that of *ornatus* but it differs in color pattern. Marlier's Julie is paler in color with the same horizontal stripes as *ornatus.* In the former species, however, there are vertical bars present extending from the dorsal fin to the midline of the body or just below it giving the appearance of a crosshatched pattern.

Spawning is similar to that of *Julidochromis ornatus.* The young are coal black with white spots and lack the electric blue lines in the fins that the parents exhibit.

Temperatures should be in the upper seventies and the water should be towards the alkaline side.

Julidochromis ornatus. The Julie comes from Lake Tanganyika, Africa. It is a rather smallish cichlid reaching a size of about 4 inches although spawning may occur at a smaller size. The males and females are similarly colored both being bright yellow with horizontal brownish-black bands along the upper sides of the body. An electric blue stripe extends along the length of the vertical fins near the edge. The color resembles somewhat the pattern of another African lake cichlid, *Pseudotropheus auratus.* The female is slightly larger and possesses a rounder belly.

Spawning is typical of the group, a nest site being prepared on the rocks, flower pot, coconut shell, etc. where the eggs are deposited. The spawning pair is very secretive and sites are selected where there is minimum disturbance. Many times the eggs, less than 50 in number,

The author (HRA) went diving with Pierre Brichard in Lake Tanganyika. Brichard is shown above with a squeeze bottle of quinaldine dissolved in acetone (quinaldine is available from Kodak). This drug stuns but usually does not kill the fishes, enabling Brichard to collect them for export. The photo below shows a typical scene at 30 feet depth in Lake Tanganyika, near Bujumbura, Burundi. Photos by Dr. Herbert R. Axelrod.

A pair of Julies, *Julidochromis ornatus*, getting ready to spawn under the flat rock. The eggs are hung in the most protected area and then guarded aggressively from all intruders. Photo by Hans Joachim Richter.

The color pattern of this Mbuna, *Pseudotropheus auratus*, is similar to some degree to that of *Julidochromis ornatus*. However, this is superficial. *Pseudotropheus auratus* is endemic to Lake Malawi, and its breeding and feeding habits are entirely different also. Photo by Dr. Herbert R. Axelrod.

Julidochromis marlieri from Lake Tanganyika is now regularly imported and regularly bred by some hobbyists. Photo by H. Hansen, Aquarium Berlin.

are not seen, the first proof of spawning being the young fish peeking out from their nest. Water conditions suggested are a temperature of from 78° to 80° and a pH tending towards the alkaline.

Male and female share the guard duty. During spawning the Julies will often place the eggs on the roof of the nest site, an upside down position apparently not causing any problems to them. The eggs are yellowish to greenish colored.

Hybridization between this species and *Julidochromis marlieri* has been reported. The young produced were apparently sterile.

Lamprologus brichardi. The beautiful Lyretail Cichlid occurs in Lake Tanganyika, Africa. It reaches a length of about 3½ inches. The Lyretail Cichlid is of a brownish pink color, with the dorsal, anal and caudal fins marked with orange dashes. A black mark extends from the eye to the gill cover setting off the distinctive bright yellow spot at the upper edge of the operculum. A greenish mark is present above each eye and the face has a bluish vermiculated pattern. The most extraordinary feature of this cichlid is the extension of the tips of the dorsal, anal, and caudal fins into filaments, hence the name Lyretail Cichlid. These fins are edged with electric blue.

The Whiptail, *Loricaria parva.* Photo by G. J. M. Timmerman.

Spawning the Lyretail Cichlid follows the typical cichlid pattern. The actual spawning sites are usually protected and actual spawning is difficult to observe in these secretive fish. The fry may be free-swimming by the fifth to seventh day and do well on baby brine shrimp. The parents care for the young for about two weeks after which they are ready to spawn again and the parents or fry should be removed.

It has been said that the Lyretail Cichlids spawn in different spots in the aquarium on successive days similar to reports of this habit for *Julidochromis ornatus*. Number of fry ranged from 20 to 75.

Loricaria parva, the Whiptail, comes from Paraguay and Southern Brazil. Size attained is 5 inches; here we have one of the catfishes which breeds like the cichlids. The body is long and slender, and the under-slung mouth is adapted for cleaning algae from rocks and plants or picking things off the bottom. The body is a mottled, grayish brown, and the upper rays of the tail are considerably elongated. The males are distinguished by their broader heads.

Although they have often been spawned, the first published account is that of Carroll Friswold, of Altadena, California. He conditioned his breeders on dried foods only; the temperature varied from 73° to 78°, with aeration. The water was 13 inches deep and a piece of petrified wood was selected as the site for spawning after much preparation. Courtship lasted about 72 hours, after which the female laid about 40 eggs on the wood. The male then drove off the female and took full charge of the incubation, fanning and mouthing the eggs cichlid fashion. The eggs hatched in 8 days at 78°, and the fry were unmolested by the parents, growing up rapidly on a diet of rotifers, mashed white worms and fine dried foods.

Mogurnda mogurnda, the Purple-striped Gudgeon, is one of the few aquarium fishes which come from Australia, where it is native to the north and central regions. Largest size attained is reputed to be 8 inches, but we have never seen any that big. The body color is grayish, and there is a horizontal line which is composed of red and black dots, some of which also sprinkle the fins. There are several stripes on the gill-plates. The double dorsal fin identifies this fish as one of the gobies. These dorsal fins and the anal are larger in the males.

Eggs are deposited on rocks or glass sides, where they hang by sticky threads. Temperature best suited is about 72°. The male then takes over, and the female should be removed at this point. Eggs are fanned for 9 days, after which they hatch. At this time the male should be removed. After about a week of infusoria feeding, the fry will grow rapidly on brine shrimp and larger foods. This fish is not a peaceful citizen in the community aquarium.

A pair of Lyretail Cichlids, *Lamprologus brichardi*. Notice the pinkish eggs laid in the concavity of the rock. Photo by Hans Joachim Richter.

412

A female Leaf Fish, *Monocirrhus polyacanthus*, in upside down position laying eggs on a broad leaf. Photo by Hans Joachim Richter.

Mogurnda mogurnda, the Purple-striped Gudgeon. Photo by G.J.M. Timmerman.

Monocirrhus polyacanthus, the Leaf Fish, comes from the Amazon and Rio Negro basins. It attains a length of 3 inches; it is brown in color with a dark lateral line. Its shape and peculiar habit of "drifting" on its side, its fins apparently scarcely moving, provides it with a means of protection by camouflage against predators. It looks for all the world like a dead leaf, drifting near the surface. In order to keep this fish in top shape, much food in the form of small fishes must be provided. It will put away a surprising amount of them in the course of a day. Sexes are distinguished in the Leaf Fish by the larger fins of the male.

The usual spawning site is, aptly enough, the surface of a broad leaf. Usually the under surface is chosen. When spawning is completed, the male surrounds the eggs with a mass of bubbles resembling nests made by the anabantids. The female may interfere at this point and should be removed. Three days later, at a temperature of 80°, the male cleans a depression in the gravel under the nest; hatching begins on the fourth day. Fry are always guarded by the watchful male. Two days after hatching, the fry absorb their yolk-sac and the hunt for food begins. Brine shrimp is well suited to their needs. At this time the male may be removed. The fry should get an occasional sorting, or the smaller ones will be swallowed by the larger.

Nanochromis nudiceps. The Congo Dwarf Cichlid is from the Congo River drainage. The males reach a size of almost 3 inches while the females reach only to $2\frac{1}{4}$ inches. They are basically greenish yellow in coloration with electric blue spots on head and body. The lower portions of the body are greenish with a pinkish coloration above the anal fin (more pronounced near spawning time). There is a white band in the dorsal fin and much like species of *Pelvicachromis* the caudal fin has a double pattern, the upper portion black and white striped and the lower portion spotted or barred.

The Congo Dwarf Cichlid is shy and spawning sites are usually in caves, flower pots, coconut shells, or other places where the eggs and young may be hidden from view. Temperatures should be in the upper 70's and the water should be acid (pH 6).

In about a week to 10 days the female will emerge from the nest site followed by up to 150 young. At this time both parents take part in the protection of the young fishes. In about three weeks these young fishes grow to about $\frac{3}{4}$ of an inch.

Pterophyllum scalare, the Scalare or Angelfish, comes from the Rio Negro and Amazon basins and attains a length of 5 inches. Their unusual shape, graceful movement and attractive coloring make the Angelfish one of the perennial favorites among aquarists. The body is compressed. Body color is silvery. The iris of the eye is red, and a black vertical bar passes through the eye to the base of the gill-plate. A second black bar descends from the first dorsal rays to the first anal rays, and a heavier bar passes through from the middle rays of these fins, extending well into both. There is another bar at the caudal base and some faint ones cross the tail fin itself. The top and bottom rays of the tail are elongated into threadlike filaments. The fins are the unusual feature: the dorsal fin is almost as high as the body is deep and is rounded on top. The anal fin is even deeper than the

A female *Loricaria parva* spawning on a leaf. Unlike some *Corydoras* species, this catfish takes care of the eggs. The male will guard the eggs until the young are hatched. Photo by Dr. W. Foersch.

Eggs of *Loricaria parva* in different stages of development.

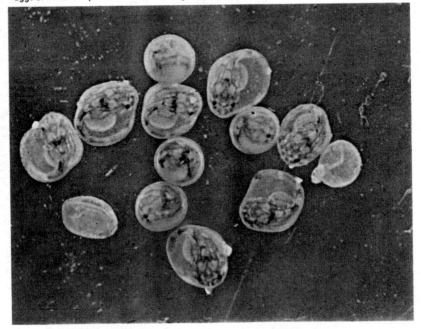

The Purple-striped Gudgeon, *Mogurnda mogurnda*, is not too easy to find because it originates from Australia. Photo by Hilmar Hansen.

A pair of Congo Dwarf Cichlids, *Nanochromis nudiceps*, surrounded by free-swimming young. Photo by Hans Joachim Richter.

A tank-raised variety of *Pterophyllum scalare*. Photo by G. J. M. Timmerman.

dorsal is high, and the first ray also forms a long filament which extends beyond the tail. The ventral fins consist of only a few rays, which in some specimens are longer than the overall size of the fish. Sexes are very difficult to distinguish. Careful observation, however, will disclose that the female has a larger vent; a few days before spawning, a short tube will be extended from the vent. The female's tube has about twice the diameter of the male's.

Breeders have succeeded in developing many strains of this beautiful fish. One of these strains is known as the Black Lace Angelfish; the color is dusky throughout, and there are several extra black bars. Incidentally, members of this strain have been found to be very scrappy, even among themselves. By selective breeding of the duskiest specimens, a pure black strain has also been developed. These are a solid, velvety black all over, and a tankful of these is a sight to behold. It has been our sad experience that these latter fish are not as hardy as their forebears. A sort of "happy medium" strain has been developed by European aquarists which is of normal coloration in the front half of the body, while the last half is solid black. Gold, albino, and long-finned varieties are also available.

Breeding follows the general pattern of the other cichlids. There are several methods used, which will be gone into here. The first and most simple method is to put a mature, well-conditioned pair in a large, well-planted aquarium and let nature take its course. The pair select a wide, stiff plant stalk or leaf and after much cleaning, attaches a great many eggs in rows to its surface. The eggs are fanned and mouthed by both parents and hatch in 4 days at a temperature of 80°. The helplessly wriggling fry are secured to the leaf by a fine, sticky thread which is attached to the head. In 3 or 4 days the contents of the yolk-sac have been absorbed and the thread disappears. The fry then drop to the bottom, and feeding with infusoria is begun and the parents are removed. Brine shrimps supplant this food in a few days and the fry soon attain the size of newly-born guppies. From here on it is just a matter of feeding generously with predominantly live foods. A charming picture of family fish life is often gotten by leaving the parents in with the young after they become free-swimming, but there is the ever-present danger, as with the other cichlids, of the fry being eaten by their own parents. Commercial breeders, who raise this fish by the thousands, cannot afford to take this chance, and do not even leave the parents to tend the eggs before hatching. They use a bare tank, with a 3-inch wide piece of slate leaning against the top edge of the tank. The fish almost inevitably spawn against this slate. When egg-laying and fertilization is completed, the breeders are either netted out, or the slate containing the eggs is removed to another tank. An air-stone is placed so that a steam of bubbles rises near, but not on, the eggs. Eggs which turn white may be picked off with an eye dropper and discarded. There are usually few losses, and the headache of having a good batch of young eaten by their parents is eliminated.

Spawnings are large, and for this reason a large tank, at least 15 gallons in capacity, should be used. As the fry grow they must be divided into other tanks to prevent crowding.

Pyrrhulina vittata, a fanning characin from Brazil, attains 2 inches in length. Body color is dark brown on the back, shading to lighter on the sides. Belly is white. There is a dark line from the tip of the mouth to the edge of the gill-plates which continues as a zigzag line to the

419

A pair of *Pterophyllum scalare*, Marble Angels, looking over a possible spawning site. Photo by Mrs. Hans Joachim Richter.

The eggs are guarded by the parents after they are laid. However, it is advisable to remove the parents as soon as the young have hatched to prevent predation of the fry. Photo by Mrs. Hans Joachim Richter.

Close-up view of Marble Angelfish eggs. The eggs are of course susceptible to fungus growth, and precautions should be taken to maintain them under the most hygienic conditions. Photo by Mrs. Hans Joachim Richter.

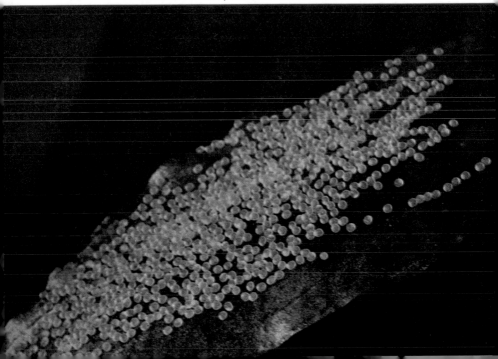

Pterophyllum dumerilii, a 2-inch specimen collected by the author (HRA) in the Rio Purus, Brazil. Note the odd angle of its head, especially when compared with *Pterophyllum altum* on the facing page. Photo by Dr. Herbert R. Axelrod.

Pterophyllum altum, one of the largest of the genus *Pterophyllum.* There have been many imports of this species but as of 1974 no one has succeeded in spawning them! Photo by Dr. Herbert R. Axelrod of a fish supplied by Kyle Swegles.

These Angelfish are two months old. The fish to the left is an All Black while the fish to the right is a Lacetail. Both fish were bred by Ludwig in Detroit. Photo by Herbert R. Axerod.

Color changes in Angelfish are common. By feeding hormones look what happens to an otherwise colorless fish. The fish in the background is colorless. The one in the foreground was fed color food.

An Angelfish cleaning off the spawning site prior to actual spawning.

The Angelfish spawning.

Bud Goddard, a professional fishbreeder, produced this albino Angelfish which was too blind to spawn. Since that time several strains of albino Angelfish have been produced. Photo by Dr. Herbert R. Axelrod.

A strain of stripeless Angelfish was produced by Connie and Lester Boisvert in Connecticut. They called their fish the Con-les Blushing Angelfish, but the trade preferred to call them "Ghost Angels." Photo by Dr. Herbert R. Axelrod.

Pyrrhulina rachoviana, male.

tail base. The dorsal carries a black spot; in the males this spot appears near the tip, while the females have theirs nearer the center. The males also have some small orange dots on the sides. There are three large blotches on the sides.

This fish may be spawned in a small aquarium of as little as 2 gallons capacity. There should be some broad-leaved plants provided. Spawning temperature should be around 78°. The pair selects a broad leaf and the eggs are deposited on it. The female is chased away when she has finished and is best removed at this point. The male takes charge, fanning the eggs which hatch in about 24 hours and fall to the bottom. At this point the male has finished his duties, and he is taken out, lest he make a meal of the fry. After 3 or 4 days, the fry will put in an appearance near the top, looking for food. Infusoria is the best first food, but a small pinch of very fine prepared food daily may also be used. Young will soon be large enough to take brine shrimp.

Pyrrhulina rachoviana, female.

Steatocranus casuarius, the Lionhead Cichlid, is a fairly peaceful cichlid from the Congo area of Africa. It is brownish to greenish often with an indistinct mottled pattern on its sides. The most conspicuous aspect of this fish is the fleshy protuberance which appears on the male fish as it nears maturity. It grows larger with age and becomes quite exaggerated in older fish.

Spawning follows the cichlid pattern for egg anchorers though like some other cichlids they are very secretive and actual spawning is rarely observed. The usual caves, flower pots, cocoanut shells, etc., should be provided. Success has been achieved with soft, slightly acid water although this species does not seem to be sensitive to water conditions. The usual gravel rearranging and plant removing occurs before the parents spawn. Both parents guard the 100 or so eggs and are said to bring food to the fry after they hatch.

Symphysodon aequifasciata axelrodi, the Brown or Common Discus, comes from the Rio Negro and Amazon Basins and grows to a length of 9 inches. This fish, sometimes dubbed the "King of Aquarium Fishes," has been the pride and also despair of aquarists the world over. Besides being a bit difficult to capture, their large size makes them require a lot of water and sends shipping charges sky-high. It is the dream of every breeder to be able to turn them out by the thousands like Angelfish, but few are able to do so. More and more home-bred fish are now available on the market, and the species no longer commands such high prices as were common twenty years ago, but the Discus is still far from commonly bred and has not yet yielded its secrets entirely.

Breeding the Discus is far from being an impossibility, as it breeds in exactly the same manner as *Pterophyllum scalare*, the Angelfish. The difference involves the rearing of the fry through the first few weeks of life. The parents spawn and fan the eggs exactly like a pair of Angelfish. After the fry are hatched and absorb the yolk-sac, they are dependent on the parent for food, feeding on the mucus secreted by the parent's skin. Thus they must either be left with the parents and take their chances of being eaten or raised by complicated artificial methods. If you intend to try your hand at the tricky business of breeding this fish, it is suggested that a very large aquarium be used and that there be as little disturbance as possible. A piece of slate, similar to that used for Angelfish, will be accepted as a spawning site, sometimes in preference to a large-leaved plant. The best food for Discus, in fact the only one which they can be counted on to eat, is tubifex worms. The fact that a pair devours their fry once does not necessarily mean that they will always do the same; they may be model parents next time, under exactly the same conditions.

Pyrrhulina vittata spawns in the same general manner as Angelfish. Photo by Dr. Herbert R. Axelrod.

The frontal protuberance of the male Lionhead Cichlid increases with age. Females lack such enlargement of the head. Photo by Dr. Herbert R. Axelrod.

A pair of Brown Discus, *Symphysodon aequifasciata axelrodi*. Photo by Miloslav Kocar.

A couple of Brown Discus in front of their spawn. Photo by D. Terver.

Close view of the eggs of the Brown Discus. Note the presence of a few opaque eggs which will not develop. Photo by Dr. D. Terver.

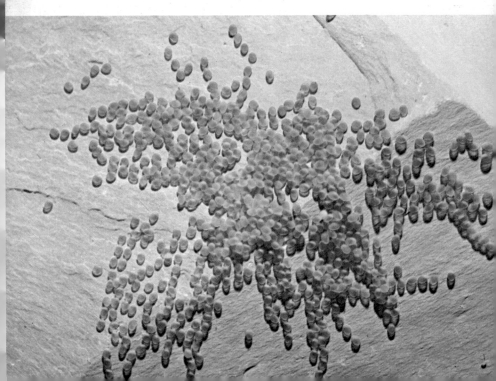

The distinctive feature of *Symphysodon discus* is the central body bar, which is darker and more distinct than the other body bars. Photo by Hilmar Hansen.

A mature *Symphysodon discus*. Photo by Dr. D. Terver.

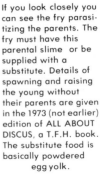

If you look closely you can see the fry parasitizing the parents. The fry must have this parental slime or be supplied with a substitute. Details of spawning and raising the young without their parents are given in the 1973 (not earlier) edition of ALL ABOUT DISCUS, a T.F.H. book. The substitute food is basically powdered egg yolk.

As the baby Discus grow they continue to feed off the parent's body, though at about one month of age they will begin to take newly hatched brine shrimp. Photos by Gene Wolfsheimer.

The overall shape of this fish is its greatest claim to distinction. It is compressed laterally and almost perfectly round, like a large saucer. The basic color is a rich, deep blue and brown. Three vertical bars of darker hue cross the body between gill-cover and caudel base. The dorsal and anal fins are short, but travel most of the way around the body, ending just short of the tail. These fins are deep blue near the body and red at the edges; there is an area of yellow between the blue and red near the tail. The body of the male is a bit duskier in color, and there are many wavy bright blue lines around the head and in the back and belly region. The female has some of these wavy blue lines as well, but only a few. The tail is almost colorless, with a few blue dots in both sexes.

SECOND GROUP

B. THE EGG SPLASHER

Copeina arnoldi, the Splashing Tetra, comes to us from the Brazilian Amazon to Venezuela. It attains a size of 3 inches, and is peaceful in disposition. The back is chocolate brown, shading to a bluish sheen on the sides. Anal and ventral fins are orange in color at the base, and the tail is yellow, tipped with orange; in the male, the upper lobe of the tail is elongated and edged with black. The dorsal fin carries a black, triangular spot, and is tipped with black; this fin is much longer in the males, making them easy to distinguish.

This fish has one of the most unusual breeding procedures of all fishes. Spawning is accomplished by finding an overhanging leaf or stone which it can reach by jumping, and placing its eggs there. Why don't the eggs dry out? Because the parents keep them wet by swimming under them and splashing water up at them! When the youngsters hatch, they fall into the water and swim unconcernedly away.

Copeina arnoldi, the Splashing Tetra. Two males are shown here. They have much longer dorsal fins and are easily identified. Photo by G.J.M. Timmerman.

Splashing Tetras, Copeina arnoldi, are not difficult to keep, but it is very necessary to have an aquarium cover at all times. Photo by Hilmar Hansen.

Harald Schultz discovered this beautiful fish and Dr. Jacques Gery named it C. *vilmae* in honor of Harald's wife, Vilma Chiara Schultz. Since Schultz died the influx of new fishes from Brazil has all but ceased. Photo by Dr. Herbert R. Axelrod.

There are many *Copeina-Copella*-like fishes in Brazil. Almost every body of shallow, grassy water contains them, even when there are no other fishes to be found. The author found this fish in Brazil and its body is lying at the U.S.N.M. waiting to be described. Photo by Dr. Herbert R. Axelrod.

Unlike the Splashing Tetra, the Red-spotted Copeina, *Copeina guttata*, spawns on the bottom. The male excavates the bottom where the eggs are laid. Photo by Rudolf Zukal.

A male Splashing Tetra, *Copeina arnoldi*. Photo by G. J. M. Timmerman.

Breeding the Splashing Tetra is not the difficult job it would seem to be at first; it breeds willingly and accepts substitutes for the over-hanging leaf. A planted tank of at least 10 gallons capacity is used. The water should be well aged, soft, and neutral to slightly acid in character. Temperature should be between 82° and 84°. A small amount of salt should be added to the water, a heaping tablespoonful for 10 gallons. Of course, the tank should be completely covered, as with all fishes which jump. The cover glass may be treated in several ways to imitate the overhanging leaf or stone. Some aquarists slip a strip of green frosted glass, rough side down, under the cover glass. A strip of slate, cemented under the cover glass, will also serve the purpose. The surface of the water must be brought within exactly 2 inches of the spawning surface. The pair, which has been brought into condition with generous feedings of live foods, preferably daphnia, is then placed into the tank. When ready for her egg-laying duties the female allows herself to be coaxed under the spawning site. They then assume a side-by-side position with their bodies bent in opposite directions and leap out of the water to land alongside each other under the spawning site, where the female releases several eggs which are immediately fertilized by the male and remain hanging there when the parents drop back. This is repeated until the female is depleted. The male then assumes his job of splashing water up at the eggs until they hatch, a process which takes from 2 to 3 days. If they are well-fed, the parents pay no further attention to their offspring, but removing them at this point makes feeding the fry easier.

SECOND GROUP

C. THE EGG HIDERS

Apistogramma agassizi, Agassiz's Dwarf Cichlid
    corumbae
    ortmanni, Ortmann's Dwarf Cichlid
    pertense, the Yellow Dwarf Cichlid
    ramirezi, Ramirez's Dwarf Cichlid
    reitzigi, Reitzig's Dwarf Cichlid
Badis badis
Brachygobius xanthozonus, the Bumblebee Fish
Bunocephalus coracoideus, the Banjo Catfish
Nannacara anomala, the Golden-eyed Dwarf Cichlid
    taenia, the Lattice Dwarf Cichlid
Pelvicachromis pulcher (previously *Pelmatochromis kribensis*), the
    Kribensis
    taeniatus (previously in *Pelmatochromis*)
Thysia annectens (previously *Pelmatochromis annectens*)

There is only a very fine dividing line between this group and the Egg Anchorers. The difference is that, where members of the first group generally place their eggs right out in the open, this group seldom does, preferring to hide them out of sight. In their natural environment, they probably search for a pocket between rocks or scoop out a hole alongside a rock which takes them underneath. The smaller size of the dwarf cichlids tends to make them resort to stealth rather than aggressiveness where their eggs and fry are concerned; this is not to say that there is a lack of aggressiveness when the safety of their brood is threatened. We have seen many a tiny dwarf cichlid mother charge furiously at a fish many times her size and make him beat a hasty retreat.

There are included in this group the genera *Apistogramma*, *Nannacara* and *Pelvicachromis*. These are the so-called "dwarf cichlids." Because of their small size, plus the fact that they have practically the same breeding habits as the larger cichlids, this group includes some fishes which are particularly dear to the hearts of aquarists whose space is too limited for keeping the larger cichlids. The dwarfs can be bred comfortably in an aquarium of 5 gallons capacity and we have bred smaller ones like the *Nannacara* species in aquaria as small as 2 gallons. Because of their preference for hiding their eggs, there is less likelihood of plants being uprooted, as the majority of larger cichlids do so annoy-

Both the male and female Agassiz's Dwarf Cichlid guard the eggs, shown here laid in the interior of a halved coconut shell. Photo by Rudolf Zukal.

After spawning is accomplished it is best to remove the male and leave the female by herself to take care of the eggs until hatching time. Photo by Rudolf Zukal.

A pair of Agassiz's Dwarf Cichlid, *Apistogramma agassizi*. The male, upper fish, is larger and has a very distinctive caudal fin. Photo by Rudolf Zukal.

ingly. An overall optimum temperature, unless otherwise specified, is 78° to 80° if breeding is desired. For conditioning, it is better to reduce the temperature somewhat, say to about 76°. A planted tank gives the fish a greater sense of security than an empty one; give them besides a number of rocks, a small flowerpot on its side in a dark corner. Turn the open end of the flowerpot away from the light and you will probably find that this site is usually chosen for spawning, either inside or underneath, working in a hole which is laboriously scooped out beforehand, the male spitting out a few grains of gravel outside of the excavation site then picking up more and doing the same until all is taken care of to his satisfaction. Then the female is sought out, and woe betide her if she is not ready! When the male is observed to be making preparations, check the female and remove her for further conditioning in another tank if her sides are not well filled out. Otherwise she may get a bad beating from her mate. The female, if ready, will soon allow herself to be coaxed to the spawning site. She deposits her eggs in a group, the male following and fertilizing them. As soon as spawning is completed a strange thing takes place in the female: instead of her usual shy, timid self she becomes a tigress. The male, who is often twice her size, is butted and bitten until he beats a hasty retreat. If left in her company, he is in danger at this time. Left to her own devices, the female often takes excellent care of her eggs and young, but the unhappy fact remains that sometimes, especially when there are too many disturbances, she will suddenly decide that her eggs or babies are pretty enough to eat, and proceeds to eat them. Here again, if we want to assure a safe hatching, artificial methods must be used. As with the large cichlids, the eggs are removed or, if more convenient, the parents are fished out and a constant, fine stream of air is placed near the eggs, but not so near as to touch them. Eggs hatch in 4 or 5 days, after which time the fry lie helplessly squirming on the bottom. Yolk-sacs are absorbed in another 3 days or so and the fry, in the case of the *Apistogramma* or *Nannacara* species, are started on infusoria or, as a poor second choice, finely powdered dry food. The fry of *Pelvicachromis* species are large enough to be started on brine shrimp or sifted daphnia at once; this food, of course, follows after a few days of infusoria feeding for the other two groups. Once they have started growing, the rest is easy; in 6 months, the youngsters will begin pairing off to raise families of their own.

Apistogramma agassizi comes from the Amazon Basin; the male attains a size of 3 inches, and the female about an inch less. The colors of this fish are extremely variable. Generally, the body color is yellowish brown, with a bluish sheen on the sides and reddish on the belly. A black

These *Apistogramma agassizi* are about to lock jaws. The winner eventually becomes the mate of the female.

A mature male *Apistogramma agassizi*.

Ortmann's Dwarf Cichlid, *Apistogramma ortmanni*, guarding the eggs laid underneath the large rock. Photo by Stanislav Frank.

Apistogramma ortmanni guarding eggs in an empty flowerpot. Photo by Stanislav Frank.

Ramirez's Dwarf Cichlid, *Apistogramma ramirezi*, of the wild form. Photo by Dr. Herbert R. Axelrod.

A pair of *Apistogramma ramirezi*. The male, to the left, is a golden form while the female, lower fish, is a wild color form of *A. ramirezi*. Photo by Hans Joachim Richter.

stripe passes horizontally from the mouth, through the eye to the tip of the tail. The male has dorsal, anal and ventral fins which are bluish with a bright orange to red edge. The edge of the tail fin, which comes to a single point, is black. The fins of the female are more brownish in color, much smaller and rounded, and her body is more yellow in appearance.

Breeds as described for the group.

Apistogramma corumbae comes from parts of Brazil and Paraguay, and attains $2\frac{1}{2}$ inches in length, with the female slightly smaller. This fish is a little stubbier in the body and fins than the rest of the group. Body color is a muddy yellow, with a faint horizontal stripe, and a more definite diagonal bar which runs from the eye to the bottom of the gill plate. There are faint horizontal stripes in the lower part of the body, and also faint suggestions of wide vertical bars throughout the body. Fins are tinged with red, and there is a red edge on the upper part of the dorsal fin. The female is a bit smaller, with plain fins and a lighter body.

Breeds like the rest of the group.

Apistogramma ortmanni, Ortmann's Dwarf Cichlid, comes from the Guianas. Males attain a length of 3 inches and the females 2 inches. Body color is brown, with a yellow belly. The diagonal bar from the eye to the lower part of the gill plate is also present here, but the horizontal line is usually quite faint. There are a few irregular yellowish bars. The male's fins are light rosy pink, with vertical streaks in the anal and tail. The female has yellow fins and a black edge on the front of her ventrals. At breeding time, her entire body becomes golden yellow, and a horizontal black line is very much in evidence.

This fish breeds like the others; the female is often found to be a very good parent.

The eggs of *Apistogramma ortmanni* enlarged about 12 times. Photo by Arend van den Nieuwenhuizen of Heemstede, Holland.

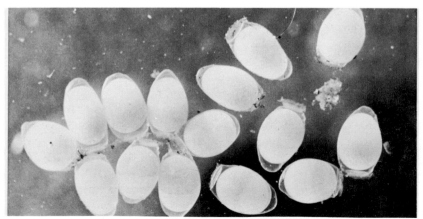

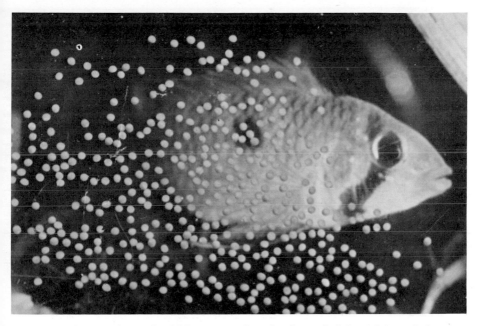

Eggs of Ortmann's Dwarf Cichlid were pasted on the glass wall of the tank instead of a hidden place elsewhere. Photo by A. van den Nieuwenhuizen.

Apistogramma pertense, the Yellow Dwarf Cichlid, comes from the Amazon Basin. The male is 2 inches in length, the female a bit smaller. The body color varies and is usually olive to yellowish brown. There is a dark horizontal stripe which extends from the snout, through the eye, to a dark spot in the center of the body, and then continues to another dark spot at the caudal base; sometimes the line fades and the two spots remain. The short dark bar from the eye to the base of the gill-cover is also present in this species. There are green and brown wavy lines and dots on the head and gill-covers. The dorsal fin is gray with an orange edge, and the anal is yellow. The tail is gray, with alternating light and dark bars. The female has less color and her anal and dorsal fins are rounded.

Breeds like the others and is usually prolific.

Apistogramma ramirezi, Ramirez's Dwarf Cichlid, is also known to some aquarists as the Butterfly Dwarf Cichlid. It is native to the Orinoco Basin in Venezuela. Maximum size is 3 inches, but specimens this size are unusual. Body color is blue, with a violet overcast, and deep blue spots cover the body. At times there are 5 or 6 vertical bars, but they are never prominent. The black band which is characteristic of the *Apistogramma* species passes through the eye and down across the gill-

451

The male and female *Apistogramma ramerizi* clean the spawning site very carefully before laying the eggs. Photo by Hans Joachim Richter.

A female *Apistogramma ramirezi* laying eggs as the male eagerly waits for his turn to fertilize the eggs. Photo by Hans Joachim Richter.

A male *Apistogramma pertense* photographed at the height of its breeding coloration.
Photo by Hans Joachim Richter.

A pair of *Apistogramma ramirezi*. The male, the fish on the left, is readily identified by his longer dorsal fin rays. Photo by G.J.M. Timmerman.

cover. The snout is bright red, a shade brighter in males. The large dorsal fin is edged with orange, and the males show elongated second and third rays, which are black. There is a large black spot in the center of the body; in the females, this spot is dotted with gold. A golden variety is also available.

This lovely fish seems to be a bit more "touchy" than the others; it spawns readily as a rule, but frequently is guilty of eating its own eggs. A pair which raises a family is an outstanding exception. Temperature should be slightly higher than for the rest, about 82°F. Artificial incubation is strongly recommended.

Apistogramma reitzigi, Reitzig's Dwarf Cichlid, comes from the Amazon Basin. Maximum size is 2½ inches. This fish is easily recognized by the large, sweeping dorsal and anal fins, the last rays of which reach almost to the tip of the tail. Body color is slate gray, and the dark edges of the scales form a reticulated pattern. Belly is yellowish and there are gleams of blue around the head. Spawns like the others.

Badis badis is native to India and Burma, and attains a size of 2 inches. Although it looks and acts like a dwarf cichlid, this fish together with the Leaf Fish is a member of the Nandid family. The colors of *Badis badis* are practically impossible to describe; they change com-

Eggs of *Apistogramma reitzigi* laid on the glass in a darkened aquarium. Photo by G.J.M. Timmerman.

A pair of *Apistogramma reitzigi*. The male is the upper fish. Photo by Chvojka Milan.

A pair of *Apistogramma reitzigi* fighting for the privilege of breeding with the female. Photo by A. van den Nieuwenhuizen.

A male *Apistogramma reitzigi* chasing the female. Note the beautiful coloration of the male on the left. Photo by Rudolf Zukal.

A female *Apistogramma reitzigi* in an almost upside down position attaching eggs on the surface of a big rock. Photo by Rudolf Zukal.

Badis badis is also known as the Dwarf Chameleon Fish on account of its changes of color. Photo by Hilmar Hansen.

The attractive coloration of the Bumblebee Fish makes up for its diminutive size. Photo by G. J. M. Timmerman.

Badis badis burmanicus, from Burma, of course, is an old favorite which is rarely seen any more. J.P. Arnold, the famous German aquarist, spawned this fish in 1920 when a shipment arrived via a German sailor from Rangoon. Photo by Dr. Herbert R. Axelrod.

The Banjo Catfish, *Bunocephalus coracoideus*. Photo by Harald Schultz.

Bunocephalus coracoideus, the Banjo Catfish, is native to the Amazon Basin, Ecuador and the Rio Negro. Maximum size attained is 6 inches. This fish has a thin, elongated body and a large, flat head. Body color is a mottled brown and gray. It is peaceful and makes an excellent scavenger. Females have a fuller, more rounded body.

There have not been many instances of this odd catfish breeding in captivity, but it has been done. A breeding tank of about 10 gallons capacity is provided with clean sand to a depth of about 3 inches, and a number of flat rocks are placed there. The tank is then planted heavily, and a temperature of 76° is maintained. The water should be slightly alkaline (pH 7.6). A pair of fish which have been fed generously on tubifex worms or chopped earthworms is then placed in the tank. The male will begin to scoop out holes under the flat rocks, tearing out some of the plants in the process. Spawning then takes place under the rock. The parents do not eat their eggs or young as a rule, but there is no great amount of parental care either, so removing the parents after spawning does no harm. When the young become free-swimming, infusoria and powdered dried foods are provided such as brine shrimp until they become large enough to handle more substantial foods.

Nannacara anomala, the Golden-eyed Dwarf Cichlid, is native to Guyana. Males attain a size of $2\frac{1}{2}$ inches and females an inch less. Body color of the male is a metallic green, with each scale showing a blue edge, giving a reticulated pattern. Sometimes a dark horizontal stripe is in evidence. The dorsal and anal fins are large and flowing. The female, on the other hand, besides being an inch smaller, shows the horizontal stripe more plainly and has a series of dark bars extending into the dorsal fin in the upper part of her body.

A small tank may be used to spawn this fish, if it is well planted. The procedure used for the *Apistogramma* species is applicable here.

Nannacara taenia, the Lattice Dwarf Cichlid, is native to the Amazon Basin, and resembles the preceding species in size. The body color is a light brown, and besides the horizontal line which is described for *N. anomala*, there are 6 other smaller lines, 3 above and 3 below the center. At times, a number of vertical bars appear, giving a latticed, checkerboard effect. As in the preceding species, the females are an inch smaller, with smaller fins.

This fish also spawns like the *Apistogramma* species.

Thysia annectens comes from the Niger Basin in West Africa. The female attains a length of about 4 inches, the male is considerably smaller. Body color is a yellowish brown, bluish on the back and with a pink glow beneath. The sides have 3 horizontal stripes and 6 vertical bars, and a bright green spot appears at the point of the gill-covers. The dorsal and anal fins are a dark olive toward the forward region and lighter toward the rear, peppered with red dots. The ventral fins are bluish black. Besides being a bit larger than her mate, the female is of a more sombre coloring and has a white spot directly above her vent.

Spawning is similar to that of the *Apistogramma* species; this one is inclined to be a bit shy and should have a well-planted tank of at least 10 gallons, and few disturbances. An arrangement into which the *Thysia* species like to spawn is an upright flowerpot, with a notch cut out of the upper rim which is large enough to permit the passage of the fish's body. A flat piece of slate covers the flowerpot. This provides a dark little cave which is particularly acceptable as a spawning site. When the fish spend a lot of time in it, lift the slate cover to check for eggs, and unless you are willing to risk them being eaten, resort to artificial hatching procedure.

Pelvicachromis pulcher is one of the more popular introductions from the Cameroons in West Africa. Size attained is 3 inches for the males, an inch less for the females. The upper part of the body is brown, with

Two males of *Nannacara anomala*, the Golden-eyed Cichlid. The fish on the left is starting to challenge the other fish into a fight. Photo by Rudolf Zukal.

Pelvicachromis pulcher, the Krib. This is a male fish. Photo by Dr. Herbert R. Axelrod.

A female Krib depositing her eggs on the inner wall of a flowerpot.

Pelvicachromis taeniatus has a distinctive color pattern which is not too difficult to recognize. Photo by Dr. Herbert R. Axelrod.

A male specimen of a pink variety of *Pelvicachromis pulcher*. Photo by Dr. Herbert R. Axelrod.

a golden stripe. The forehead is crossed by 3 dark lines. The lower part of the body is golden, with a brilliant wine-red spot covering the entire belly region. The dorsal and anal fins have a violet sheen, edged with gold and red. The female has one or more eye-spots on the after end of the dorsal fin, and the male has a number of eye-spots along the upper edge of the tail. Ventral fins are deep red, edged with violet in front. When breeding, the female becomes dark brown posteriorly and coppery in front.

This fish spawns quite readily in the same manner as the preceding species. It has an unsavory reputation as an egg-eater, and to have a pair raise their young without eating them is an exceptional performance. Artificial incubation is therefore strongly recommended.

Pelvicachromis taeniatus comes from the lower Niger River in West Africa. Size attained is $3\frac{1}{2}$ inches, slightly smaller for females. In color it is a little lighter than *P. pulcher*, with 5 or 6 faint bars on·the sides. The big difference is in the upper part of the male's caudal fin, which instead of showing a series of dots, shows a number of streaks. Other coloration is very similar.

A pair of *Pelvicachromis pulcher*. The male is to the right.

Breeding habits for this species are exactly as for *P. pulcher*.

Spawns are usually large, so it is best to use an aquarium of about 15 gallons or more. Water should be about neutral, temperature 76°. The male will soon go to work on a depression in the gravel, and after she has finished egg-laying, the female will be driven away and should be taken out. The male will fan and protect the eggs until they hatch, in about 48 hours. After they become free-swimming, there is little further parental attention and the male may be taken out to insure the safety of the fry. The youngsters are hardy, and will soon outgrow their need for infusoria and be able to handle brine shrimp and other larger foods.

SECOND GROUP

D. THE EGG SCOOPERS

Copeina guttata, the Red-spotted Copeina
Etroplus maculatus, the Orange Chromide
Jordanella floridae, the American Flagfish
Mesogonistius chaetodon, the Black-banded Sunfish

This group, which we call the "Egg Scoopers," breeds in a manner similar to the North American sunfishes, of which one, *Mesogonistius chaetodon*, is a member and many Lake Malawi cichlids. Spawning is simple: a site is chosen by the male and a depression is scooped out by swirling the water while swimming in a circle; particles of sand and other debris which cannot be cleared away in this manner are picked up in the mouth and deposited outside of the depression. The female takes no part in the procedure, but lets herself be coaxed there when the work is finished. The eggs are deposited at the bottom of the depression and guarded by the male until they hatch and the young can fend for themselves.

Copeina guttata, the Red-spotted Copeina, attains a size of 4 inches and comes from the Brazilian Amazon and the Rio Negro. The body color is a bluish gray, becoming white on the belly. The male has 6 rows of red dots crossing the body horizontally. The dorsal fin is yellowish with a large dark spot and the ventral, anal and caudal fins are light orange. Females are lighter and lack the rows of red dots. A strange thing about this species is that the tank-raised specimens become larger than wild, imported ones. This is the only known instance where the opposite is not true. Keep a cover-glass on an aquarium which contains these fish; they are not very fast movers, but are adept at jumping.

Etroplus maculatus, the Orange Chromide, attains a size of 3 inches and is a native of India (the Malabar coast and Madras) and Sri Lanka. The body is golden in color, with a blue spot in the center. There are many horizontal lines composed of tiny red dots. The eyes are red. The dorsal fin is orange and the tail yellow. The ventrals are sooty, as is the fore part of the anal fin. When this fish is ready to spawn, the sooty color appears on the body and dorsal fin. Females have fewer red dots and a bit less color.

Spawning is performed by digging down into the gravel until the bottom is reached; there are deviations, however, which might entitle them to a place elsewhere. Sometimes they prefer to spawn in a flower-pot or on or under a rock. Eggs and fry are held by a filament which anchors them until they are strong enough to break it. Incubation takes

Etroplus maculatus with
fry. Photo by Rudolf Zukal.

A female (lower fish) *Jordanella floridae* releasing her eggs not too far from the bottom of the tank. Photo by Vojtech Elek.

The female Copeina *guttata* lays her eggs in the shallow pit on the sand scooped earlier by the male. Photo by Rudolf Zukal.

This pair of Orange Chromides, *Etroplus maculatus*, prefer to lay their eggs on the side of a rock instead of in a shallow pit. There is considerable controversy about exactly how these fish spawn and care for their young. Photo by Rudolf Zukal.

Apeltes quadracus, the Four-spined Stickleback (above), and *Gasterosteus aculeatus*, the Three-spined Stickleback (below) are very ingenious nest-building species. They utilize whatever materials are on hand. Upper photo by Aaron Norman, lower photo by Klaus Paysan.

Riccia leaves were utilized by this pair of Comb-tails, *Belontia signata*, to reinforce the weak bubblenest. Photo by Rudolf Zukal.

This spawning pair of Comb-tails preferred to build a small nest under an Amazon Sword plant leaf. Notice the eggs floating towards the leaf. Photo by Hans Joachim Richter.

Apeltes quadracus, the Four-spined Stickleback, attains a length of 2 inches and ranges from Labrador to Virginia where it inhabits salt, brackish and sometimes fresh waters. Body color is green, with a mottled light and dark irregular pattern. Belly region is silvery; in the spring the males may be distinguished by their red ventral fins.

As the sticklebacks are practically salt-water fishes, there should be a generous addition of salt to their water; a tablespoon per gallon. Sticklebacks breed in the springtime, and efforts to get them to breed at any other time are usually fruitless. A net pulled through a grassy bottom in almost any body of brackish water which is not contaminated will generally yield one or more species of stickleback, which can be acclimated to aquarium life by gradually freshening the water from which they come. Only living foods are accepted. Keep the aquarium in a cool place and do not heat the water. A 60° temperature is perfect. There should be aeration and a generous planting provided. A 10-gallon aquarium may be used; do not put in any more than one male, or there will be fights. Several females, however, may be added. The male first signifies his desire to spawn by developing bright red ventral fins. He soon begins to search around for a proper location and begins constructing his nest. The female has no part in these operations. Her only job is to be ready with the eggs when they are required.

A Stickleback's nest partially demolished to show the eggs.

A pair of Comb-tail Paradise Fish, *Belontia signata*. They are very nasty fish, but are equally as hardy. Not too difficult to breed, either. Photo by G.J.M. Timmerman.

When the nest is woven to his satisfaction, the male turns his attention to the female of his choice. She is wheedled, bullied, bumped, pushed and steered until she enters, and the male squeezes in beside her. There is a quivering and trembling that threatens to shatter the nest to pieces until finally some eggs are expelled and the female swims out for a rest. She is finally coaxed back, however, and the process is repeated. Sometimes, if several females are available, a vigorous male will choose one or two additional mates after the first is depleted. When the females are driven off, they should be taken out, lest they be harmed. Eggs hatch in 3 to 4 days, and the youngsters are soon able to graduate from infusoria to newly hatched brine shrimp.

Belontia signata, the Comb-tail, is native to Sri Lanka and attains a length of 5 inches. Body color is brick-red, fading to a brown mottled pattern when the fish is unhappy or frightened. The rays of the tail fin are separated at the ends, giving its popular name. The fish is hardy and has a healthy appetite. Unfortunately it is also scrappy and is not recommended for the community aquarium.

Temperature for breeding should be around 80°. The male builds a haphazard bubble-nest of sorts, which serves to keep the floating eggs in place. Hatching occurs in 3 days, and the fry become free-swimming 2 days later. They are large and able to take brine shrimp at once.

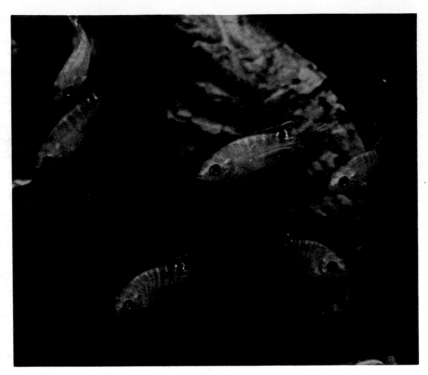

The young *Belontia signata* differs in markings from the adult. In time the dorsal spot disappears. Photo by Hans Joachim Richter.

Betta bellica is also known as the Slender Betta. This is a male fish. Photo by Herbert R. Axelrod.

A female Siamese Fighting Fish, *Betta splendens*. Photo by Hilmar Hansen.

A male *Betta splendens*. Notice the greater development of the fins and more brilliant coloration. Photo by Dr. Herbert R. Axelrod.

Betta bellica is native to Malaysia and gets to be 4 inches long. Body color is metallic green and there is a series of dark bars. The dorsal fin is a rusty red with a greenish edge. The anal and lower part of the caudal fin are a bright red. Females are less gaudy and have shorter fins.

This species spawns in a manner similar to *B. splendens*, which follows.

Betta splendens, the Siamese Fighting Fish, is native to Thailand and attains a length of 2½ inches. This is the famous Fighting Fish about which so much has been written. Two males put together in a confined space will attack each other so viciously that in a short time one may be so mutilated that he is unable to continue fighting. The gorgeous specimens available to aquarists everywhere today would scarcely be recognizable as the same species if compared to the original wild strains. These latter are a dull brownish or greenish gray, sometimes with dark horizontal stripes. The fins are very short when compared with the huge dorsals, anals and caudals of domesticated specimens.

Here we have one of the finest examples of the breeder's art. We have at present reds, blues, greens, orchids, albinos and even a strain which is almost totally black. There are all sorts of combinations of body and fin colors, for instance a strain which has a white body and bright red fins. The males have had their ferocity tamed very little with all the domestication. Putting two of them together is still sure to provoke a bloody battle. There is one fortunate thing: being an anabantoid, the bettas breathe atmospheric air and are not dependent on the oxygen content of the water in which they live. For this reason, it is possible to keep individuals in separate small containers, such as pint jars. With only a minimum of attention such as feeding them and keeping the water clean, a male can be raised to maturity in these close confines. Females are no problem; they will grow up together with very little lack of harmony.

Males begin to show their sex when a little under an inch long, and are recognizable by longer fins and their "chip on the shoulder" attitude. It is time then to begin picking them out and giving them their individual quarters.

Let us take the breeding procedure from the beginning: we have a male and a female of characteristics which we wish to combine. The male is fully grown and healthy, and the female's belly is almost bursting with eggs. A large aquarium is put into use, one of about 20 gallons being good. This aquarium is filled to a depth of 4 to 5 inches and the water brought to 82°. A glass cover should be kept in place at all times. There need be no gravel on the bottom; the male has an easier time finding dropped eggs without it. A few floating plants are placed in the water. The male is then introduced; he will soon begin to build a nest of bubbles, either in a corner or between the floating plants. Now is the time to introduce him to his mate. Watch them at first, to make sure that the female does not get badly damaged. The male will soon show her the nest, and when he gets her under it, will wrap his body around hers in such a way that their vents are close together. Both will roll over in what is known as the "nuptial embrace." This is usually repeated a few times before any eggs are released. Here is a much discussed point as to what goes on in this embrace: some breeders claim that the eggs are squeezed out of the female's body in this act, and others brand this as nonsense, and say that the pressure, if there is any at all, is so gentle that it has no appreciable effect.

A trio of Fighting Fish breaking the surface of the water to breathe atmospheric air.
Photo by Robert E. Gossington.

A beautiful red variety of Betta. Photo by Dr. K. Knaack.

This blue Betta has very little red coloration showing. Photo by Dr. Karl Knaack.

A pair of Bettas in typical
nuptial embrace under their
bubble-nest.

The male squeezes the eggs
from the female and they
slowly fall to the bottom of
the aquarium.

The male immediately leaves the benumbed female and catches the eggs in his mouth. Most of the eggs are caught before they reach the gravel bottom.

Then he blows the eggs into his nest and stands guard over them lest they fall out of the nest or some intruders try to eat them.

A male *Betta* spawning with a female *Macropodus*. Hybrids produced from such crossings may or may not be fertile. Photo by Hans Joachim Richter.

The same male Fighting Fish shown on the opposite page picking up the eggs dropped by the female *Macropodus*. Photo by Hans Joachim Richter.

The jars against the wall are for isolating male Bettas. The tanks on the right are used for spawning. The fish are then sexed and dumped into the pools to mature. This is the setup that Orville Tutwiler uses in Florida.

There are anywhere from 10 to 40 eggs released and fertilized at each embrace, once things get started. The female sinks exhausted after each embrace, and the male straightens out and picks up the eggs, catching some of them before they drop to the bottom. These he spits into the bubble-nest. The female recovers shortly, and the act is repeated until her egg supply is exhausted. She is then driven away and may be injured if not removed at this point. The male then takes up his post under the nest, which he keeps in repair by blowing more bubbles when needed. Once in a while an egg drops out; his sharp eye spots it, and it seldom falls more than an inch before he retrieves it and replaces it in the nest. Incubation is completed in 30 to 40 hours, after which time it is possible to see a great many tiny tails quivering below the nest. Once in a while, an individual becomes dislodged and begins to spiral down to the bottom; he is quickly picked up by the busy male and replaced. In 3 to 4 days, however, the fry become free-swimming and try as he might, the male can no longer keep his family in the nest, which he abandons at this time.

490

Now is the time to put him back into his old quarters. You will probably find that you have a large number of young; remember this when feeding with infusoria and make the feedings as frequent as possible. Another necessity at this stage is the introduction of a gentle stream of air. For the first 3 to 5 weeks of their lives, the organ known as the "labyrinth" (which makes it possible for anabantoid fishes to breathe atmospheric air) is not developed and the young fish must get his oxygen from the water; when this organ is first put to use is a critical time for the growing fish. There must be no oily scum on the surface, and the air temperature above the surface must be equal to the water temperature below. This explains the need for the glass cover and the stream of air, which breaks up any surface scum. No matter how perfect their attention has been, there will always be a few individuals whose labyrinths do not develop properly. Some losses will be experienced and should be expected. Once this critical period has been passed, growth becomes very rapid with proper feeding. Live foods are of course best, but prepared foods with a high meat content may be used to fill in.

Callichthys callichthys, the Armored Catfish, ranges from eastern Venezuela and Trinidad to Buenos Aires. Size is 5 inches. Body color is a muddy gray to light brown, with small dots on the fins. The head is flat and provided with two sets of barbels, and there are series of large

The famous Tutwiler Butterfly Betta. Unfortunately the strain was never fixed and no one has ever been able to duplicate this fish. In the late 1960's Tutwiler retired from the fish business to raise tropical plants.

To prevent great damage to the fins of male Bettas they are usually isolated from each other by glass partitions. This is a convenient method of keeping them in one display tank.

This close-up photograph of an Armored Catfish, *Callichthys callichthys*, clearly shows the arrangement of the head and body plates. Photo by Hilmar Hansen.

A colorful male *Colisa fasciata* guarding the nest. Photo by Hans Joachim Richter.

Hoplosternum is another Armored Catfish that builds bubble-nests under floating leaves. New York Zoological Society photo.

bony plates in two overlapping rows which run the length of the body.

The main item necessary to spawn this fish is a very large tank of at least 20 gallons. Some floating plants are provided, and a pair is well conditioned with generous feedings of chopped earthworks or large quantities of tubifex worms. Females may be distinguished by their heavier bodies when viewed from above. It is claimed that in their natural habitat this fish always spawns after a shower, so when your pair is conditioned, try removing some of the water into a watering-can and providing them with a "shower" every day. Sounds silly, but it works. The male builds a bubble-nest under a floating plant leaf or piece of floating *styrofoam*, and a huge number of eggs are deposited by the female. She is then driven off and the male stands guard under the nest, which he may be permitted to do until the young begin to swim freely.

Colisa fasciata, the Giant Gourami, is native to India and attains a size of 5 inches. Body is light brown, with a series of blue lines running diagonally down the sides. Throat is blue, and there are some blue markings in the belly region. Males have a white -tipped dorsal fin, the anal is tipped and edged with red, and the tail is a light yellow with orange dots. Females have much less color, and round fins.

Breeding is similar to that for the *Belontia signata*, but the eggs hatch in 2 days instead of 3.

Colisa labiosa, the Thick-lipped Gourami, is native to Burma and gets to be 3 inches long. The body is brown, and a horizontal line runs from the gill-cover to the tail base. This line is more prominent in the females. The males show some blue bars on the sides. The dorsal fin is blue, tipped with orange, and the anal fin is yellow at the base, then blue, and edged yellowish. The tail is blue. Females lack these colors in the fins, and have only the brown on the sides, with the horizontal line.

The same set-up as for breeding *Betta splendens* is used here. The male builds a bubble-nest, and the same "nuptial embrace" is performed; a big difference, however, is that the gouramis release an egg which floats, and the male has a much easier job tending the nest, because the eggs do not drop out. Hatching takes place in a little more than a day, but it may be a week before the fry become free-swimming. The female is taken out right after spawning, and the male when the fry begin to swim freely.

A pair of Giant Gouramis, *Colisa fasciata*. The male is to the left. Photo by G.J.M. Timmerman.

Colisa lalia, the Dwarf Gourami, is native to India and attains a length of $2\frac{1}{2}$ inches. This is the most popular of the three species. The male's body is a beautiful blue with an indigo patch on the throat and belly region during spawning. A series of narrow red bars cross the sides diagonally. The dorsal fin is red with blue dots, and the anal and tail fins are orange with blue dots.

The Dwarf Gourami has one spawning characteristic which distinguishes it from the Thick-lipped Gourami. It should be provided a little more generously with floating plants, as it likes to include bits of plants in its nest. Otherwise, all other instructions apply.

Giant Gouramis, Colisa fasciata, surrounded by a shower of eggs spawned a few moments earlier. The male on the left is attempting to retrieve as many eggs as possible to deposit into the nest. Photo by Hans Joachim Richter.

Thick-lipped Gouramis, *Colisa labiosa*, in a spawning embrace. Photo by Rudolf Zukal.

A pair of Thick-lipped Gouramis, *Colisa labiosa*, male on the right. Photo by G.J.M. Timmerman.

A pair of Dwarf Gouramis, *Colisa lalia*, male on the bottom. Photo by G.J.M. Timmerman.

Eucalia inconstans, the Brook Stickleback, is native to the middle western States and Southern Canada. It grows to 2½ inches. Unlike the other sticklebacks, this is a strictly fresh-water species, and the heavy addition of salt recommended for the others would not be beneficial here. The sides are green, with a mottled pattern. During the breeding season, the male develops bright red ventral fins; otherwise, the males are distinguishable by their slimmer, slightly smaller bodies.

Spawns exactly like *Apeltes quadracus*.

Gasterosteus aculeatus, the Three-spined Stickleback, is found in the Temperate Zone of the Northern Hemisphere in the coastal waters of the world. Normally the sides are greenish, with a mottled pattern; the belly is silvery, with a light pink tinge. In the spring months the sides become metallic blue and the throat and belly region are bright red. Females have silvery bellies and are more heavily built.

All the rules of keeping and breeding this fish are exactly like those given for *Apeltes quadracus*.

A male Dwarf Gourami, *Colisa lalia*. Photo by Rudolf Zukal.

A male *Colisa labiosa*. Dwarf Gouramis are produced by the millions in Florida where they spawn in outdoor pools, never bothering each other or their fry. No one has been able to do the same thing with C. *labiosa*. Photo by Rudolf Zukal.

Colisa labiosa in spawning embrace directly beneath the nest. Photo by Rudolf Zukal.

Upon uncoiling from the tight embrace, eggs are scattered violently around. These will be gathered by the male soon afterwards. Photo by Rudolf Zukal.

A typical bubble-nest of the Dwarf Gourami, *Colisa lalia*.

Macropodus chinensis is found in eastern China, Formosa and Korea. Length attained is 2½ inches. It is known as the Round-tailed Paradise Fish. The body is a reddish brown with a series of darker bars on the sides. Fins are rusty in color and dark edged. Anal and dorsal fins of the male are pointed, and of the female, rounded.

This species is seldom bred because there is a very limited demand for them. A 10-gallon aquarium is set up without gravel on the bottom, but with a few floating plants. Temperature is brought to 76°, and a well-conditioned pair is introduced. Some breeders prefer to introduce the male first and wait until he builds the bubble-nest. Keep an eye on them at first to make sure that no damage is done to the female. If the male chases her so vigorously that she is forced to hide in a corner, place a glass partition between them until they calm down a bit. Spawning itself is done betta-fashion, the male wrapping his body around the female while she expels a number of non-buoyant eggs which the male picks up and spits into the nest. When she is done, remove her at once. The male guards the nest, and the eggs hatch in a little more than a day.

The young become free-swimming a week later. The male is then taken out, and the young are given the same attention as other anabantoid fry.

Macropodus cupanus dayi, the Spike-tailed Paradise Fish, is found in Sri Lanka, Sumatra and Malaysia. It attains a size of 3 inches. Body is reddish, with two wide brown horizontal stripes. Fins are reddish, and the pointed tail is red with a gleaming blue edge. Some of the caudal rays are extended beyond the edge of the fin. Females have shorter fins and less color.

Spawns at 78° in a manner similar to *M. chinensis*, but the bubble-nest is sometimes built beneath the surface of the water, under a leaf or rock.

Macropodus opercularis, the Paradise Fish, is native to southern China, Cochin China and Formosa. It attains a length of 3 inches. The body is beautifully marked with alternating red and blue bars. Dorsal fin is large, blue in color, and edged and spotted with white. The anal fin is blue anteriorly, becoming red posteriorly. The tail is large and forked, red in color with blue spots.

Spawns at 74° in a manner similar to that described for *M. chinensis*.

Macropodus chinensis. Photo by Sam Dunton, New York Zoological Society.

The Three-spined Stickleback, *Gasterosteus aculeatus*. During the breeding season the males develop red on the throat and belly. Photo by Aaron Norman.

The Spike-tailed Paradise Fish *Macropodus cupanus dayi*. Photo by Hans Joachim Richter.

A male Paradise Fish, *Macropodus opercularis*, constructing the bubble-nest. Photo by Hans Joachim Richter.

A black variety of *Macropodus opercularis*. This male fish is blowing an egg into the nest. Photo by Rudolf Zukal.

A pair of the black variety of Paradise Fish. The female fish is to the left. Photo by Rudolf Zukal.

A pair of African Leaf Fish. The female is slightly paler in coloration. Photo by Karl Knaack.

The main drawback of keeping *Osphronemus gouramy* is that these fish can grow very large. They also are greedy fishes.

The beautiful and dainty Pearl Gouramis, *Trichogaster leeri*. The female is to the right and she has less elongated fins than the male. Photo by G.J.M. Timmerman.

Trichogaster leeri, the Pearl or Mosaic Gourami, comes from Sumatra, Borneo, Malaysia and Thailand. Maximum size of this beautiful fish is 5 inches. The sides are light blue with a definite violet overcast. The entire body is covered with pearl-gray dots which form a mosaic pattern. There is a zigzag black horizontal line which starts at the lips, runs through the eyes, and then fades out three-quarters way to the tail. During spawning time the male's belly and throat regions become a brilliant orange.

Spawning is similar to that of the Dwarf Gourami, *Colisa lalia*, with one exception: the female is treated more politely, and will share the male's duties if left after spawning. They both should be removed, however, after the fry begin to swim.

Trichogaster pectoralis, the Snake-skinned Gourami, comes from Indochina and Thailand, and gets to be 10 inches long. Body is olive-colored, with a dark broken horizontal line. A series of slightly slanting gold bars adorn the sides. The anal fin is amber-colored. Males have slightly larger fins.

Spawns like the above species.

Trichogaster trichopterus, the Blue, or Three-spot Gourami, is native to Malaysia and gets to be 5 inches long. The back is blue, shading to olive on the belly. There is a series of indefinte blue vertical bars in the after half of the body. A large black spot occurs in the center of the body, and another at the tail base. Whoever named this fish the "Three-

The first stage in the development of the Cosby Blue Gourami took place in Holland in 1953 when this photo was taken by Timmerman.

A pair of Snakeskin Gouramis, *Trichogaster pectoralis*. Photo by Dr. Herbert R. Axelrod.

A pair of Pearl Gouramis, *Trichogaster leeri*, in breeding condition. Intense red coloration develops in the male during this period. Photo by Rudolf Zukal.

During the spawning embrace the eggs are released from the genital aperture of the female as illustrated in this photograph of a spawning pair of Pearl Gouramis. Photo by Hans Joachim Richter.

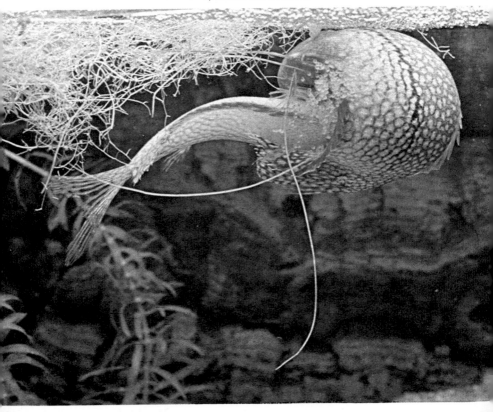

The Snakeskin Gourami, *Trichogaster pectoralis*, is one of the more difficult fish to spawn.
Photo by Hans Joachim Richter.

The Three-spot or Blue Gourami, *Trichogaster trichopterus*. Numerous color variations
of this species are also available today. Photo by Dr. Herbert R. Axelrod.

Because Blue Gouramis, *Trichogaster trichopterus* are so hardy and easy to breed, millions are produced every year in Florida where they are spawned indoors and the fry placed outdoors in huge pools about 25 feet by 100 feet, with a depth of about 6 feet. Amongst these inbred fish (no one bothers to import the wild ones from Indonesia), color sports are bound to appear. The fish above is the "old" Three Spot Blue Gourami. The fish shown below is just called a Blue Gourami because it lost its spots. These two varieties, however, interbreed and produce fish with and without spots. Photos by G.J.M. Timmerman.

The absence of pigmentation on the anterior half of this *Trichogaster trichopterus* is due to an abnormal condition or some form of disease. It is not genetic in character. Photo by Rudolf Zukal.

spot Gourami" included the eye as the third spot. Fins have pink dots. Males are distinguished by their larger anal and dorsal fins.

Spawns like the rest of the group.

Trichopsis vittatus, the Croaking Gourami, is found in Java, Borneo, Sumatra, Malaysia, Indochina and Thailand. Size attained is $2\frac{1}{2}$ inches. This is one of the few fishes which is capable of producing a sound. Body color is brown, with three horizontal dark stripes. The belly is yellowish. Fins are reddish brown, with many red and green dots.

Spawns like the *Trichogaster* species.

This beautiful fish named the Golden Gourami is a variety of *Trichogaster trichopterus*. Photo by Hans Joachim Richter.

A male Croaking Gourami, *Trichopsis vittatus*, photographed while displaying beside a receptive female. Photo by Hans Joachim Richter.

Croaking Gouramis build small bubble-nests under the leaves of plants. Photo by Hans Joachim Richter.

A mass of newly hatched Croaking Gouramis. The parents return any fish that stray from the nest during the early stages of guarding the young. Photo by Hans Joachim Richter.

The Javanese Medaka, *Oryzias javanicus*. The female is the lower fish as evidenced by her heaviness. Photo by G.J.M. Timmerman.

The Medaka, *Oryzias latipes*, found by the author (HRA) in Indonesia. Photo by Dr. Herbert R. Axelrod.

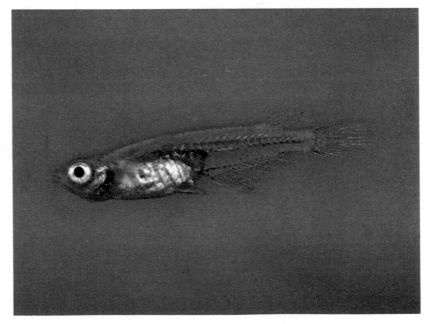

A pair of Cuban Killies, *Cubanichthys cubensis*. Photo by Stanislav Frank.

A well-planted tank is recommended for spawning Cuban Killies. The eggs can easily get snagged in fine-leaved plants like the Java Moss shown here. Photo by Rudolf Zukal.

A Javanese Medaka with eggs still attached to the genital opening.

Oryzias javanicus, the Javanese Medaka, is native to Java and Malaysia and attains a length of 1½ inches. The sides are silvery, with some iridescence in sunlight. Males have deeper dorsal fins, with a blue edge.

Spawns like *Cubanichthys cubensis*, but temperature should be higher, around 80°.

A pair of Medakas, *Oryzias latipes*. The male is the upper fish. Photo by G.J.M. Timmerman.

Oryzias latipes, the Medaka, comes from Japan, Korea, and neighboring China. Size attained is 2 inches. The body color is grayish, with a silvery horizontal stripe. Males have deeper anal fins. Most of the ones seen nowadays are a golden variety of this fish, which are a pleasing yellow in color.

Both color varieties spawn like *Cubanichthys cubensis*.

THIRD GROUP

B. THE MOUTHBROODERS

Betta brederi, the Mouthbrooding Betta
Chromidotilapia guentheri (previously *Pelmatochromis guentheri*)
Geophagus balzani, the Parana Mouthbrooder
Haplochromis philander (previously *H. moffati*)
 multicolor, the Egyptian Mouthbrooder
Labeotrophus fuelleborni, Fuelleborn's Cichlid
Pseudotropheus auratus, Nyasa Golden Cichlid
Sphaerichthys osphromenoides, the Chocolate Gourami
Tilapia macrocephala, the Black-chinned Mouthbrooder
 mossambica, the Mozambique Mouthbrooder

The members of this group have the interesting instinct of holding their eggs and young in the oral cavity, not only during incubation but also after the young are able to swim. When danger threatens, the parent opens up his (or her) mouth and the fry dash madly into it. After they have grown a few days, an amusing situation takes place whenever they all try to crowd in, somewhat reminiscent of the New York subway during rush hour.

Betta brederi, the Mouthbrooding Betta, is native to India and attains a length of $3\frac{1}{2}$ inches. It is amazing that a close relative of the Siamese Fighting Fish should have a method of breeding which is so dissimilar. Body color is light brown to gray, lighter on the belly. The scales on the sides each carry a light green dot, forming several horizontal lines. Fins are reddish, edged with gold. The males may be distinguished by the longer fins.

The method of spawning is unusual, even for a mouthbrooder. A tank of 5 to 10 gallons capacity may be used; planting should not be too heavy. Recommended temperature: 80°. A nuptial embrace, such as has been described for the Siamese Fighting Fish, occurs. The eggs, instead of being allowed to fall, are caught by the male in his anal fin and fertilized. The female then picks them out in her mouth and spits them

The Parana Mouthbrooder, *Geophagus balzani*. This female has just laid her eggs in an area which has not been too carefully cleaned. Photo by Hans Joachim Richter.

A pair of *Betta brederi*. The male is the upper fish. Notice his longer and more pointed fins. Photo by E. Roloff.

Chromidotilapia guentheri, previously known as *Pelmatochromis guentheri*. Photo by Rudolf Zukal.

Tilapia mossambica during their spawning process. In the upper photo you can barely discern a few large eggs being fertilized by the male as the female pecks at his anal fin. This signals the male to leave the spawning pit (lower photo) so she can gather the eggs in her mouth. Photos by Chvojka Milan.

A young pair of *Betta brederi*; the male is the top fish. Photo by G.J.M. Timmerman.

at her mate, one by one, who deftly catches them in his mouth; sometimes the "ball game" goes on for a while, an egg traveling back and forth for several trips before it finally comes to repose in the mouth of the male. When he has all the eggs stuffed in his mouth, the female may be removed. Incubation period is 4 to 5 days. The male may then be taken out when he releases the fry. Newly hatched brine shrimp may then be fed at once; the young are large enough to handle them and grow very rapidly.

Haplochromis philander (previously known as *H. moffati*), Moffat's Mouthbrooder, comes from the Congo tributaries and attains a length of 4 inches. Body color is olive, becoming silvery on the belly. The point of the gill-cover has a bright blue spot, and there are sometimes some vertical bars to be seen on the sides. There are copper-colored dots on the upper part of the body and blue ones on the lower part. The dorsal and tail fins are green and are marked with red and blue spots. The anal fin is red with blue dots. Males may be distinguished by a red spot at the tip of the anal fin.

A 10-gallon aquarium should be provided for spawning. Planting is not important nor does there have to be gravel on the bottom. The pair will pick out a spot, usually in a corner, and swim around in slow circles. If there are other fish in the tank with them, they will be driven

Geophagus balzani. Upon a given signal, usually a rapid trembling of her body, the fry rush to the safety of the mouth of the mother for protection against imminent danger. By tapping on the glass of the aquarium, these fish rushed back to their mother's mouth. Photo by Hans Joachim Richter.

A female Egyptian Mouthbrooder, plump and ready for spawning. Photo by Hilmar Hansen at the Berlin Aquarium.

Egyptian Mouthbrooders spawn in shallow depressions on the bottom. Photo by Rudolf Zukal.

Haplochromis philander in breeding coloration. Photo by Hilmar Hansen.

A female *Haplochromis philander* (?) with distended buccal cavity full of developing eggs. Photo by Rudolf Zukal.

The mouth cavity of *Tilapia mossambica* can accomodate an amazingly large number of fry. Photo by Gerhard Marcuse.

Geophagus balzani, the Parana Mouthbrooder, was first brought into America by Heiko Bleher and Thomas Horeman in 1972. It was first bred by Hans Joachim Richter of Leipzig, DDR and all present stocks resulted from the breeding pair of Richter.

The Parana Mouthbrooder serves as a good example for a fish which is both an egg anchorer and a mouthbrooder, for the fish first spawns on a flat rock which has been carefully cleaned and scrubbed by both parents and then, a day or so later, the female picks up the eggs in her mouth and keeps them there for about a week or 8 days until they are finally released and search for food. The female *balzani* continues to protect her young for several weeks and they come fleeing back to the safety of her mouth as soon as she signals danger is at hand by extending her fins and wriggling in a very meaningful manner.

The male loses all interest in spawning once the female is depleted of her several hundred eggs and he should be removed from the spawning aquarium as soon as spawning is completed. The female may be left with the fry for several weeks; this isolation from other large fishes is advantageous so she can regain her strength since she doesn't eat while the eggs are developing in her mouth.

Labeotropheus fuelleborni, Fuelleborn's Cichlid, is one of the mbuna cichlids of Lake Malawi (Lake Nyasa) of the rift lakes of Africa. It reaches a size of about 4 to 5 inches. The normal color pattern of Fuelleborn's Cichlid is a background of blue crossed by 6 to 8 dark vertical bars. The female in this color phase is generally paler and may have a more greenish cast, the bands being paler. A second color phase is present in the female of this species in which she exhibits a mottled pattern of black, orange, and white. Bright orange to yellow spots are present in the anal fin (and dorsal at times).

Spawning preparations are similar to those of *Pseudotropheus auratus*. Since these are sensitive fishes sudden changes are to be avoided. Courtship is active to the extent that plants are uprooted and the bottom is stirred up (do not use very fine sand as a substrate). About 50 eggs are

A newly hatched *Tilapia*. Photo courtesy of the American Museum of Natural History.

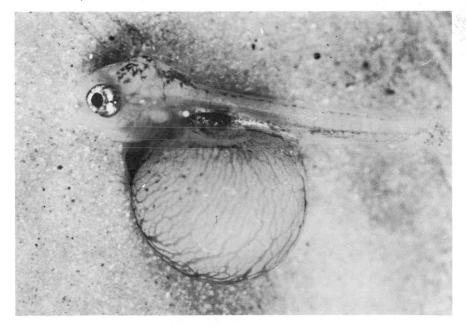

A female Haplochromis philander (♀) and its young. Photo by Rudolf Zukal.

Pseudotropheus auratus, the Nyasa Golden Cichlid. Upper photo, male. Middle photo, female. Photos by Dr. D. Terver. Lower photo, brooding female. Photo by Anthony Orsini.

Fuelleborn's Cichlid, *Labeotropheus fuelleborni*. Notice the prominent spots on the anal fin. Photo by Dr. D. Terver.

The typical habitat of *Labeotropheus* in Lake Malawi. Photo by Dr. Herbert R. Axelrod.

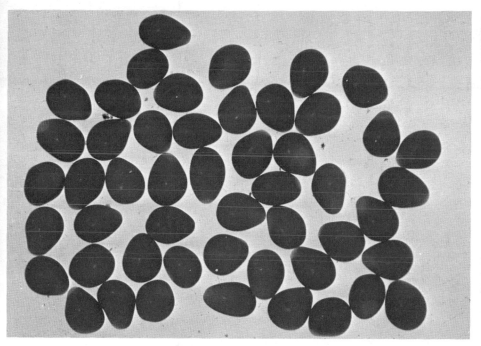

Magnified eggs of *Labeotropheus fuelleborni*. Photo by Dr. D. Terver.

Labeotropheus fuelleborni fry measuring about 10 millimeters in length. At this size they are free to swim about and can live by themselves. Photo by Dr. D. Terver.

A school of *Tilapia macrocephala*, the Black-chinned Mouthbreeder. Photo by Sam
Dunton, New York Zoological Society.

A beautiful *Tilapia mossambica*. Tilapias can live long in captivity and become "friendly" to their caretaker. Photo by L. E. Perkins.

harboring eggs. Richter never raised any fish but was able to get some baby Chocolate Gouramis which died within a week. Will you be the first one? For a very complete account of what happened with Richter see BREEDING AQUARIUM FISHES, Book 3 by Axelrod and Burgess, 1973 edition pages 154-184.

Tilapia macrocephala, the Black-chinned Mouthbrooder, is found on the Gold Coast of Africa and attains the respectable size of 8 inches. In color it is silvery, with several black blotches in the region of the lower lip and belly; there is also a black spot on the tip of the gill-cover. Fins are light pink. The females are distinguished by a pink spot on the gill-cover.

A large tank should be used, about 50 gallons in capacity. Spawns exactly like *Chromidotilapia guentheri*.

Tilapia mossambica, the Mozambique Mouthbrooder, is native to East Africa as far as Natal, and attains a length of 6 inches. This fish is immediately recognizable by its tail, which has a bright orange border. Normally the body color is metallic green, but under excitement, becomes much darker. At this time, the male sometimes shows 4 white spots on his side and a white lower lip.

Again, a large tank is necessary; spawning procedure is like *C. guentheri*, with one important difference: the female carries the eggs in her mouth.

Tilapia mossambica is a highly adaptable species and is now distributed in many tropical areas of the world. Photo by Dr. Herbert R. Axelrod.

The Chocolate Gourami, *Sphaerichthys osphromenoides*. Photo by Stanislav Frank.

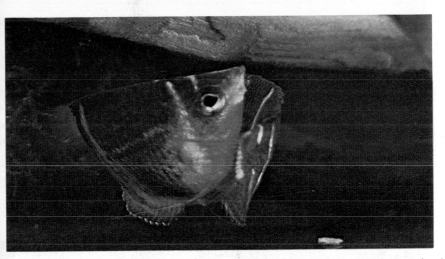

A spawning pair of Chocolate Gouramis with their bodies tightly coiled about each other. Photo by Hans Joachim Richter.

The only known photograph of a female Chocolate Gourami picking up her recently released eggs. The eggs are huge! Photo by Hans Joachim Richter.

THIRD GROUP

C. THE LIVE BEARERS

Alfaro cultratus, the Knife Live Bearer
Belonesox belizanus, the Pike Top Minnow
Brachyrhaphis episcopi, the Bishop
Brachyraphis terrabensis
Cnesterodon decemmaculatus, the Ten-spot
Dermogenys pusillus, the Half-beak
Gambusia affinis, the Mosquitofish
    nicaraguensis
    punctata, the Blue Gambusia
Girardinus metallicus, the Girardinus
    falcatus, the Yellow-belly
Heterandria formosa, the Midget Live Bearer
Jenynsia lineata
Poecilia branneri, Branner's Live Bearer
    caucana, the South American Molly
    heterandria, the Dwarf Limia
    latipinna, the Sailfin Molly
    melanogaster, the Black-bellied Limia
    nigrofasciata, the Humpbacked Limia
    ornata
    parae, the Two-spot Live Bearer
    reticulata, the Guppy
    sphenops, the Marbled Molly
    velifera
    vittata
    vivipara, the One-spot Live Bearer
Neotoca bilineata, the Two-lined Neotoca
Phallichthys amates, the Merry Widow
Phalloceros caudimaculatus, the Caudo
Phalloptychus januarius
Priapella intermedia
Xiphophorus helleri, the Swordtail
    maculatus, the Platy
    montezumae, the Montezuma Swordtail
    variatus, the Variegated Platy

It has been found that the various species of *Xiphophorus* will inter-breed quite readily. This knowledge gave the breeders, both amateur and professional, a field-day, and provided the basis for establishing many beautiful body and color variations which in many cases have become commonplace. Certain species of mollies, guppies, poecilias and limias have been hybridized to produce "new" fish, though few have ever become popular with aquarists.

Livebearers, like this *Belonesox*, have gonopodiums with which the males inseminate the females. This male is rotating his gonopodium and the camera "stopped" the action halfway through the rotation. Photo by Rudolf Zukal.

One thing the breeder of live-bearing fishes must know is the funda-mentals of their reproductive characteristics. The embryo of a mammal is attached to the mother via the placenta and umbilical cord. Food and oxygen are passed through the placenta and wastes are in turn thrown off. Though many live-bearing fishes have very similar embryonic arrangements, most of those fishes belonging to the Poeciliidae are known to have but the simplest arrangements for supplying the develop-ing young with their nutritional needs. Basically the female poeciliid provides protection for her young by carrying them within her body.

Another important way in which many live-bearing fishes differ from mammals is that the sperm cells are retained by the female and these

Belonesox belizanus, the Pike Top Minnow. The male is the lower fish with the gonopodium. Photo by Rudolf Zukal.

Pike Top Minnows are very voracious feeders and will eat only large live food. The Guppy on the right side of this picture will inevitably be eaten. Photo by Rudolf Zukal.

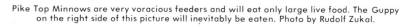

The Half-beak, *Dermogenys pusillus*, is a well known aquarium fish from Southeast Asia.

A pair of *Brachyrhaphis terrabensis*. The smaller fish to the left ·is the male. Photo by Dr. Martin Brittan.

The males of this subspecies of Mosquitofish, *Gambusia affinis holbrooki*, may appear very black, partially black or yellow to orange. Females are never black, however. Photo by G. J. M. Timmerman.

Gambusia affinis, the Mosquito-fish. This fish has been "planted" all over the world as a natural mosquito control. They are, however, equally as destructive of small fishes and should never be introduced into any water system without proper authority.
Photo by Rudolf Zukal.

Cnesterodon decemmaculatus, the Ten-spot, is native to southern Brazil to the Rio de la Plata and attains a size of 1½ inches, with the males smaller. Body is yellow, green above and silvery on the belly. There are 5 to 12 spots in a horizontal row on the sides. A peaceful fish, which may be kept in the community tank.

Females should be provided with plenty of plants when about to give birth. They are very nervous at this time.

Dermogenys pusillus, the Half-beak, is found in the brackish waters around the Malay Peninsula. Females attain 3½ inches in length and males about 1½ inches. Body color is bluish, brown above and silvery below. What makes the fish unmistakable is a beak-like projection of the lower jaw. The fish will not do well in fresh water; one-third sea water is recommended or the addition of a tablespoonful of salt per gallon of water. Males are very scrappy among themselves and will lock jaws and drag at each other furiously until one dominant fish is found. He will then proceed to make life miserable for the other males but seldom does them a direct injury.

Only living foods are taken from near the surface, making them difficult to keep. Parents should be separated from the young as soon as possible, to prevent cannibalism.

This is a female Half-beak, *Dermogenys pusillus.* She is giving birth to a youngster tail-first.

Now two youngsters at a time — tail-first — but one is nearly out and the other just starting to come out.

This time the female Half-beak drops two tail-first babies at the same time. Photos by G. J. M. Timmerman.

The Girardinus, *Girardinus metallicus*. The males are normally very much smaller than the females. Photo by Hilmar Hansen.

Heterandria formosa, the Midget Live-bearer. The small fish is a male, while the other two fish are double his size and females. The Midget Live-bearer may be the smallest fish usually kept in an aquarium! Photo by Rudolf Zukal.

Gambusia affinis, the Mosquitofish, is native to the Gulf states of this country. Females attain 2½ inches in size, males an inch less. Body is silvery and the fins are peppered with black spots. The species is used widely by introducing it into waters for mosquito control; unfortunately this is the best thing that can be said for it. It is a poor aquarium fish, often tearing the fins of the others to shreds. In Spanish, they are called "Gambusino," which means "worthless." Some individuals have a few black blotches on the body or they may be almost solid black. These fish are becoming rare in the southern part of Florida for they seem to be the food of choice for the newly established colonies of *Belonesox*.

Gambusia nicaraguensis is found in the Atlantic drainage from southern Mexico to Panama. Size of females is 2½ inches, males an inch smaller. The body color is grayish olive with a slight blue sheen on the sides. The body and unpaired fins are covered with black spots..As with the other gambusias, they will tear fins.

The Mosquitofish, *Gambusia affinis*. Upper fish is the male. Photo by G.J.M. Timmerman.

Not only *Gambusia* but numerous other species of fish can be collected from a typical brackish water habitat like this. Photo by Dr. Herbert R. Axelrod.

During low tide Mosquitofish seek cover among the exposed roots of mangrove plants. Photo by Dr. Herbert R. Axelrod.

Paul Hahnel was the first of the great guppy breeders. He said he had no secrets except that he fed his fish often with very highly nutritious foods and changed the water as often as possible. He raised some very beautiful fish and when the author (HRA) visited him and asked for his "best" fish to photograph he was told "I sell my best fish because they are getting too old to breed. But take a picture of this youngster only four months old. He'll be typical of the Hahnel strain." Here is the fish. Photo by Dr. Herbert R. Axelrod.

Girardinus metallicus. The male is to the left. Photo by Rudolf Zukal.

A pair of Snakeskin Triangle Guppies from Singapore. Photo by Dr. Herbert R. Axelrod.

Two male Guppies with characteristics of the wild form of *Poecilia reticulata*. Photo by Dr. Herbert R. Axelrod.

This was a prize-winning guppy in Europe in the late 1960's. The prize in most Guppy Shows is for fish with the most color, very intense pigmentation and long fins. Photo by Hilmar Hansen at the Berlin Aquarium.

A pair of Mosquitofish (also called the Midget Live Bearer, *Heterandria formosa.* The female is the top fish. Photo by G.J.M. Timmerman.

get to be an inch in length, and males only three fourths this size. Body color is a light brown with a dark horizontal line and a series of vertical bars running into it from above, sometimes crossing it.

Coming from a cooler climate, this fish should be kept in an unheated aquarium; 65° suits it well. Instead of giving birth to all her litter at once, the female will drop 1 or 2 daily for about 10 days, taking a rest after this time for several weeks. If well fed, especially with *Daphnia*, parents will scarcely ever eat their young. Because of its size, this species should have a small aquarium of their own.

Jenynsia lineata is a native of southern Brazil and northern Argentina. Females attain the size of 5 inches, and the males are fully grown at 1½ inches. Body color is gray, with dark horizontal bars adorning the sides.

Here we have a real oddity: the males have a gonopodium which swings sideways *in one direction only,* either to the left or the right. Females, it has been said, can accept the gonopodium from only one side or the other. Therefore it is possible only to mate a left-handed male with a right-handed female or vice-versa. This fish is not peaceful enough for the community aquarium.

Poecilia reticulata, the Guppy, is native to Trinidad, the Barbados, Venezuela, the Guyanas and probably parts of Brazil. Females attain $2\frac{1}{2}$ inches in size and males $1\frac{1}{2}$ inches. The Guppy has been the object of so much inbreeding, crossing of color strains, and selective breeding that scarcely any of the original chracteristics remain recognizable. Hardly a year goes by that some breeder does not come up with a new (and sometimes expensive) Super-Guppy. Lately the trend has been toward developing a long, flowing tail. This has been done, and with amazing results; we have seen males with tails almost as long as their bodies, some of them fanning out and displaying dazzling colors. Others have greatly elongated rays in the upper or lower edge of the tail. These are known as "Top-swords" and "Bottom-swords." Those which have elongated rays both above and below are called "Lyre-tails." Some have elongated middle rays in the tail. These are called "Pin-tails." Then there are others which have been developed for body color rather than finnage; here we have the Golds, Blues, Greens, Reds, Lace-tails, English, Trinidad and other color variations. Females of most strains are drab in color, being almost uniformly gray, with the exception of

A pair of *Girardinus falcatus*. Note the huge gonopodium on the male (upper fish). Photo by Sam Dunton, New York Zoological Society.

Bottom Sword male Guppy. Photo by Karl Knaack.

Round Tail male Guppy. Photo by Karl Knaack.

Pintail male Guppy. Photo by Karl Knaack.

568

Top Sword male Guppy. Photo by E. Schmidt.

Double Sword male Guppy. Photo by Dr. W. Foersch.

Cannibalism among Guppies can be substantially reduced by avoiding overcrowding and providing some plants for refuge of smaller fish. Photo by Chvojka Milan.

the Gold strain, which is yellow in color. Some of the other strains have streaks of black or blue in the dorsal and tail fins.

Breeding this fish requires nothing more than a clean, uncrowded aquarium with a temperature of 75°. A varied diet which contains a good proportion of live foods will result in large, beautifully colored, healthy specimens, provided of course that the original stock is desirable. Females are segregated when they become heavy with young and may be returned when the babies are born. Feeding the youngsters with a predominance of newly hatched brine shrimp for the first week or two will make a great contribution to their size and beauty later on when they grow up.

A female Guppy eating her own young. Photo by Mervin F. Roberts.

Four male Lyretail Guppies. Photo by Mervin F. Roberts.

Gold female Guppies showing tail markings. At one time Guppy breeders would use male hormones (testosterone) to test their females. The females would be dosed with testosterone until they developed color patterns which, the breeders assumed, would be the patterns passed on to their sons. Photo by Dr. Herbert R. Axelrod.

Unborn embryos of a Guppy. Photo by A. van den Nieuwenhuizen.

A pair of *Poecilia vittata*. Photo by G.J.M. Timmerman.

Poecilia nigrofasciata; the female is the upper fish. Photo by K. Quitschau.

This photograph shows a male Guppy with his gonopodium rotated forward and ready to enter the female. Photo by Dr. Myron Gordon.

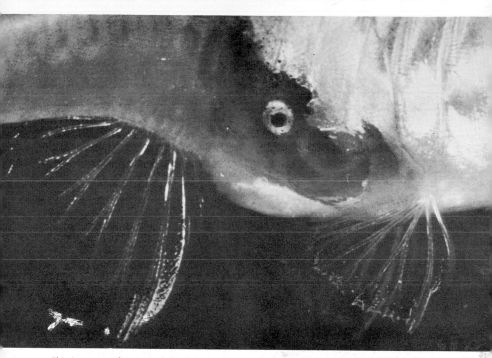

This is a magnification of the 'gravid spot' of the female Guppy. Notice the eye of the unborn fry inside the mother fish. Photo by Le Cuziat.

A Guppy fry a few moments after birth. Within seconds it escapes from the thin membrane by uncoiling the body. Photo by Le Cuziat.

Poecilia ornata collected by the author (HRA) in Haiti in 1957. The shallow, cool streams in Haiti are filled with interesting live bearers. Photo by Dr. Herbert R. Axelrod.

A pair of Black-bellied Limias, *Poecilia melanogaster*. Photo by Rudolf Zukal.

Poecilia latipunctata is another *Poecilia* species found in Central America and Mexico. Photo by Dr. Herbert R. Axelrod.

Poecilia caucana, the South American Molly. The middle fish in the photo is the female. Photo by Dr. Herbert R. Axelrod.

This enlargement shows the detail of the structure of the male gonopodium (anal fin). The sperm is injected into the female through the duct formed by this fin. Photo by Le Cuziat.

Poecilia heterandria, the Dwarf Limia, comes from Venezuela. Females attain 2 inches in length and the males 1 inch. Body color is muddy, with a white belly. Males show several dark vertical bars. A peaceful fish.

Poecilia melanogaster, the Black-bellied Limia, is a native to the island of Jamaica. Females are 3 inches long, and the males 2 inches. The body has a metallic blue sheen; there are 5 or 6 vertical bars in the after half of the body. The dorsal and caudal of the male are yellow, edged with black, and the females have a large triangular spot on the belly. A peaceful species.

Poecilia nigrofasciata, the Humpbacked Limia, comes from Haiti. Females attain 2½ inches in length, males 1½. Body is olive-colored and a series of black vertical bars adorn the sides. There are numerous golden flecks on the sides and the dorsal fin of both males and females are spotted. A strange thing takes place when the males get older. The lower part of the body, between the gonopodium and the caudal base, and the fore part of the back, to the end of the dorsal fin, take on extra tissue, giving the fish an appearance of having a spinal curvature, which it does not have. At this time, the dorsal and caudal fins also take on a yellow color. A peaceful species.

Poecilia nigrofasciata, the Humpbacked Limia. The male (upper fish) develops a humpback upon reaching sexual maturity. Photo by Chvojka Milan.

A pair of tank-bred Black Mollies. This strain probably originated from a *Poecilia sphenops* and *Poecilia latipinna* crossing. Photo by Rudolf Zukal.

Poecilia latipinna, male, marbled variety. Photo by Dr. W. Foersch.

In addition to the large flowing tail, this Lyretail Sailfin Molly, *Poecilia latipinna*, has delicately fringed pelvic fins also. Photo by Hilmar Hansen.

Poecilia ornata also comes from Haiti. Maximum size for females is 2½ inches and males 1½ inches. This fish has an overall marbled pattern of dark spots and blotches on a lighter background. Males have yellow dorsal fins. Peaceful.

Poecilia vittata is native to Cuba. Females are fully grown at 4 inches, and males at 2½ inches. Males are yellowish in color, with an orange-colored belly. There are several vertical bars and a horizontal stripe. Fins are deep yellow, attractively spotted with black. They are peaceful if not kept with small fishes.

This species established some kind of record when a female in the Shedd Aquarium in Chicago delivered 242 youngsters. Because of this great fecundity, plus the fact that they seem to take a great delight in catching and eating their own young, fertile females who are about to deliver young should be placed in large thickly planted tanks. Feeding these females heavily on live foods at this time also helps save many of the youngsters.

Poecilia branneri, Branner's Live Bearer, comes from the Amazon Basin in the vicinity of Para. Females grow to a size of 1½ inches, males to 1 inch. Back is olive, becoming silvery on the sides and white below. There are 7 to 9 vertical bars on the sides, and a beautiful ocellus at the tail base. A rather shy fish, it does best when kept with its own kind.

Poecilia parae, the Two-spot Live Bearer, is native to the Amazon

A pair of *Poecilia vittata*. The male is on the left. Photo by G.J.M. Timmerman.

Because of hybrid vigor a Sailfin Molly can grow larger than the parents. Such fish do best in a pool. Photo by G.J.M. Timmerman.

Basin and the Guianas. Females attain $1\frac{1}{2}$ inches in length, and males 1 inch. The sides have a bluish sheen, and there are two spots on the body, one at the upper center and the other at the vent. The dorsal fin of the male is marked with red, tan and black, and the tail is a greenish brown. This fish is also best kept with only its own kind.

Poecilia caucana, the South American Molly, is native to Venezuela. Females are $1\frac{1}{2}$ inches in size and the males 1 inch. This little fish is very attractively colored: the body is reddish purple with bright blue gill-covers. The dorsal and caudal fins are edged with black, and reddish in color. Peaceful, but should not be kept with fishes bigger than itself.

Poecilia latipinna, the Sailfin Molly, occurs from South Carolina to Mexico and attains a size of 4 inches. Males are slightly smaller. The body is greenish, with 6 or 8 rows of dots forming horizontal lines. There is a streak of bright blue in the lower part of the tail. The dorsal fin is tremendous, running almost along the entire back, and as wide as the entire body. A melanistic form of this fish has been segregated and bred for the black color; the result is the famous and popular Black Sailfin Molly. This gorgeous fish is now being pool-raised in Florida by the millions, resulting in a stock of fish which is far more beautiful than those which are raised in tanks. A Lyre-tail variety has also been developed.

There have been several color varieties of Mollies produced over the years. This rust-colored strain never became popular. Photo by Glen Takeshita.

Poecilia latipinna, male. Lyretail Black Sailfin Molly. Photo by Burkhard Kahl.

Poecilia latipinna, male. Black Sailfin Molly. Photo by Dr. Herbert R. Axelrod.

Poecilia latipinna, male. Albino Lyretail Sailfin Molly. Photo by Dr. Herbert R. Axelrod.

A pair of wild Green Sailfin Mollies collected in Louisiana. Photo by G. J. M. Timmerman.

Not only *Poecilia latipinna* is available in black form but also other species like this *P. sphenops*. Photo by G.J.M. Timmerman.

These Sailfin Mollies were collected in the ocean, miles away from the shore, by Dr. Charles Breder Jr. Photo by Sam Dunton, New York Zoological Society.

Many people have a great deal of trouble keeping and raising this fish. This is usually the result of disobeying a few simple rules which can be briefly laid down here. In the first place, it must be remembered that the molly is a fish which sometimes inhabits brackish and salt water; for this reason, the addition of a certain amount of salt is a necessity for keeping the molly in the best of health. A tablespoonful per gallon is the proper amount. The molly is a fish which depends largely upon vegetable matter for its food. The average foods sold for tropical fishes do not contain enough vegetable matter to satisfy this need; there are however some foods specially prepared for feeding to mollies. Many hobbyists like to keep their mollies in a community aquarium, and for good reason. They look especially beautiful with other fishes to set them off. Needing the special care they do it is obvious that the same things good for the general run of aquarium fishes are not necessarily the same which are good for mollies. There is one more thing which the Black Molly requires: a high temperature, around 80°. Given these things, plus a large tank with plenty of plant life and a sunny location, the molly will thrive. Well-fed parents will leave their fry alone.

Poecilia sphenops ranges from Mexico to northern South America. Size attained is 4 inches for females, slightly less for males. Sides are bluish, some specimens showing a few black dots on the sides. Dorsal

Phalloceros caudimaculatus reticulatus, the Caudo. Lower fish is the male. Photo by Rudolf Zukal.

A pair of *Phalloceros caudimaculatus reticulatus* with a slightly different color pattern. Photo by Dr. W. Foersch.

Phallichthys amates, the Merry Widow. Female to the right. Photo by G.J.M. Timmerman.

Poecilia vivipara, the One-spot Live Bearer. The female is the fish to the right. Photo by G.J.M. Timmerman.

and tail fins vary from yellow to red. Another color variety has marbled sides, with black spots peppered all over the body and fins and an orange edge on the tail.

This molly also needs the addition of salt in the water, but the high temperatures recommended for the Black Sailfin are not necessary here; 76° is ample. A much easier fish to handle than the Black Molly.

Poecilia velifera is native to Yucatan. Females often grow to 5 inches, a little less for males. In appearance this fish is greatly similar to *P. latipinna*, but the sides are a little more blue and the belly is yellow. The big difference, however, is that the magnificent dorsal fin of this species is even bigger and more sail-like than in the other.

All that was specified for the Black Molly also applies here, except the temperature requirements: 76° is also ample here.

Neotoca bilineata, the Two-lined Neotoca, comes from the Mexico plateau. Females are 2 inches in length, males a bit smaller. Body color is green. There is a black line which begins at the gill-cover, curves downward and then straightens out to the caudal base. Another line starts further down on the gill-cover and runs back to the end of the

A pair of wild type Green Swordtails, *Xiphophorus helleri*. The male has the caudal prolongation.

A pair of Wagtail Swordtails, a strain of *Xiphóphorus helleri* first developed and bred by Dr. Myron Gordon. Dr. Gordon was responsible for developing many strains of Swordtails and Platies which are still popular today. Photo by Dr. Herbert R. Axelrod.

A pair of Green Sailfin Mollies, *Poecilia velifera*. The upper fish is the male. Photo by Rudolf Zukal.

A pair of *Poecilia petenensis*, a species which greatly resembles *Poecilia velifera*. These fish were collected by Dr. Myron Gordon in Lake Peten in Flores, Guatemala in 1954. Photo by Sam Dunton, New York Zoological Society.

belly region. Here there is a downward bar which begins at the center of the body and ends at the vent.

This is a live bearer which does not look like one: instead of the well-formed gonopodium, the male merely shows a notch separating the first few anal rays from the others. Peaceful and may be placed with others.

Phallichthys amates, the Merry Widow, comes from Guatemala and Honduras. Females grow to 2 inches and males 1 inch. There is a dark crescent-shaped bar which crosses the eye; males have about a dozen narrow vertical bars: The dorsal fins are edged with black. The male has a very long gonopodium. A peaceful, hardy fish.

Phalloceros caudimaculatus, the Caudo, is native to southeastern Brazil and Paraguay. Females grow to $2\frac{1}{4}$ inches, males $1\frac{1}{4}$. Body color is olive green, mottled with black spots all over the body and fins. There is also a golden variety of this fish. It is peaceful and hardy.

Phalloptychus januarius comes from southeastern Brazil. Females are 2 inches, and males $1\frac{1}{4}$ inches. Sides are silvery, and the back olive-colored. A number of dark vertical bars adorn the sides.

The young of this fish are very small and difficult to keep alive. Like the Midget Live Bearer only a few are delivered each day over a period of time.

Poecilia vivipara, the One-spot Live Bearer, comes from the Leeward Islands and the north coast of South America. Females grow to 3 inches, males to 1¾ inches. There is a prominent black spot in the center of the body of both sexes. Sides are silvery in the male, with a golden blush in the belly region and a bright orange dorsal fin, which has a dark band near the base. A peaceful fish.

Xiphophorus helleri, the Swordtail, occurs from Mexico to Honduras. Females grow to 4 inches, males a little smaller. Here we come to another of the popular live-bearing species. The original wild-type, which are still available, are a bluish green in color. There is a horizontal maroon stripe which begins at the gill-covers and ends at the top of the sword, which is a very long, pointed extension of the lower caudal rays. Another horizontal stripe runs along the lower edge of the body and ends as the lower edge of the sword. This extension occurs only in males. There is a golden area above the upper horizontal stripe and another below. The dorsal fin is spotted with red. Females have the stripe on the body, but lack the sword and most of the dorsal spots. There is an albino variety with pink eyes, light yellow bodies and red stripes with a yellow sword.

A pair of Merry Widows, *Phallichthys amates*. The male is the fish to the left with the modified anal fin (called a 'gonopodium') with which he fertilizes the female. Photo by G.J.M. Timmerman.

A male Green Wagtail Swordtail, *Xiphophorus helleri*. Photo by K. Quitschau.

Xiphophorus helleri, Highfin type of the Hamburg form of Swordtail, male. Photo by K. Quitschau.

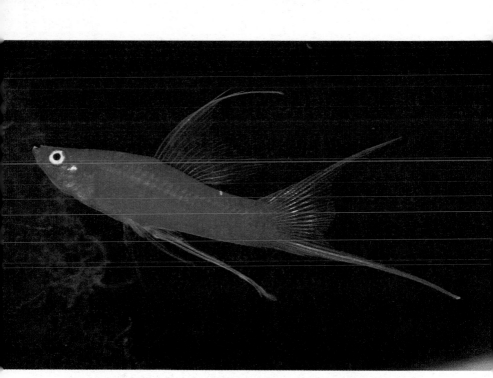

A male Lyretail Swordtail, *Xiphophorus helleri*. Photo by Rudolf Zukal.

Xiphophorus helleri guentheri is a supposed subspecies of Swordtail which is found in Mexico, Guatamala and British Honduras. This fish and all live-bearers, have been fully treated in Kurt Jacobs' book on LIVEBEARING AQUARIUM FISHES. Photo by K. Quitschau.

Dr. James W. Atz assists Dr. Myron Gordon (right) collecting Swordtails and Platyfish in a small pool along the Rio Axtla, San Luis Potosi, Mexico. Photo courtesy of the late Dr. Myron Gordon.

Crossing *X. helleri* with *X. maculatus* has produced many "new" types, such as the Green Wag, the Red Wag, the Brick Red, the Velvet Red, the Tuxedo, the Black, etc. A peaceful species which sometimes chases other fishes playfully but hardly ever hurts them. Very hardy and prolific. Mrs. Thelma Simpson developed a high dorsal variety. There has also been developed a Lyretail Swordtail.

Xiphophorus maculatus, the Platy, grows to 3 inches in the female and 1½ inches in the male and occurs from Mexico to British Honduras. The original wild specimens of this fish are brown in color with a few blue blotches on the sides. Males sometimes show a little red in the dorsal fin. From this modest beginning, breeders have patiently developed the many beautiful color varieties on the market today: Red, Red Wag, Gold, Gold Wag, Black, Blue, Salt-and-Pepper, Bleeding Heart, Berlin, Tuxedo, Mixed, etc. All these are pretty and desirable speci-

These *Xiphophorus helleri* were collected in Mexico by Dr. Gordon. Different spots appeared on fish taken from different areas. Some wild Swordtails had no spots at all. Photo by Sam Dunton, New York Zoological Society.

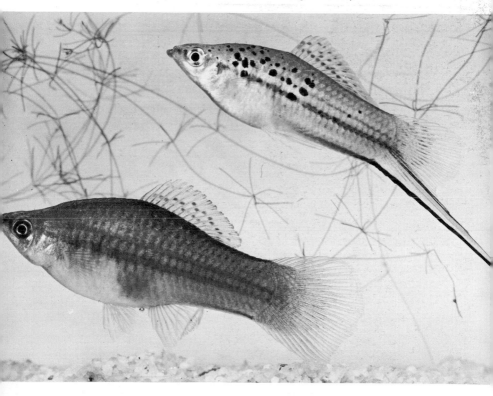

Salt and Pepper Platies, *Xiphophorus maculatus*. Female, upper fish. Photo by Dr. Herbert R. Axelrod.

Pearl Albino Platy, *Xiphophorus maculatus*, male. Photo by Dr. Joanne Norton.

Xiphophorus maculatus. This Highfin Platy is also called Topsail by some breeders and dealers. Photo by Joanne Norton.

A pair of Marigold Platies, *Xiphophorus variatus.* The male is the uppermost fish and has the most color. Normally females and males have equal coloration in Platies and Swordtails, except for *variatus* species.

Pseudoxiphophorus bimaculatus. The male, the lower fish, has a huge gonopodium in comparison to its size. Photo by Sam Dunton, N.Y.Z.S.

Mr. Orville Tutwiler developed a strain of true-breeding Hybrid Swordtails which he developed from Dr. Myron Gordon's famous Red Jet Swordtail. Unfortunately this strain broke down as the fish developed cancer.

This male Platy is called a "Moon" because of the pattern on the caudal peduncle. Photo by G.J.M. Timmerman.

A Golden Comet Platy. The Wagtail pattern was developed from this kind of fish by Dr. Gordon.

Xiphophorus montezumae montezumae, male. Photo by Dr. W. Foersch.

Albino *Xiphophorus variatus*, male. Photo by Dr. Herbert R. Axelrod.

Bill Hearin developed this beautiful strain of Topsail Variatus.

A pair of young Montezuma Swordtails. Photo by G.J.M. Timmerman.

mens, but it must be remembered that if they are mixed and kept together there will also be a mixture in the offspring. A platy of one color will not hesitate to mate with other platies of different colors, so if you have a preference and desire to breed a particular color strain, do not expose them to other color strains. This of course applies equally to the different swordtails. Peaceful and hardy, the platy is an ideal aquarium fish.

Highfin platies are commonplace now. William Hearin was a pioneer with these fancy platies, though he used *variatus* stock primarily.

Xiphophorus montezumae, the Montezuma Swordtail, comes from the Rio Panuco in Mexico. Females attain $2\frac{1}{2}$ inches in length, males 2 inches. This is a drab, olive-green fish with a zigzag horizontal line, dark-edged scales in the upper portion which gives the fish a reticulated pattern, and dark spots in the dorsal fin. The male has a very short sword. A peaceful species.

Xiphophorus variatus, the Variegated Platy, also comes from Mexico. Females grow to 3 inches, males 2 inches. Colors vary greatly: the body color is bluish to yellowish in the males; some have canary yellow dorsals and tails, others red tails and yellow dorsals, and others combine these colors. Females are a muddy brown, with a zigzag horizontal line. This fish has been hybridized successfully with the Black Platy, giving a fish which has much black in the body and fins. Highfin *variatus* are magnificent.

X. variatus is a peaceful, prolific fish, though in many color varieties it takes a long time for the males to get their red coloration.

The normal Sunset Variatus Platies which are basically yellow and red. These fish are very prolific in outdoor pools. Photo by G.J.M. Timmerman.

Xiphophorus xiphidium. Lower fish is a male. Photo by Dr. W. Foersch.

Xiphophorus pygmaeus. Male lower fish. Photo by Dr. Herbert R. Axelrod.

Redtail Black Platy Variatus, the rarest of the species. Photo by R. Zukal.

A pair of *Xiphophorus pygmaeus*, female above. Photo by Dr. C. D. Zander.

INDEX

Page listings in **bold** face refer to photographs; page listings within parentheses refer to spawning data.

A

F

G

Gymnocorymbus ternetzi, 142, (187), **188**

H

Hair Grass, 50, **51**
Half-banded Barb, 143, **260, 267, 269,** (270)
Half-beak, 546, **549,** (554), **554-555**
Haplochromis moffati, 523, **527**
    multicolor, 523, (531)
    philander, 523, (527), **530, 533, 536**
Harlequin, 295, (326)
Hart's Rivulus, 295, (331)
H-Barb, **268**
Head-and-tail Light Tetra, 142, (195), **196-197**
Heater, **19**
Helostoma temmincki, 142, **189,** (190), **191**
Helxine, **63**
Hemichromis bimaculatus, 363, (403), **404**
    bimaculatus II, 363, (406)
Hemigrammus armstrongi, 142, (191), **191-192**
    caudovittatus, 142, **193,** (194)
    gracilis, 142, (207), **213**
    nanus, 142, (195), **197**
    ocellifer, 142, (195), **196-197**
    pulcher, 142, **198,** (198)
    rhodostomus, 142, (199), **201**
    unilineatus, 142, (199), **200, 202**
Herringbone Rivulus, 295, **336**
Heterandria formosa, 546, **557,** 563, **566**

Highfin Platy, **601**
Hood, **19**
Hoplias malabaricus, **127**
Hoplosternum, **494**
Hornwort, 55, **58**
Humpbacked Limia, 546, **579,** (579)
Hydra, **89**
Hygrophila polysperma, 50, **51, 61**
Hyphessobrycon callistus, 142, (202), **203, 205-206**
    eos, 142
    flammeus, 142, (207), **208**
    herbertaxelrodi, 142, **210,** (210), **213**
    heterorhabdus, 142, **209,** (210)
    (Paracheirodon) innesi, 142, (211), **216**
    peruvianus, **220**
    pulchripinnis, 142, **215,** (215), **220**
    rosaceus, 142, **218,** (218), **221**
    rubrostigma, **221**
    scholzei, 142, **217, 219,** (219)
    serpae, **206, 208**
    simulans, 142, **217**

I

Infusoria, 90, **91,** 139
Infusoria (Culture), 94, 138
Italian Val, 35

M

N

T